Upgrading to WordPerfect 6

GEORGE R. BEINHORN

Screen reproductions in this book were created with Collage Plus from Inner Media, Inc., Hollis, NH.

Upgrading to WordPerfect 6 is based on WordPerfect Version 6.0. Commands and functions detailed in this book may work with other versions in which the pertinent features are available.

Publisher: David P. Ewing

Associate Publisher: Rick Ranucci

Operations Manager: Sheila Cunningham

Publishing Plan Manager: Thomas H. Bennett

Marketing Manager: Ray Robinson

CREDITS

Title Manager
Elden Nelson

Acquisitions Editor
Rick Ranucci

Product Development Specialist
Kathie-Jo Arnoff

Production Editor
Anne Owen

Editors
Jane A. Cramer
Virginia Noble

Technical Editor
Tish Nye

Book Designer
Amy Peppler-Adams

Production Team
Danielle Bird
Julie Brown
Jodie Cantwell
Laurie Casey
Brad Chinn
Brook Farling
Heather Kaufman
Caroline Roop
Linda Seifert
Michelle Worthington

Indexer
Johnna VanHoose

Composed in *Cheltenham* and *MCPdigital* by Que Corporation

George R. Beinhorn is a writer, editor, and commercial photographer. He is the author of Que's *Using Professional Write Plus for Windows, Look Your Best with WordPerfect for Windows, Look Your Best with WordPerfect 5.1, Word for Windows Hot Tips*, and is the revision author of *Using Q & A*, 4th Edition. He writes the "Pro Tips" word processing column and is a contributing editor for *PC Computing* magazine.

Beinhorn serves as a document design consultant for business clients and may be reached through Que Corporation.

CONTENTS AT A GLANCE

TABLE OF CONTENTS

I WordPerfect's New Look

II Formatting and Editing Tools

III Special Features

Introduction

Relax. If you're familiar with WordPerfect 5.1, or an earlier version of WordPerfect, you will have little trouble learning the new features of WordPerfect 6. You will find that the new graphical user interface in Version 6 makes it easy and fun to learn.

WordPerfect 6 looks different—definitely! When you first run the program, the first thing you notice is the menu bar at the top of the screen. You can turn off the menu bar and make WordPerfect 6 look just like Version 5.1. Or you can keep the menu bar and add Ribbon and Button Bars, horizontal and vertical scroll bars, an Outline Bar, and document window frame. In keeping with established WordPerfect tradition, the Version 6 editing screen remains highly customizable.

If you're tempted to grumble about how WordPerfect Corporation has "broken something that didn't need to be fixed," consider the advantages of the new graphical interface. With the Button and Ribbon Bars enabled, you can choose many important WordPerfect commands with a single mouse click instead of having to search through several layers of menus. And desktop publishing has never been easier, thanks to WordPerfect 6's editable graphics views.

When you type a familiar WordPerfect 5.1 keyboard command, WordPerfect displays a dialog box instead of a menu. For example, pressing F5 and Enter displays the File Manager List dialog box instead of the File Manager List screen.

In deciding which features to change, the WordPerfect 6 programmers have exercised excellent judgment. In some cases, change was clearly overdue. For example, F1 is now the Help key, reflecting its function in most programs; and you can now exit dialog boxes by pressing Esc or by using the familiar F7 (Exit) key. F3 is now the Repeat key.

Many improvements in user convenience are evident throughout the program. WordPerfect Corporation clearly listens to its users! For example, you can split and join adjacent tables much more easily, and you can add a new table row by simply pressing Tab in the last cell of an existing table.

The outline feature now includes the capability to collapse and expand headings and rearrange entire outline families simply by moving their collapsed headings. (At last!)

The merge, styles, envelope and label printing, and graphics features have all been greatly improved. The File Manager function has a powerful new QuickList option that displays frequently used file lists instantly. The new QuickFinder indexes document files for lightning-fast retrieval. And a new Directory Tree command displays a DOS-like visual list of directories.

You can open up to nine separate document windows and arrange them on-screen in overlapping (cascaded) or side-by-side (tiled) fashion. Macro users will be delighted to find that they can edit macros in the WordPerfect document screen.

Desktop publishing has suddenly become much easier now that you can write and edit in a graphical view, with fonts and page layouts displayed exactly as they will appear when printed.

With a fax modem installed in your computer, you can send and receive documents from within WordPerfect 6. You can check grammar with the popular Grammatik software that now comes with the program. You can easily create hypertext buttons that enable readers to search long documents by clicking with the mouse. And with the proper hardware installed, you can attach audio messages and sounds to your document files.

These are just a few of the many improvements and additions of this program. WordPerfect 6 is a tremendously impressive product—and best of all, it's easy and fun to both learn and use.

What This Book Does

The purpose of *Upgrading to WordPerfect 6* is to get you up and running with WordPerfect 6 as quickly as possible. Most readers will first want to learn about basic changes, then study a few specialized areas in which they spend the most time (mail merge, for example, or graphics and tables). Chapters 1 through 3 give you a quick tour through the basics of the new interface. Chapters 4 through 11 review the new formatting and editing features—including the new grammar checker, the many changes in styles, the new envelope printing, hypertext, subdivided pages, and File Manager. It is recommended, therefore, that you read those sections through.

Chapters 10 and 11 describe printing and font operations. If you're upgrading from WordPerfect 5.1, you can probably skip these chapters until you need specific information. The WordPerfect 6 installation procedure handles routine printer and font installation. You will have no trouble recognizing the old, familiar printing and font options in the appropriate dialog boxes.

Chapters 12 through 18 describe advanced features: graphics, index and TOC, merge, macros, tables, outlines, fax, and sound. You will probably want to read just the chapters from those sections that apply to your daily work.

Conventions Used in This Book

Certain conventions are used in this book for selection of menu and dialog box items. You can select most commands by clicking the appropriate menu or dialog box item with the mouse or by highlighting the command name with the arrow keys and then pressing Enter; or you can press the boldfaced letter in the command name. To access the menus in the menu bar, press Alt and the underlined letter in the menu's name.

In this book, commands are given by name, with the appropriate letter boldfaced. Separate instructions for the mouse and keyboard are not given. Where shortcut keys are available, they are generally listed with the equivalent menu commands—for example, "Choose **F**ile, **P**rint; or press Shift+F7."

PART

I

WordPerfect's New Look

OUTLINE

Learning WordPerfect's New Interface

This chapter gives new and veteran WordPerfect users a quick tour of the essential features of WordPerfect 6. Through step-by-step instructions, you learn how to start WordPerfect and open and save files. The chapters that follow provide in-depth explanations of WordPerfect's new and changed features.

Some of the most significant changes in WordPerfect 6 are in the user interface. But don't worry—most WordPerfect 5.1 commands work the same way in WordPerfect 6; only the visual surroundings have changed. You will quickly come to enjoy WordPerfect 6's more visually pleasing graphical user interface.

The first thing you discover about WordPerfect 6 is that Microsoft Windows-like dialog boxes replace most WordPerfect 5.1 menus. Dialog boxes have two important advantages over menus: by organizing commands more clearly, they make the program easier to learn; and check boxes, radio buttons, and lists make it easier and quicker to select commands with the keyboard or mouse.

You also find that certain commands have been relocated in WordPerfect 6. More logical command placement makes it easier to find the functions you need, whether you're a long-time user or a novice.

If you're a veteran WordPerfect user, you can skip lightly through this chapter, because most of the familiar WordPerfect 5.1 function-key commands work the same in WordPerfect 6. Newcomers may want to take time to reproduce the step-by-step procedures at the keyboard in order to familiarize themselves with the various basic menu, keyboard, and dialog box options.

 NOTE   Installing WordPerfect 6 doesn't update an earlier version of the program; it installs an entirely new copy of Word-Perfect 6. The default installation directory is c:\wp60.

Installing WordPerfect 6

WordPerfect 5.1 users will find the installation program quite familiar, except for the replacement of menus with dialog boxes, in keeping with new graphical appearance of WordPerfect 6.

The steps for starting the installation procedure are the same as for WordPerfect 5.1:

1. Insert the Install 1 disk in drive A.

   If you're using 3.5-inch disks, you may be inserting the disk into drive B.

2. Type **a:install** (or **b:install**) at the C:\ DOS prompt.

3. Press Enter.

The WordPerfect Installation dialog box appears (see fig. 1.1).

Options 1 through 3 (**S**tandard Installation, **C**ustom Installation, and **N**etwork Installation) are the same as before.

If you choose Option 4 - **D**evice (Printer, Sound, Graphics) Files, the install program prompts you for the drive and directory to install device files from, and the location of the WordPerfect Program files. Answer the prompts and press Enter. WordPerfect displays the Install: Device dialog box, with options for installing a sound board, graphics card, or printer. Choose an option, and WordPerfect prompts you to insert the appropriate installation disk.

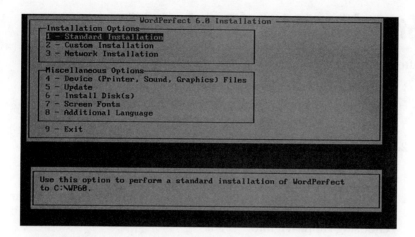

```
┌─────────────── WordPerfect 6.0 Installation ───────────────┐
│ ┌─Installation Options──────────────────────────────────┐  │
│ │ 1 - Standard Installation                              │  │
│ │ 2 - Custom Installation                                │  │
│ │ 3 - Network Installation                               │  │
│ │                                                        │  │
│ ┌─Miscellaneous Options─────────────────────────────────┐  │
│ │ 4 - Device (Printer, Sound, Graphics) Files            │  │
│ │ 5 - Update                                             │  │
│ │ 6 - Install Disk(s)                                    │  │
│ │ 7 - Screen Fonts                                       │  │
│ │ 8 - Additional Language                                │  │
│ └────────────────────────────────────────────────────────┘ │
│   9 - Exit                                                  │
│                                                             │
│                                                             │
│ ┌─────────────────────────────────────────────────────────┐│
│ │ Use this option to perform a standard installation of    ││
│ │ WordPerfect to C:\WP60.                                  ││
│ └─────────────────────────────────────────────────────────┘│
└─────────────────────────────────────────────────────────────┘
```

FIG. 1.1

The WordPerfect Installation dialog box.

The rest of the device installation process is very similar to installing printers with WordPerfect 5.1. Insert the installation disk and press Enter. WordPerfect displays a list of sound boards, graphics cards, or printer files, depending on the type of device you choose to install.

Use the arrow keys to select a device from the list, and then press Enter. WordPerfect copies the appropriate files from the installation disk and asks whether you want to install another driver. Press N to return to the Install: Device dialog box; or press Y to install another device.

Another new option is Option 7 - **S**creen Fonts. If you are using printer fonts that WordPerfect's fonts don't match very well, you may be able to obtain better screen fonts from the font manufacturer or an independent vendor. You use this option to install screen fonts.

After choosing 7 - **S**creen Fonts, you are prompted for the location of the screen fonts. Type the disk and/or directory path and the filename of the screen font file. Press Enter to complete the installation process.

Choosing Option 8 - **L**anguage, installs files for using the Speller and Thesaurus features with foreign-language dictionaries. Foreign language modules aren't included with the program and must be purchased separately from WordPerfect Corporation. The language modules also enable you to display menus and dialog boxes in the foreign language.

After you complete the options for a standard installation, WordPerfect installs the printer files you choose, prompting you to insert the printer installation disks as needed. The installation program then returns to DOS.

Starting WordPerfect 6

After installing WordPerfect, follow these steps to run the program:

1. At the DOS prompt, type **cd\wp60** and press Enter.

   If WP.EXE file is located in another directory, type the directory name instead of wp60.

2. Type **wp** and press Enter.

   The first time you run WordPerfect, you are prompted for your registration number. You find this number on the Certificate of License Registration card that comes with WordPerfect. You can then display the registration number from within WordPerfect by choosing **Help**, **WP** Info.

3. Type the registration number and choose OK.

The WordPerfect editing screen appears in Text mode, with the pull-down menu bar displayed (see fig. 1.2). If you prefer to edit in a "clean screen," with the menu bar turned off, you can do so by following the instructions in the Chapter 2 section, "Customizing the Display."

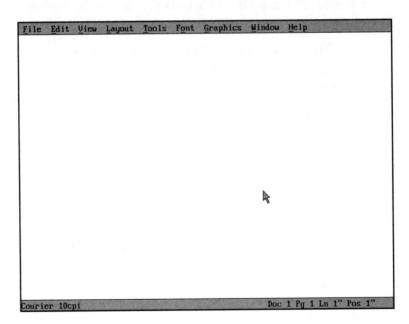

FIG. 1.2

The WordPerfect 6 editing screen as it appears after installation.

You may wonder why WordPerfect now runs by default with the menu bar displayed. The single, most all-encompassing change in the program is the new, Microsoft Windows-like optional graphical user interface. If you have used WordPerfect 5.1, you know that using function-key commands is much faster. Fortunately, you can tailor the program to work the old way, with all menus permanently hidden, or you can set WordPerfect to display all menus. You can also compromise between mouse and keyboard commands, turning on only those features that make your work go easier. For example, you can hide the menu bar and Outline Bar but turn on the Ribbon and Button Bars, both of which enable you to choose commands with a single mouse click.

 NOTE Screens in this book show the WordPerfect 6 document window in Graphics mode. WordPerfect's display modes are described fully in Chapter 2.

Using Function-Key Commands

Most WordPerfect 5.1 function-key commands work the same in WordPerfect 6. The most immediately noticeable differences appear in the following table:

Key	WordPerfect 5.1	WordPerfect 6
F1	Cancel	Help
F3	Help	Repeat
Esc	Repeat	Cancel

The Exit (F7) key functions as it did in Version 5.1.

If you prefer to use the old, familiar WordPerfect 5.1 assignments for these keys, you can restore their original meanings (see Chapter 3).

Using Menus and Dialog Boxes

Users who are familiar with Microsoft Windows will feel right at home with WordPerfect's pull-down menus and dialog boxes.

Choosing Menu Commands

You can pull down a menu by clicking its name or by pressing Alt plus the underlined letter in the menu name in Graphics mode or the highlighted letter in Text mode. Figure 1.3 shows the Font menu.

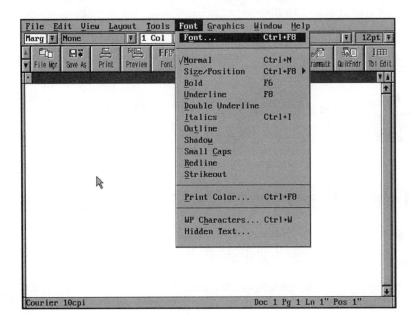

The Font menu.

You can select most commands by clicking the appropriate menu or dialog box item with the mouse, or by highlighting the command name with the arrow keys and then pressing Enter. Or you can press the boldfaced letter in the command name. To access the menus in the menu bar, press Alt and the underlined letter in the menu's name in Graphics mode or the highlighted letter in Text mode.

In this book, commands are given by name, with the appropriate letter boldfaced. Separate instructions for the mouse and keyboard are not given. Where shortcut keys are available, they are listed with the equivalent menu commands: "Choose **F**ile, **P**rint; or press Shift+F7."

Dialog box commands followed by ellipses (...) display another dialog box when selected. Text entry boxes that have up and down arrows display a pull-down list when you press the up- or down-arrow key or click an arrow indicator with the mouse.

Responding to Dialog Boxes

Choosing Font, Font or pressing Ctrl+F8 displays the Font dialog box, shown in figure 1.4. (The figure is shown for illustration; the Font feature is fully described in Chapter 13.)

FIG. 1.4

The Font dialog box.

List Boxes

Notice in figure 1.4 that the Size list is displayed. To display a list box, type the underlined letter in its name, or click the down-pointing arrow at the right end of the box. Or press Tab to highlight the name of the list box and press Enter to drop down the list.

Check Boxes

In figure 1.4, the Appearance section contains check boxes for text attributes such as bold and underline. (To move between dialog box sections with the keyboard, use Tab to move forward and Shift+Tab to go backward.)

To select a check box, click it or type the section number or the underlined letter in the section title, then type the check box number that appears. Alternatively, you can use the arrow keys to move to the check box and press the space bar or Enter to select it. You can select any number of check boxes in a section.

Radio Buttons

Notice in figure 1.4 that the Normal radio button is selected in the Relative Size area. You can select only one radio button in a given area at a time. For example, you cannot select both Normal and Fine in the Relative Size area. To select a radio button, click it or, with the keyboard, type the section number or the underlined letter in the section title, then type the check box number. Alternatively, you can use the arrow keys to move to the check box and press the space bar to select it.

Notice that when you change the Font, Size, Appearance, Position, Relative Size, or Underline options, your changes are reflected in the Resulting Font window.

Using the Mouse

The following terms are used in this book to describe basic mouse functions:

Term	Meaning
Click	Quickly press and release the left mouse button
Double-click	Click the left mouse button twice rapidly
Drag	Hold down the left mouse button and move the mouse
Point	Move the mouse until the pointer rests on the chosen item

To change the way the mouse works from within WordPerfect 6 (for example, to switch the left and right buttons for left-handed users), see Chapter 3.

Using Help

Remember that in WordPerfect 6, F1 is the Help key, Esc is the Cancel key, and F3 is the Repeat key. (To restore these keys to the Word-Perfect 5.1 meanings, see Chapter 3.

Using Help Options

Choosing **H**elp, **C**ontents or pressing F1 displays the Help dialog box. The following sections describe the options listed in the Help dialog box. To return to the Help dialog box after using any of these options, choose **C**ontents from the dialog box. To exit from any Help dialog box and return to the document window, press Esc or choose Cancel.

Template

Notice that pressing F1 twice doesn't display a function-key template, as pressing F3 twice does in WordPerfect 5.1. To display the function-key template in WordPerfect 6, choose **H**elp, **C**ontents; or press F1 and double-click Template; or choose Template, **L**ook. WordPerfect displays the Template dialog box, shown in figure 1.5.

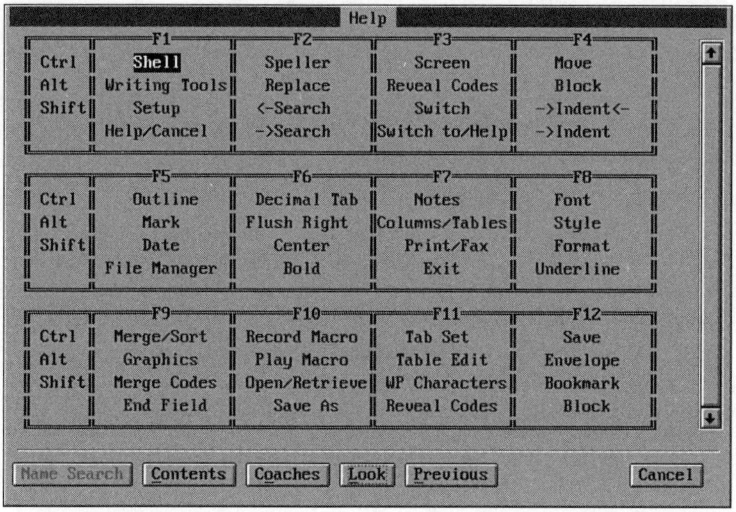

FIG. 1.5

The Template dialog box.

Index

To find help for a feature by name, choose Index. WordPerfect displays the Help Index list dialog box.

To find Help for a specific feature:

1. Choose **N**ame Search and type the name of the feature. WordPerfect highlights the feature name in the list.

2. Press Enter or double-click the name. WordPerfect displays information about the feature.

3. Press Esc to return to the document window.

How Do I

To get step-by-step help for the most common WordPerfect tasks, choose How Do I in the Help dialog box. WordPerfect displays the How Do I List dialog box.

Notice that the tasks are grouped under the following sections:

> Basics
> Basic Layout
> Advanced Layout
> Writing Tools
> Graphics/Equations
> Macros
> Merge

To display Help for a particular topic, double-click it or highlight it with the arrow keys and press Enter. For example, if you choose the Use Help topic, WordPerfect displays the Using Help dialog box.

The WordPerfect 6 Help screens include underlined "hypertext" buttons (the WordPerfect User's Guide calls them "pop-up terms") that you can select to move instantly to topics related to the current subject. For example, pressing PgDn at the Using Help dialog box displays a second screen with a hypertext button labeled Context-Sensitive Help. To display information about the topic in a hypertext button, double-click the button or highlight it with the arrow keys and press Enter; or choose **L**ook. To return to the previous screen, choose **P**revious.

Using Coaches

Choosing Coaches in any Help dialog box displays the Coaches dialog box, shown in figure 1.6.

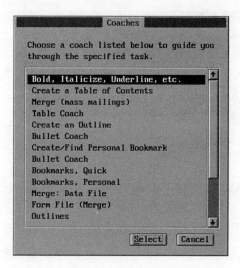

The Coaches dialog box lists topics for which WordPerfect can display detailed, step-by-step Help. To choose a coach, double-click the name of a Coach or highlight the name with the arrow keys. Then press Enter or choose Select; or type the name of a topic and press Enter. Word-Perfect displays the corresponding Coaches dialog box.

Glossary

WordPerfect 6 can provide explanations of common computer and WordPerfect-related terms. When you choose Glossary in the Help dialog box, the Glossary Help list dialog box appears.

To choose an item in the Glossary list, double-click the item or highlight it with the arrow keys and press Enter; or choose Look. Word-Perfect displays the glossary screen for the item.

Keystrokes

Choosing Keystrokes at the Help dialog box displays the Keystrokes list dialog box, shown in figure 1.7.

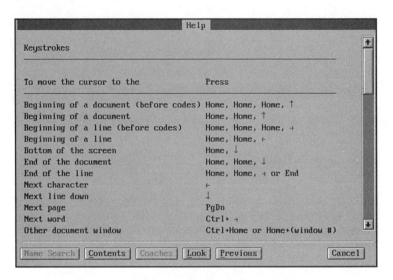

FIG. 1.7

The Keystrokes list dialog box.

The Keystrokes list shows the actions of key combinations in Word-Perfect 6. Notice that you cannot select a keystroke from the list and choose **L**ook or **C**oaches to display further help, as you can with other Help lists. This is the "end of the line" for Keystrokes Help. Choosing Coaches displays a list of topics for which you can display step-by-step Help, and choosing Look displays the WordPerfect 6 default function key template.

Shortcut Keys

Choosing Shortcut Keys at the Help dialog box displays the Shortcut Keys list dialog box, shown in figure 1.8. As with the Keystrokes list dialog box, this is the "end of the line" for Shortcut Keys Help.

About Help

Choosing About Help in the Help dialog box displays the Using Help dialog box.

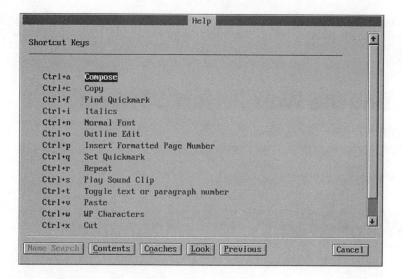

The Shortcut Keys list dialog box.

Using Macro Help

Choosing **Help, Macros** displays the WordPerfect Online Macros Manual dialog box. The WordPerfect Online Macros Manual can save you a tremendous amount of time if you create lots of macros. Instead of looking up a macro command in the User's Guide, for example, just choose **Help, Macros,** Macro Commands Index to display the Macro Commands Index list dialog box, shown in figure 1.9.

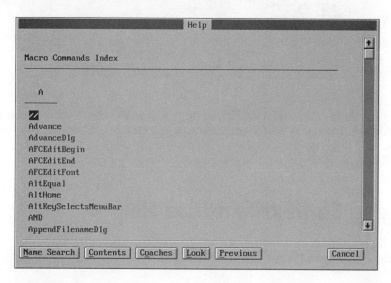

The Macro Commands Index dialog box.

To display more information about a command, double-click its name or highlight it with the arrow keys and press Enter; or choose Look. For further discussion of the Online Macros Manual, see Chapter 17.

Using the WordPerfect 6 Tutorial

With WordPerfect's new online tutorial, you can learn to use many program features interactively, without having to look them up in the User's Guide. To start the tutorial, choose Help, Tutorial and follow the instructions in the dialog boxes.

WordPerfect System Information

Choosing Help, WP Info displays the WP Info dialog box, shown in figure 1.10.

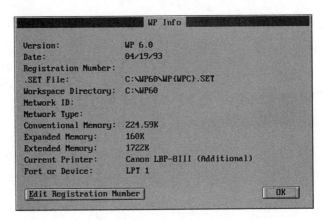

WP Info	
Version:	WP 6.0
Date:	04/19/93
Registration Number:	
.SET File:	C:\WP60\WP{WPC}.SET
Workspace Directory:	C:\WP60
Network ID:	
Network Type:	
Conventional Memory:	224.59K
Expanded Memory:	160K
Extended Memory:	1722K
Current Printer:	Canon LBP-8III (Additional)
Port or Device:	LPT 1

Edit Registration Number   OK

FIG. 1.10

The WP Info
dialog box.

The contents of the WP Info dialog box change to reflect your current hardware, DOS, and WordPerfect setup options. Notice especially the Date and Registration number, which you may need to supply when calling WordPerfect technical support.

Using Context-Sensitive Help

To display context-sensitive Help for a menu or dialog box option, press F1 (Help) with the menu or dialog box displayed.

Retrieving a File

WordPerfect 5.1 users should be aware that in WordPerfect 6, the following three options for retrieving and creating a file replace the WordPerfect 5.1 Retrieve command (Shift+F10):

■ *File, New has no function-key equivalent.* Choosing this option opens a new, untitled document. The title bar displays the document number and the word Untitled—for example, 3-(Untitled).

You can open up to nine document windows in WordPerfect 6, compared to only two with the Switch command (Shift+F3) in WordPerfect 5.1. Pressing Shift+F3 in WordPerfect 6 still opens a second document, but pressing Shift+F3 again switches you back to the first document.

■ *File, Open (Shift+F10) is the WordPerfect 6 equivalent of the Retrieve command in WordPerfect 5.1.* Choose this command to open a document in its own, separate document window. For example, if you're working in Document 1 and retrieve a file with the Open command, WordPerfect 6 loads the file into the Document 2 window. From this point forward, the term *Open* is used instead of *Retrieve*.

■ *File, Retrieve retrieves a file and inserts it in the current document at the cursor.*

To retrieve a file, press Shift+F10, just as you do in WordPerfect 5.1. WordPerfect displays the Open Document dialog box. For now, ignore any unfamiliar options such as QuickList. New features are described in later chapters.

In the Open Document dialog box, type a filename and press Enter. Or, to open one of the last four files you have worked on, click the arrow at the right end of the Filename text box; or press the down arrow and use the arrow keys to highlight a filename, then press Enter.

To use the File Manager (the WordPerfect 6 equivalent of the Word-Perfect 5.1 List Files screen), press F5 and Enter, highlight a filename, and press Enter again. WordPerfect opens the file in the document window.

Saving Files

Saving files in WordPerfect 6 is similar to saving in WordPerfect 5.1, except that you work with dialog boxes instead of menus. Also, the Save command in WordPerfect 5.1 has been split into two commands in WordPerfect 6: Save and Save As.

Saving the On-Screen File

Follow these steps to save the on-screen file:

1. If you're saving the file for the first time, choose File, **S**ave (Ctrl+F10); or **F**ile, Save **A**s (F10). WordPerfect displays the Save Document dialog box, shown in figure 1.11.

2. Notice that the cursor is in the Filename text box. Type a filename and choose OK or press Enter.

   If the filename already exists, WordPerfect displays the dialog box shown in figure 1.12.

3. Choose Yes to replace\overwrite the previous version of the file, or choose No to return to the Save Document dialog box and type a different filename.

WordPerfect displays a Saving message box while it saves the file, then returns to the editing screen.

Using Save As

You can use the File, Save As command to save the on-screen file under a new name after you have saved it once already. Save As works the same as File, Save but displays the previously saved name in the Filename text box.

Printing a File

Follow these steps to print the on-screen file:

1. Choose File, Print/Fax; or press Shift+F7, just as in WordPerfect 5.1. WordPerfect displays the Print dialog box shown in figure 1.13.

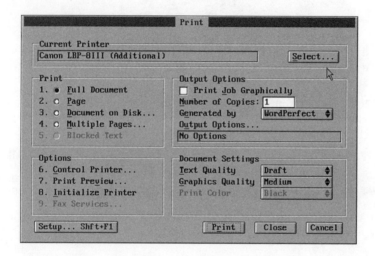

FIG. 1.13

The Print dialog box.

Notice that the dialog box is similar to the Print menu in Word-Perfect 5.1, except for a few new options that are described in Chapter 10.

2. To print the entire document, accept the default settings in the Print dialog box and choose Print or press Enter.

3. To choose print options 1 through 4 and 6 through 8, which are the same as in WordPerfect 5.1, press the number of the option, or press the underlined letter in the option name; or click the option's radio button, then choose Print or press Enter. (The remaining options are fully described in Chapter 10.)

WordPerfect begins printing.

Exiting WordPerfect 6

Exiting WordPerfect 6 works similarly to WordPerfect 5.1. Follow these steps:

1. Choose **File**, **Exit**; or press F7 as in WordPerfect 5.1.

   WordPerfect displays the Exit WordPerfect dialog box, shown in figure 1.14.

```
┌──────────────── Exit WordPerfect ────────────────┐
│                                                   │
│         Save     Filename                         │
│   A.    □     1. C:\WPDOCS\TRAV2.WP               │
│                                                   │
│   B.    ⊠     2. C:\WP60\60BOOK\TRAVEL2.WP        │
│                                                   │
│   [(Un)mark All]        [Save and Exit] [Cancel]  │
└───────────────────────────────────────────────────┘
```

If you have made changes to the file since the last time you saved it, the Save check box is marked, as shown in figure 1.14, and the Save and Exit button is displayed.

If you haven't made any changes since the last Save, the Save check box is unmarked and the Exit button is displayed, instead of the Save and Exit button.

2. To mark or unmark the Save check box, choose (Un)**mark** All.

3. Choose Exit to return to DOS without saving the file, or choose Save and Exit to save the file and return to DOS.

If you choose Save and Exit, WordPerfect does not ask you whether or not you want to overwrite the existing disk copy of the file.

A Powerful New Graphical Look

The most notable change in WordPerfect 6 is the graphical user interface, which gives WordPerfect, in its Graphics modes, a strong resemblance to Microsoft Windows.

Is this merely window dressing? Hardly. You can still work in a WordPerfect 5.1-like screen. (In fact, you may find Text mode quicker and easier on the eyes.) But the new graphical modes solve an irritating problem with Version 5.1: the torturous necessity to switch back and forth to Print Preview in order to check the results of your document formatting. As you will see, WordPerfect 6's easy-to-edit graphic views make desktop publishing a breeze.

Working in Graphics and Text Modes

The new WordPerfect 6 Graphics mode is a lot like Print Preview in WordPerfect 5.1—but with a major difference: Graphics mode not only shows fonts and graphic elements as they will be printed, which Print Preview also does, but *you can write and edit in the Graphics mode screen,* which you cannot do in Print Preview in WordPerfect 5.1.

Many WordPerfect 6 users may feel more comfortable writing and editing in Text mode, either because they find a graphics screen harder on the eyes, or because the Graphics mode screen refreshes as you type, making the text appear to "jiggle." Dialog boxes and menus pop up faster, and program functions that rewrite the screen operate more quickly in Text mode. And if you have upgraded from WordPerfect 5.1, old habits die hard.

A common practice among users of programs that have Text and Graphics modes is to create text in Text mode, then switch to Graphics mode to view the results of formatting commands.

Turning on Graphics Mode

To turn on Graphics mode, choose **View, G**raphics mode. Figure 2.1 shows a document displayed in Graphics mode.

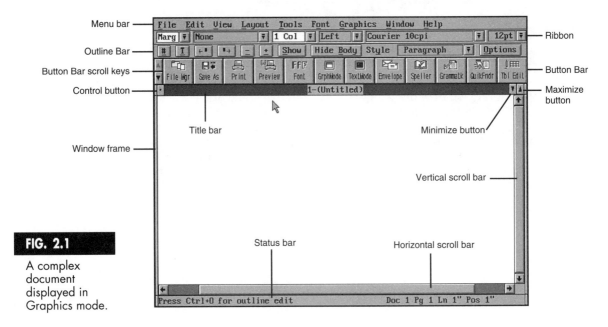

FIG. 2.1

A complex document displayed in Graphics mode.

To toggle quickly between modes, click the GphMode or TextMode buttons in the Button bar; or press Ctrl+F3, and choose **G**raphics or **T**ext from the Screen dialog box.

T I P

Some screen elements in figure 2.1 may be foreign to WordPerfect 5.1 users, though they're sure to be familiar to users of Microsoft Windows. The following list describes their functions:

- *Menu bar.* To drop down a menu, click its name with the left mouse button, or hold down Alt and press the underlined letter in the menu's name.

- *Ribbon.* From left to right, click to: change the display zoom size; insert a style; change column format, justification, font, and font size. You cannot access the Ribbon with the keyboard.

- *Outline Bar.* Click to choose outline commands. (These commands are described in detail in Chapter 16.)

- *Button Bar.* Click to choose the named commands.

- *Title bar.* Gives the number of the current document window and the current filename. If the file has not been saved, the title bar displays (Untitled).

- *Vertical scroll bar.* Click the up or down arrows or drag the inside bar in the appropriate direction to view other parts of a document.

- *Horizontal scroll bar.* Click the left or right arrows or drag the scroll bar to view other parts of a document.

- *Status bar.* Lists messages and displays the current document number and location of the cursor by page, line, and position.

- *Control button.* Click to exit the on-screen document.

- *Minimize button.* Click to reduce the document window to small size.

- *Maximize button.* Click to restore a minimized document to full-screen size.

- *Window frame.* The frame around the text area includes the title bar with the document name: 1-(Untitled) in figure 2.1. As in Microsoft Windows, you can minimize a framed window by clicking the minimize button or by choosing **W**indow, **M**inimize. Figure 2.2 shows the Untitled document window minimized.

- *Button Bar scroll keys.* Click the up -and down-pointing arrows at the left end of the Button Bar to scroll the Button Bar right or left to display buttons that are not visible on-screen.

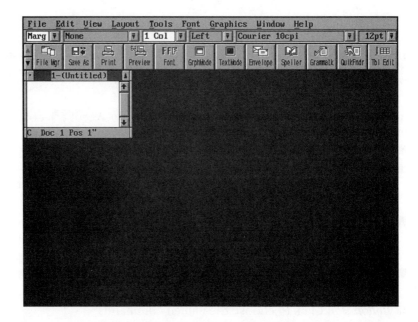

FIG. 2.2

A minimized
document
window.

You can also toggle a frame on and off for the on-screen document by double-clicking the status line at the bottom of the screen.

Notice that, unlike Microsoft Windows, WordPerfect 6 doesn't minimize a framed window to an icon but merely reduces its size. To position a minimized window, click on the title bar and drag. To resize the window, click on a corner or edge of the window and drag.

These features are quite useful when you're working with several open windows at a time and want to view the contents of each.

To switch from one window to another, choose **Window, S**witch; or press Shift+F3. Or you can click in the window. To switch to a window by the number displayed in its title bar—for example, 1 - (Untitled)— choose **W**indow, S**w**itch To; or press Home, 0. WordPerfect displays the Switch To Document dialog box. Type the number of the document; the dialog box disappears, and the window whose number you select becomes active.

If you maximize a window with the frame feature turned on, the frame disappears from the screen. To restore it, choose **W**indow, **F**ramed Window. With the frame turned on but not displayed, this action does not turn Framed Window off; it only makes the frame visible again in the document window.

Customizing the Display

You can customize the WordPerfect 6 window to your liking. You can choose a "clean screen" without scroll bars, button bars, pull-down menus, and so forth. Or you can load the screen with all the graphical tools that WordPerfect 6 has to offer. Figure 2.3 shows the screen with all on-screen options turned on except for the horizontal scroll bar.

To customize the display, choose **V**iew, Scree**n** Setup. The Screen Setup dialog box appears, as shown in figure 2.3.

FIG. 2.3

The WordPerfect 6 Screen Setup dialog box in Graphics mode, with all screen options installed.

To turn a display item on or off, select or deselect the appropriate check box. For example, to turn off the pull-down menus option, deselect the **P**ull-Down Menus check box. Most of the items are self-explanatory. Choosing **A**lt Key Activates Menus lets you move the cursor to the menu bar by pressing Alt and then pressing the menu's *mnemonic* (underlined letter), instead of holding down Alt and the menu's mnemonic. This method is helpful for those people who temporarily can use only one hand.

If you prefer to write and edit in Text mode in a "clean screen," you can turn off the menu bar and the status line display options. Figures 2.4 and 2.5 show a document displayed in Graphics and Text modes with all screen options turned off.

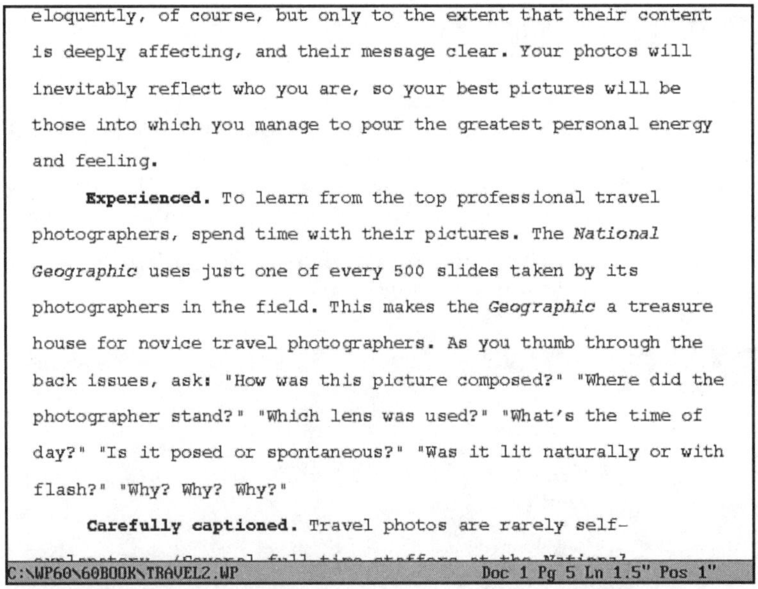

> eloquently, of course, but only to the extent that their content is deeply affecting, and their message clear. Your photos will inevitably reflect who you are, so your best pictures will be those into which you manage to pour the greatest personal energy and feeling.
>
> **Experienced.** To learn from the top professional travel photographers, spend time with their pictures. The *National Geographic* uses just one of every 500 slides taken by its photographers in the field. This makes the *Geographic* a treasure house for novice travel photographers. As you thumb through the back issues, ask: "How was this picture composed?" "Where did the photographer stand?" "Which lens was used?" "What's the time of day?" "Is it posed or spontaneous?" "Was it lit naturally or with flash?" "Why? Why? Why?"
>
> **Carefully captioned.** Travel photos are rarely self-
>
> C:\WP60\60BOOK\TRAVEL2.WP   Doc 1 Pg 5 Ln 1.5" Pos 1"

FIG. 2.4

A document in Graphics mode with screen options turned off.

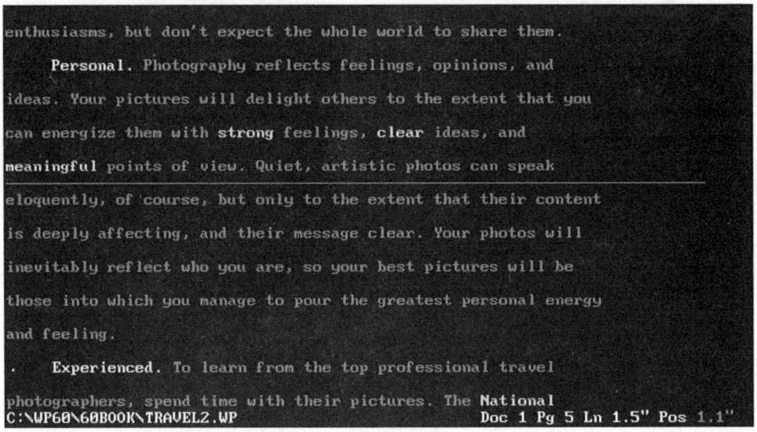

> enthusiasms, but don't expect the whole world to share them.
>
> **Personal.** Photography reflects feelings, opinions, and ideas. Your pictures will delight others to the extent that you can energize them with **strong** feelings, **clear** ideas, and **meaningful** points of view. Quiet, artistic photos can speak eloquently, of course, but only to the extent that their content is deeply affecting, and their message clear. Your photos will inevitably reflect who you are, so your best pictures will be those into which you manage to pour the greatest personal energy and feeling.
>
> . **Experienced.** To learn from the top professional travel photographers, spend time with their pictures. The **National**
>
> C:\WP60\60BOOK\TRAVEL2.WP   Doc 1 Pg 5 Ln 1.5" Pos 1.1"

FIG. 2.5

A document in Text mode with screen options turned off.

Notice that figure 2.5 looks exactly like the document screen in WordPerfect 5.1.

Using Page Mode

Page mode is exactly like Graphics mode except that headers and footers are displayed in the document screen. To turn on Page mode, choose View, Page mode (Ctrl+F3). Figure 2.6 shows a document displayed in Page mode. Notice that headers are shown in the document window.

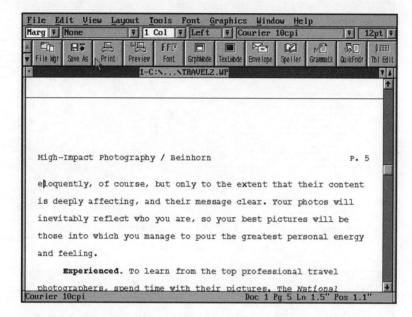

FIG. 2.6

In Page mode, document headers and footers are displayed in the editing screen.

Using Zoom

You can further customize the display by changing the size at which WordPerfect displays on-screen documents in Graphics mode. With Zoom you can display documents in a variety of sizes. To select a size, choose View, Zoom. WordPerfect displays a cascading menu with the options: 50%, 75%, 100%, 150%, 200%, Full, or Wide. Choose a size to change the display. Figure 2.7 shows the document from figure 2.6 displayed at 50% zoom reduction.

Choosing View, Zoom, Wide fills the document window with the width of the document. Figure 2.8 shows a document with the Wide option turned on. Notice that the empty area to the right of the document in figure 2.7 has been eliminated.

Choosing View, Zoom, Full Page displays a full-page view of the document, including headers and footers (see fig. 2.9).

To restore the default Graphics view document proportions, choose View, Zoom, Margin Width.

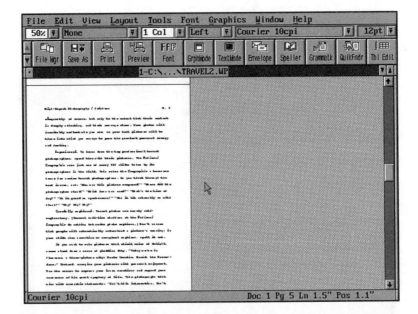

FIG. 2.7

A document
displayed at
50% zoom
reduction.

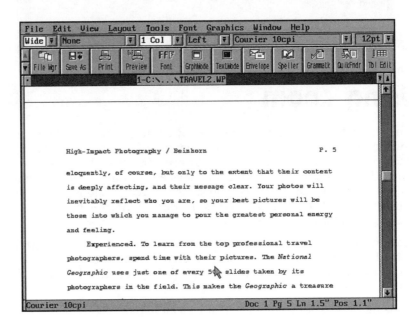

FIG. 2.8

A document in
Wide view.

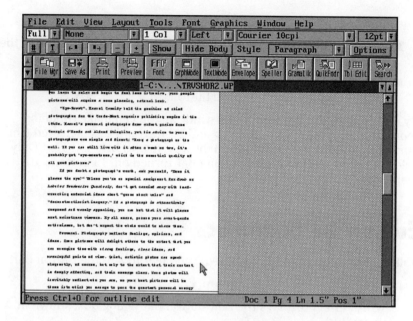

FIG. 2.9

A document in
Full view.

Customizing the Button Bar

With the WordPerfect 6 Button Bar, you can choose commands with a single mouse click. You can customize the Button Bar with buttons for commands that you use repeatedly, and you can create button bars for specialized tasks—for example, desktop publishing, report writing, and creating spreadsheets.

Positioning the Button Bar

You can change the position of the Button Bar in the document window. Follow these steps:

1. Choose View, Button Bar Setup, Options.

   WordPerfect displays the Button Bar Options dialog box.

2. Choose Position and Style options and choose OK.

The following paragraphs explain the Position and Style options:

- *Position.* Choose **T**op, **B**ottom, **L**eft Side, or **R**ight Side to move the Button Bar to the specified location.

- *Style.* Choose **P**icture and Text, Picture **O**nly, or Te**x**t Only to change the appearance of the buttons.

By customizing the WordPerfect 6 window, you can make room for more buttons. With **T**op or **B**ottom and **P**icture and Text selected (the defaults), 12 buttons are displayed; however, with **L**eft and Te**x**t Only selected, and the Ribbon and Outline Bar turned off, 15 buttons are displayed.

Editing the Button Bar

Follow these steps to add menu items and features to the Button Bar:

1. Choose **V**iew, Button Bar **S**etup, **E**dit.

   WordPerfect displays the Edit Button Bar dialog box, shown in figure 2.10.

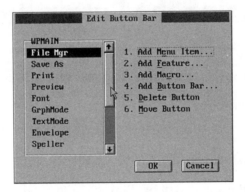

2. Choose the desired options in the Edit Button Bar dialog box, then choose OK.

The following paragraphs describe the Edit Button Bar dialog box options. Notice that as you use these options, your changes are reflected in the Button Bar, which remains visible behind the dialog box:

- *Add Menu Item.* This option highlights **F**ile in the menu bar. Choose a menu item with the mouse or keyboard. Repeat to add other menu items, then press F7 (Exit) and choose OK.

WordPerfect adds a new button by deleting the last button in the list and replacing it with the new one. To replace a specific button, highlight its name and choose **D**elete Button; then add the new button and move it as described in the Move Button option, discussed later.

■ *Add Feature.* This option displays the WordPerfect Feature Button List dialog box, as shown in figure 2.11.

FIG. 2.11

The Feature Button List dialog box.

To create a new feature button, highlight a feature and choose Select. For a list of explanations of the feature codes, press F1 (Help) with the Feature Button List dialog box displayed.

■ *Add Macro.* This option displays the Macro Button List. This dialog box lists all global macros. To assign a macro to a button, create the macro, display this dialog box, highlight the macro's name, and choose Select. Macros are described in detail in Chapter 17.

■ *Add Button Bar.* Choose this option to add a button that displays another Button Bar. This option displays the Button Bar List dialog box. Highlight a Button Bar and choose Select. For instructions on creating Button Bars, see the section "Creating a Button Bar," discussed later.

■ *Delete Button.* Highlight a button and choose **D**elete, **Y**es to remove it from the list.

■ *Move Button.* This option selects the highlighted button in the list and displays a new menu option, **P**aste Button. Move the selected button with the arrow keys and choose **P**aste Button. WordPerfect inserts the button above the cursor position in the list.

Creating a Button Bar

Follow these steps to create customized Button Bars:

1. Choose View, Button Bar Setup, Select.

   WordPerfect displays the Select Button Bar dialog box.

2. Choose Create, type a name of up to eight characters, and choose OK.

   WordPerfect displays the Edit Button Bar dialog box with the name of the new Button Bar displayed at the top of the list box, as shown in figure 2.12.

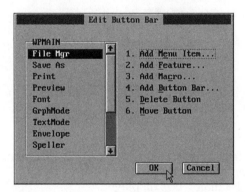

The Edit Button Bar dialog box.

3. To create buttons for the new bar, follow the directions in the preceding section "Editing the Button Bar," then choose OK.

   WordPerfect returns to the Select Button Bar dialog box and inserts the name of the new Button Bar in the Button Bars list.

4. Choose Select to display the new Button Bar in the document window.

You can create a Button Bar button that selects a different Button Bar. For instructions, see *Add Button Bar* in the previous section, "Editing the Button Bar."

Setting Program Defaults

The WordPerfect 5.1 Setup command (Shift+F1) enables you to set important program defaults without exiting WordPerfect. The major Setup options are Mouse, Display, Environment, Keyboard Layout, Location of Files, and Color Printing Palette.

In WordPerfect 6, the Initial Settings options have been moved to dialog boxes under their corresponding features or have been eliminated. For example, choosing Merge from the WordPerfect 5.1 Initial Settings menu displays options for merge-printing with delimited data files. To set these options, you now choose File, Setup; or press Shift+F1. Then choose Environment, Delimited Text Options.

To display the Setup dialog box, choose File, Setup; or press Shift+F1. If you choose File, Setup, WordPerfect displays the Setup cascading menu (see fig. 3.1).

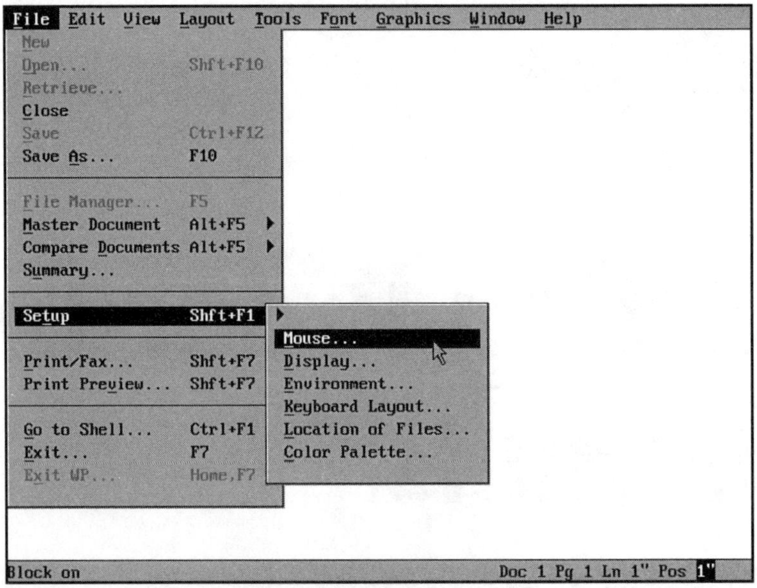

FIG. 3.1

The Setup
cascading menu.

In figure 3.1, notice the **C**olor Printing Palette item, which is new in WordPerfect 6 and is described later in this chapter. (Color printing isn't available in WordPerfect 5.1.)

To give another example, the Date Format options have been relocated to the Date Formats dialog box in WordPerfect 6 (see fig. 3.2). To change these options, you must now choose **T**ools, **D**ate, **F**ormat. The date format you select in the Date Formats dialog box becomes the default.

The following sections describe the options in the Setup dialog box. (Setup options that have been moved to their own dialog boxes are discussed in other chapters.)

Mouse

To change the way the mouse works, choose **F**ile, Setup; or press Shift+F1. Then choose **M**ouse. WordPerfect displays the Mouse dialog box. The options for setting up a mouse are exactly the same as in WordPerfect 5.1.

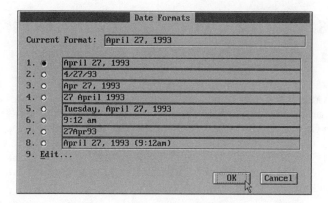

FIG. 3.2

The Date Formats
dialog box.

Display

Choosing File, Setup (Shift+F1), **D**isplay displays the Display dialog box.
Choosing **Gr**aphics Mode Screen Type/Colors displays the Graphics
Mode Screen Type/Colors dialog box (see fig. 3.3).

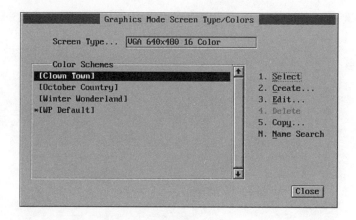

FIG. 3.3

The Graphics
Mode Screen
Type/Colors
dialog box.

Choosing a Screen Type

Choosing **S**creen Type in the Graphics Mode Screen Type/Colors dialog
box displays the Setup Graphics Screen Type dialog box. This dialog
box lists the screen types available for your graphics card and monitor.
To choose a screen type, double-click on the type, or select it with the
arrow keys and choose **S**elect to return to the Graphics Mode Screen
Type/Colors dialog box.

Choosing and Customizing a Graphics Mode Color Scheme

WordPerfect 6 comes with four, preconfigured, screen color schemes: October Country, Toon Town, Winter Wonderland, and WP Default. To select a color scheme, double-click on its name in the **Color** Schemes list in the Graphics Mode Screen Type/Colors dialog box. Using the keyboard, choose **Color** Schemes, highlight a scheme with the arrow keys, and choose **Select**. Click on Close to return to the document window. (Notice that WordPerfect doesn't change the color scheme until you're back in the document window.)

You can customize the supplied color schemes, or you can create new ones. Follow these steps to create a new color scheme:

1. Highlight a name in the Color Schemes list. (WordPerfect uses this color scheme as the default for further customizing.) Then choose **Create**. WordPerfect displays the Color Scheme dialog box.

2. Type a name for the color scheme and choose OK. WordPerfect displays the Edit Graphics Screen Colors dialog box (see fig. 3.4).

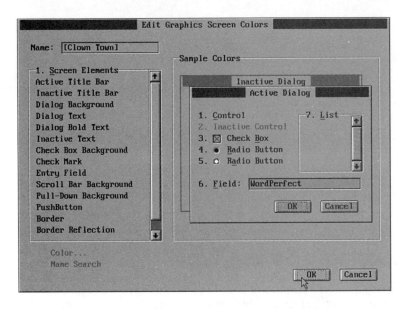

FIG. 3.4

The Edit Graphics Screen Colors dialog box.

In figure 3.4, notice that the name of the customized scheme is displayed in the Name text box.

3. In the **S**creen Elements list, choose a screen element to customize (for example, Active Title Bar). WordPerfect activates the **C**olor option at the bottom of the dialog box.

4. Choose **C**olor. WordPerfect displays the Colors dialog box.

5. To choose a color, double-click on it using the mouse, or highlight it with the arrow keys and then choose **S**elect.

   The Sample Colors area shows a sample dialog box labeled Active Dialog. This sample displays your color choice for Active Title Bar.

6. Repeat steps 3 through 5 to customize screen elements. When you're finished, choose OK to return to the Graphics Mode Screen Type/Colors dialog box.

To change a customized color scheme, highlight its name in the **C**olor Schemes list and choose **E**dit. Then follow the instructions in steps 3 through 5 on creating new color schemes.

To copy a color scheme (as a basis for a new, customized scheme), highlight the scheme's name in the **C**olor Schemes list; then choose Cop**y**. WordPerfect displays the Color Scheme dialog box. Next, type a name for the copy, make any desired changes, and choose OK. WordPerfect returns to the Graphics Mode Screen Type/Colors dialog box and inserts the name of the copy in the Color Schemes list.

To delete a color scheme, highlight its name and choose **D**elete, **Y**es. WordPerfect removes the color scheme's name from the Color Schemes list.

Choosing Text Mode Screen Type and Colors

The steps for choosing and customizing Text mode screen types and colors are exactly the same as for choosing Graphics mode screen types and colors, as described in the preceding section. However, because the WordPerfect screen looks very different in Text mode, the options in the Text Mode Screen Type/Colors and the Edit Text Screen Colors dialog boxes are somewhat different. For example, different color schemes are offered.

Also, the Sample Colors area in the Edit Text Screen Colors and Create Text Screen Colors dialog boxes shows Text mode options instead of dialog boxes (see fig. 3.5).

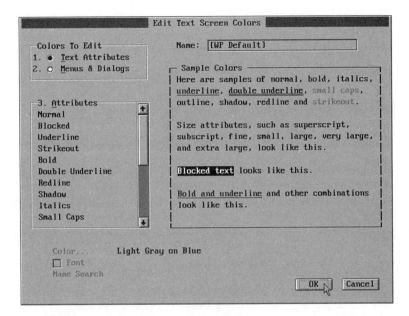

The Edit Text
Screen Colors
dialog box.

Environment

Choosing Setup (Shift+F1) and then choosing Environment displays the
Environment dialog box (see fig. 3.6).

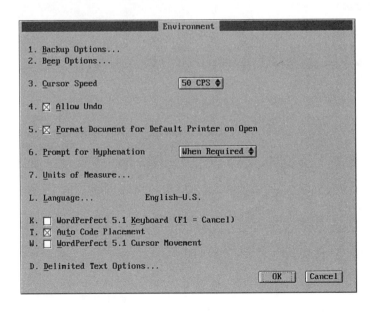

The Environment
dialog box.

Choosing **B**ackup Options or B**e**ep Options displays exactly the same options as in WordPerfect 5.1. In WordPerfect 6, however, these options are displayed in dialog boxes instead of menus.

Choosing **C**ursor Speed displays a pop-up list from which you can choose to set cursor speed to **N**ormal, **1**5 CPS, **2**0 CPS, **3**0 CPS, **4**0 CPS, or **5**0 CPS. (Normal is 10 CPS.)

The **A**llow Undo check box is new in WordPerfect 6 and enables or disables the Undo feature, which is described fully in Chapter 5.

The Format **R**etrieved Documents for Default Printer option is located on the Setup: Initial Settings menu in WordPerfect 5.1. This option works exactly the same as in the former version.

Choosing **P**rompt for Hyphenation displays the options **N**ever, **W**hen Required, and **A**lways. These options have also remained the same.

Choosing **U**nits of Measure displays the Units of Measure dialog box. Notice that in WordPerfect 6 you can set units of measure separately for the display and entry of numbers and for the status line display. Choosing **D**isplay/Entry of Numbers or **S**tatus Line Display reveals the units of measure list. Notice that the millimeters option is new in WordPerfect 6.

Choosing **L**anguage displays the Available Environmental Languages dialog box. If you have purchased and installed a foreign language module from WordPerfect Corporation, that language appears in the list box.

To use the U.S. version of WordPerfect 5.1 with a foreign language, you had to purchase and install hyphenation, thesaurus, and spelling dictionaries. To use the foreign dictionaries, you needed to insert a language code in each document, and to display WordPerfect 5.1 menus in a foreign language, you needed to purchase the separate foreign language version of the program.

Using foreign languages is much more convenient in WordPerfect 6. Installing a foreign language module translates all program menus and dialog boxes. (You must still purchase foreign language modules from WordPerfect Corporation.)

Choosing WordPerfect 5.1 **K**eyboard (F1 = Cancel) restores the WordPerfect 5.1 functions of the F1 (Cancel/Undelete), F3 (Help), and Escape (Repeat) keys. In WordPerfect 6, the meanings of these keys have changed: F1 (Help), F3 (Repeat), and Escape (Cancel/Undelete).

Choosing Auto Code Placement tells WordPerfect to automatically move to the top of the current page codes for headers/footers and other features that must be placed at the beginning of the page in order to take effect on that page. This option is especially useful for desktop publishing; you can use it when you're working in the middle of a page and want to quickly change the formatting without moving to the top of the page.

Choosing **W**ordPerfect 5.1 Cursor Movement restores the former operation of cursor-movement keystrokes that have changed in Word-Perfect 6.

Choosing **D**elimited Text Options displays the Setup Delimited Text Options dialog box. This dialog box enables you to set options for using delimited merge data files. These options were located on the Setup: Merge DOS Text File Options menu in WordPerfect 5.1.

The new options in the Setup Delimited Text Options dialog box solve certain problems that WordPerfect 5.1 users had when trying to merge with comma-delimited and other text files. For example, WordPerfect 5.1 would routinely confuse commas and double quotes used to enclose fields. Consequently, it would merge the data incorrectly. In WordPerfect 6, you use the **F**ield Delimiter and Field **E**ncapsulate Character to set these delimiters separately. The defaults are set for merging standard comma-delimited data files.

WordPerfect 6 can also strip unwanted characters from a data file during a merge. To specify the characters you want removed, type them in the **S**trip Characters text box.

With the cursor in a text box, choosing Codes (F5) lets you insert the **T**ab, **L**ine Feed, **F**orm Feed, and **C**arriage Return characters from a drop-down list. The **R**ecord Delimiter text box shows how WordPerfect formats the [CR] and [LF] characters for you. You must use the Codes feature to enter these characters; you cannot type them in a list box or press the Tab or Enter key to insert [TAB] and [CR] codes.

Keyboard Layout

Choosing **K**eyboard Layout in the Setup dialog box displays the Keyboard Layout dialog box (see fig. 3.7).

WordPerfect does not enable you to customize the default keyboard layout. If you choose [ORIGINAL], the following options aren't available: Edit, Delete, Copy, Rename, and Map.

The WordPerfect 6 Keyboard Layout feature contains subtle changes. For example, when you choose MACROS and then **E**dit, WordPerfect displays the Edit Keyboard dialog box (see fig. 3.8).

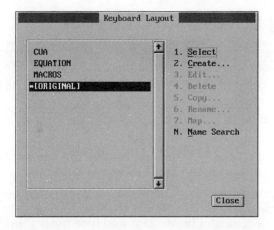

FIG. 3.7

The Keyboard Layout dialog box.

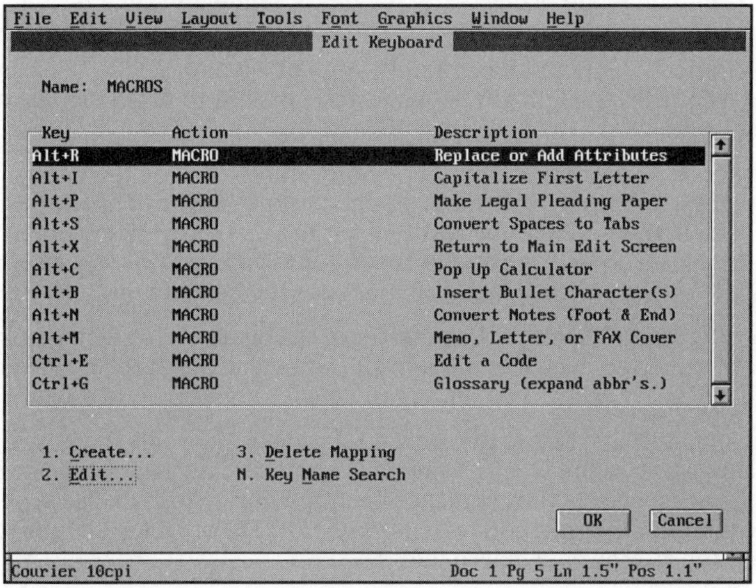

FIG. 3.8

The Edit Keyboard dialog box.

Notice that the following options from the WordPerfect 5.1 Keyboard Edit screen have moved: Action, Descrptn, Move, Macro Save, and Macro Retrieve. These options are now accessed by choosing **C**reate or by highlighting an existing key definition and choosing **E**dit in the Edit Keyboard dialog box.

Creating a Keyboard Layout

Choosing **C**reate displays the Create Key dialog box. When you press a key that you want to define (for example, Alt+F), WordPerfect inserts the key code at the **K**ey prompt and turns on the remaining dialog box options.

Choose **K**ey and press another key to change the key that you want to define.

Choose **D**escription and type the description that you want WordPerfect to display in the Edit Keyboard dialog box.

Choose an Action Type (**T**ext, **C**ommand, or **M**acro). Notice that the **T**ext action type is new in WordPerfect 6. You can now define keys that enter text in a document. Choose **T**ext and type the text in the box.

Choosing **C**ommand displays the Keyboard Commands dialog box.

The Keyboard Commands pop-up list includes special codes for WordPerfect functions (for example, AppendFilenameDlg). To learn what a code does, highlight its name and press F1 to display context-sensitive help.

To insert a code in the Action Type box, double-click on the code or highlight it and then press Enter or choose **S**elect. WordPerfect inserts the code in the Action Type text box in the Create Key dialog box. You can only insert one command in the Action Type text box. To assign multiple commands to a key, you must use the next action type, **M**acro.

Choosing **M**acro displays the Key Macro dialog box. This dialog box tells WordPerfect which macros to run when you press the newly defined key.

Choosing **R**etrieve Macro displays the Retrieve Macro dialog box. Type a macro name in the Macro Name text box. Pressing a macro Alt+key combination inserts the correct code in the box. (You can also type the Alt code.) Another method is to use File List (F5) or Quick List (F6) to locate the appropriate macro file.

Choosing **S**ave Macro displays the Save Macro to File dialog box. To save the current key macro to a file, type a file name and choose OK.

Choosing **E**dit/Create Macro displays the Macro Record window. For detailed instructions on editing macros, see Chapter 17. Edit the macro as needed and press F7 (Exit) to compile the macro and return to the Key Macro dialog box.

To assign an existing macro to the key, choose Macro File on **D**isk and type the macro's path and file name.

Editing a Keyboard Layout

To edit an existing keyboard layout, highlight its name in the Keyboard
Layout dialog box and choose Edit. The steps for editing a keyboard
layout are the same as for creating a layout. See the preceding section,
"Creating a Keyboard Layout."

Deleting, Copying, and Renaming
Keyboard Layouts

Highlighting the MACROS keyboard and then choosing the Delete option in the Keyboard Layout dialog box displays a Yes/No dialog box
with the following message: Delete MACROS.WPK? Choose Yes to proceed with the deletion, or choose No to cancel.

Highlighting a keyboard definition and choosing Copy displays the
Keyboard Name dialog box. Type a name for the copy and choose OK.
WordPerfect copies the keyboard definition and lists it in the Keyboard
Layout dialog box.

Highlighting a keyboard definition and choosing Rename displays the
Keyboard Name dialog box. Type a new name and choose OK.
WordPerfect renames the keyboard definition and lists the new name in
the Keyboard Layout dialog box.

Mapping a Keyboard Layout

Highlighting a keyboard definition in the Keyboard Layout dialog box
and choosing Map displays the Keyboard Map dialog box. Several options from the WordPerfect 5.1 Keyboard: Map menu are gone: Key,
Macro, Description, and Compose. These options are now accessed by
using the Create and Edit commands, which work as described in the
previous section "Creating a Keyboard Layout."

Except for these changes, the Keyboard Map dialog box works the
same as the Keyboard: Map menu in WordPerfect 5.1.

Location of Files

Choosing Setup (Shift+F1) and then choosing Location of Files displays
the Location of Files dialog box (see fig. 3.9).

```
╔══════════════════ Location of Files ══════════════════╗
║                                                        ║
║  1. Backup Files:              │C:\WP60              │ ║
║  2. Macros/Keyboards/Button Bar... │C:\WP60          │ ║
║  3. Writing Tools...           │C:\WPC60DOS          │ ║
║  4. Printer Files...           │C:\WPCDOS60          │ ║
║  5. Style Files...             │C:\WP60              │ ║
║                                                        ║
║  6. Graphics Files...          │C:\WP60              │ ║
║  7. Documents:                 │C:\WP60              │ ║
║  8. Spreadsheet Files...       │                     │ ║
║  9. QuickFinder Files...       │C:\WPDOCS; C:\WPDOCS │ ║
║                                                        ║
║  R. WP.DRS File and *.WFW Files: │C:\WPC60DOS        │ ║
║  F. Graphics Fonts Data Files...                       ║
║                                                        ║
║  ⊠ Update QuickList                                     ║
║                                                        ║
║  [Directory Tree... F8] [QuickList... F6]  [ OK ] [Cancel] ║
╚════════════════════════════════════════════════════════╝
```

FIG. 3.9

The Location of Files dialog box.

Notice in figure 3.9 that options 1 through 8 are the same as in Word-Perfect 5.1. However, all options except **B**ackup Files and **D**ocuments now lead to dialog boxes, and some choices have been renamed. The new names are as follows:

WordPerfect 5.1	WordPerfect 6
Keyboard/Macro Files	Macros/Keyboards/Button Bar
Thesaurus/Spell/Hyphenation	Writing Tools
Graphic Files	Graphics Files

Choosing **M**acros/Keyboards/Button Bar displays the Macros/Keyboards/Button Bar dialog box. WordPerfect 6 makes placing macros, keyboard layouts, Button Bar definitions, and styles on a network server or a local terminal easy. For example, when you set up styles, Button Bars, or printer definitions, you can save them on the network to make them available to all users, or save them on your own hard disk for personal use. Files located on the server are called *shared files*, and files saved locally are called *personal files*. To choose paths for these file types, choose **P**ersonal Path or **S**hared Path and type the corresponding path.

Choosing **W**riting Tools displays a dialog box with text boxes. You can use these text boxes to specify paths for main and supplementary dictionaries for the Speller, Thesaurus, and Grammatik programs.

Choosing **P**rinter Files displays a dialog box with text boxes for specifying personal and shared paths for printer files, as described above for choosing Macros/Keyboards/Button Bar personal and shared paths.

Choosing Style Files displays the Style Files dialog box. The Styles feature has been greatly expanded and revised in WordPerfect 6. The new Personal Library and Shared Library features are described fully in Chapter 7. Specifying the location of shared and personal style files is also discussed.

Choosing **G**raphics Files enables you to specify paths for personal and shared graphics files.

Choosing **D**ocuments moves the cursor to the text box where you can type a path name for document files. As in WordPerfect 5.1, WordPerfect 6 makes this directory the default directory when you run the program.

Choosing Spreadsheet Files enables you to choose directories for personal and shared spreadsheet files.

Choosing **Q**uickFinder Files enables you to choose personal and shared paths for Quick Finder files. Choosing Graphics **F**onts Data Files enables you to specify directories for fonts.

Choosing the new WP.D**R**S File option enables you to specify a location for device driver (WP.DRS).

Color Printing Palette

Color printing is new in WordPerfect 6. Choosing **C**olor Printing Palette displays the Color Printing Palettes dialog box (see fig. 3.10).

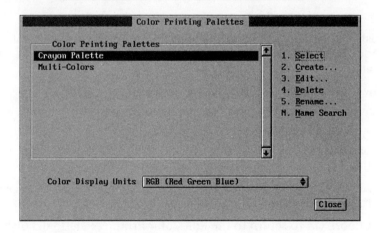

FIG. 3.10

The Color Printing Palettes dialog box.

You use the options on this dialog box to change the way WordPerfect works with a color printer.

Choosing, Creating, and Editing Color Printing Palettes

When you choose **Create**, WordPerfect prompts you for a name and inserts the name in the Color Printing Palettes list. You can then customize the name with the **Edit** function.

Highlighting a palette name in the Color Printing Palettes list and choosing **Edit** displays the Edit Color Printing Palette dialog box, shown in figure 3.11.

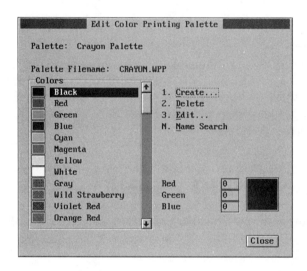

The Edit Color Printing Palette dialog box.

Choosing **Create** in the Edit Color Printing Palette dialog box displays the Add Color dialog box. This dialog box enables you to design a new, custom color to add to the Colors list (see fig. 3.12).

Follow these steps to create a custom color:

1. Type a name in the Color **N**ame text box.

2. Drag the color selection squares in the color wheel and the color bar to the appropriate area in order to choose a color and saturation.

   Alternatively, with the mouse or keyboard, adjust the settings in the **R**ed, **G**reen, and **B**lue text boxes.

3. Choose OK to return to the Edit Color Printing Palette dialog box.

To delete a color from the Colors list, choose **D**elete and then choose **Y**es to confirm the deletion.

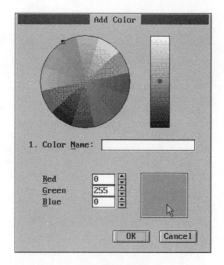

FIG. 3.12

The Add Color
dialog box.

Choosing a Color Display Type

Choosing Color Display **U**nits in the Color Printing Palettes dialog box
displays a pop-up list with three choices: **R**GB (Red Green Blue), **H**LS
(Hue Luminosity Saturation), and **C**MYK (Cyan Magenta Yellow Black).
These options tell WordPerfect how to display printed color on your
color monitor. Most monitors use the default option, **R**GB (Red Green
Blue). If your monitor doesn't display printed colors properly with this
option, consult the monitor documentation to find out which option
will work best for you.

P A R T

II

O U T L I N E

Formatting and Editing Tools

Formatting Documents

WordPerfect 5.1 users may expect to find lots of changes in formatting commands in WordPerfect 6. Formatting is, after all, one of the most basic, ordinary, word processing operations. You will, in fact, find dozens of improvements and additions, both large and small, in the new version. But the programmers have once again succeeded in adding new features without radically changing the way WordPerfect works.

Format versus Layout

In WordPerfect 6, you can still press Shift+F8 (Format) to display formatting options. When you do so, the Format dialog box appears, as shown in figure 4.1.

FIG. 4.1

The Format
dialog box.

Notice in figure 4.1 that the Line, Page, Document, and Other options
from Version 5.1 are still offered. Several frequently used features from
WordPerfect 5.1 now have their own menu options: Margins, Header/
Footer/Watermark, Date, and Character. (The Watermark feature is
entirely new and is discussed in detail at the end of this chapter.)

You can also select formatting options from the Layout menu (see figure 4.2).

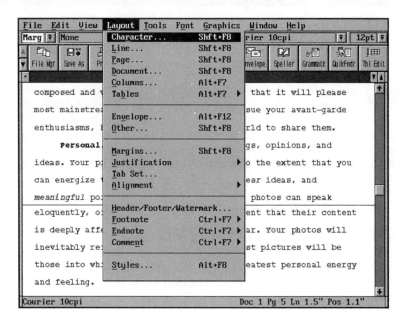

FIG. 4.2

The Layout menu.

Notice in figure 4.2 that the Layout menu includes options that are not
located on the Format (Shift+F8) menu in WordPerfect 5.1: Columns
(Alt+F7), Tables (Alt+F7), Footnote (Ctrl+F7), Endnote (Ctrl+F7), Comment (Ctrl+F7), and Styles (Alt+F8).

Notice also that you can still access these features by pressing their WordPerfect 5.1 function keys. Whether you use the Format dialog box (Shift+F8) or the Layout menu is entirely up to you. Throughout this book, command instructions refer to the pull-down menus, with function-key assignments in parentheses—for example: "Choose **Layout**, **P**age (Shift+F8)."

Some commands on the Layout menu have their own chapters in this book: Styles (Chapter 7), and Envelope (Chapter 8).

Character Formatting

To perform character formatting, choose **Layout**, **Ch**aracter. WordPerfect displays the Character Format dialog box, shown in figure 4.3.

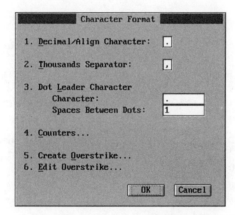

FIG. 4.3

The Character Format dialog box.

The next sections discuss the new and changed options in the order that they are listed in the dialog box.

Decimal/Align Character

This option hasn't changed. It was on the Format, Other menu in WordPerfect 5.1. To specify a decimal/align character, type it in the **D**ecimal/Align Character text box. (To create an aligned tab, you still press Ctrl+F6, as in WordPerfect 5.1.)

Thousands Separator

This option hasn't changed. It was on the Format, Other menu in WordPerfect 5.1. To specify a separator, type the separator character in the Thousands Separator text box.

Dot Leader Character

This option was on the Format, Line, Tab Set menu in WordPerfect 5.1. The new Spaces Between Dots parameter lets you vary the amount of space that WordPerfect inserts between dot leader characters. To specify a dot leader character, type the character in the Character text box. To change the spacing between dot leader characters, type a number in the Spaces Between Dots text box.

Counters

This is a new name for the graphics box numbering options in WordPerfect 5.1, which are listed on the graphics box options menus. (These menus are displayed by pressing Alt+F9, choosing a box type, and choosing Options.) WordPerfect 6 graphics features are discussed in detail in Chapter 12.

You can still change the Counters (box numbering) options by pressing the WordPerfect 5.1 Graphics key (Alt+F9) and choosing Numbering in the Graphics dialog box. See Chapter 12 for details.

Create Overstrike

This option hasn't changed in WordPerfect 6, but it's become a bit easier to use, thanks to dialog boxes. Overstrike is assigned to the Format: Other menu in WordPerfect 5.1.

Choosing Layout, Character, Create Overstrike is different from choosing Font, Strikeout. Strikeout places a dashed line through struck-out letters. With Overstrike, you can customize the overprinted characters, as described earlier. Also, Strikeout is shown in Graphics mode and struck-out characters are highlighted in Text mode. To view the effects of Overstrike, you must use Print Preview.

Choosing Create Overstrike displays the Create Overstrike dialog box. Follow these steps to create overstrike character(s):

1. To assign character attributes (bold, underline, and so on), before typing anything in the Overstrike Characters text box, choose Attributes (Ctrl+F8) to display the Overstrike Attributes dialog box.

   Any attributes you choose are assigned to the overstrike text you type in the Create Overstrike dialog box. You must first choose Attributes (F8) before typing the overstrike characters, because the attribute codes must be placed to the left of the overstrike characters.

2. Type the desired character(s) in the Overstrike Characters text box, then choose OK to return to the document window.

Edit Overstrike

This option takes you to the Edit Overstrike dialog box where you can make changes to an existing overstrike character. This dialog box is exactly the same as the Create Overstrike dialog box, described in the previous section.

Line Formatting

To change line formatting, choose Layout, Line. You can still use the WordPerfect 5.1 command Shift+F8, Line. WordPerfect displays the Line Format dialog box (see fig. 4.4).

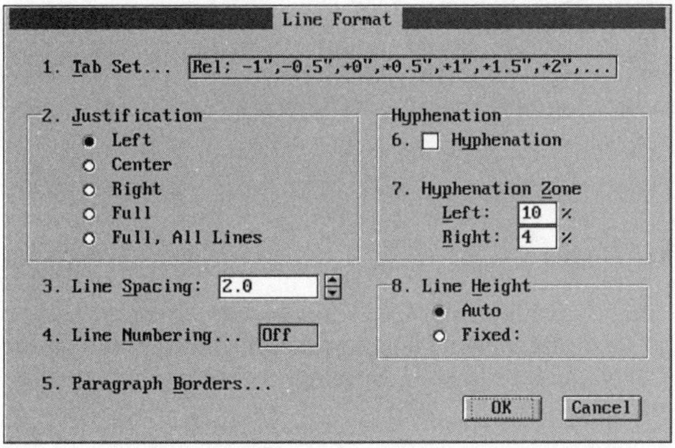

FIG. 4.4

The Line Format dialog box.

The Line Format dialog box contains the options described in the following text.

Tab Set

Choosing **T**ab Set displays the Tab Set dialog box (see fig. 4.5).

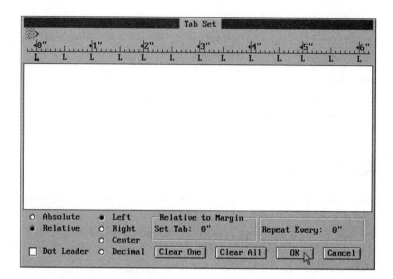

FIG. 4.5

The Tab Set
dialog box.

The basic method of setting tabs is the same as in WordPerfect 5.1, except that you use buttons, check boxes, and radio buttons, as shown in figure 4.5.

In WordPerfect 6, you can set tabs with the mouse. Click the tab ruler where you want to create a tab stop. Then click the radio button for the tab type (Left, Right, Center, Decimal).

You can only set tabs with the mouse at 1/8-inch intervals. To set tabs more precisely, type exact tab positions by using the Set Tab box. Notice that your changes are immediately reflected in Tab Set dialog box document window.

Justification

Notice the new Justification option in the Line Format dialog box: Full, All Lines (refer to fig. 4.4). Choosing this option justifies all lines in a document or in selected text, including short last lines in paragraphs.

The Full, All Lines justification option is useful for creating "designed" special effects with type, by forcing justification of a few words across a long line to add extra space between the letters. It's much quicker than adjusting the letter spacing with the Word/Letter Spacing command, which is discussed later in this chapter. To apply this effect, first make sure that the line you want to "stretch" is left-justified. Then select the text. Next, press Shift+F8 (Format) and choose Line, Justification, Full, All Lines, and choose OK, Close to return to your document. Word-Perfect justifies the line, as shown in figure 4.6.

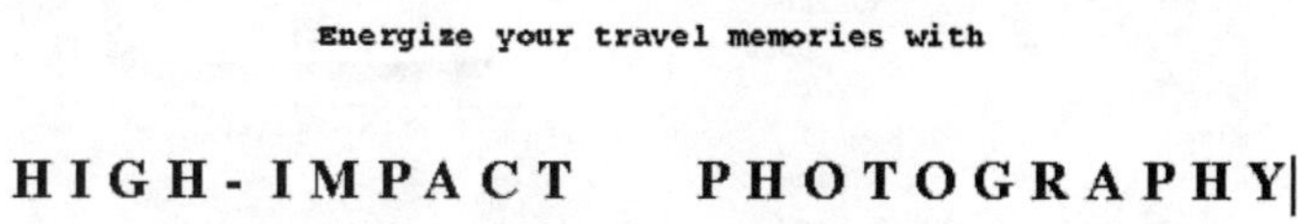

Energize your travel memories with

HIGH-IMPACT   PHOTOGRAPHY|

FIG. 4.6

A line of text formatted with Full, All Lines justification.

Paragraph Borders

The remaining Line Format options work the same as in the WordPerfect 5.1 Format: Line menu, except for Paragraph Borders, which is new to WordPerfect 6. WordPerfect can now automatically place borders around the paragraph that contains the cursor.

Choosing Paragraph Borders displays the Create Paragraph Border dialog box.

Choosing Border Style displays the Border Styles dialog box. To choose one of listed styles, double-click it or highlight it and choose Select. The other options in this dialog box pertain to styles and are discussed in detail in Chapter 7.

Choosing Fill Style from the Create Paragraph Border dialog box displays the Fill Styles dialog box. To choose a fill style from the list, double-click the style or highlight it and choose Select. You can create and edit your own fill styles. The options available on this dialog box are discussed detail in Chapters 7 and 12.

Choosing Customize in the Paragraph Border dialog box displays the Customize Paragraph Border dialog box (see fig. 4.7).

Choosing Based on Border Style displays the Border Styles dialog box, mentioned earlier.

Lines

Choosing Lines from the Customize Paragraph Border dialog box displays the Border Line Styles dialog box. The options in this dialog box are the same as the Border Line Style options in WordPerfect 5.1, except for Select All and Separator Line, which are new.

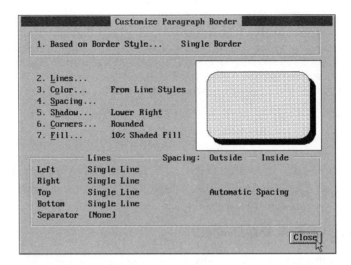

FIG. 4.7

The Customize
Paragraph
Border dialog
box.

Select **A**ll takes you to the Line Styles dialog box, which is the same as
the Border Line Styles dialog box. Selecting a line style from the list and
choosing **S**elect returns you to the Border Line Styles dialog box, with
the selected line style assigned to all four sides of the box and the separator line.

Choosing **L**eft Line, **R**ight Line, **T**op Line, **B**ottom Line, or **S**eparator
Line also takes you to the Line Styles dialog box. From here, you can
choose a line style from the list box, then choose **S**elect to return to the
Border Line Styles dialog box.

Choosing **S**eparator Line opens the Line Styles dialog box. Using styles
is discussed in detail in Chapter 7.

Color

Choosing C**o**lor at the Customize Paragraph Border dialog box displays
the Border Line Color dialog box.

Choosing **U**se Color From Each Line Style assigns to each line the
color assigned to that line's style. (Styles are discussed in detail in
Chapter 7.)

Choosing **C**hoose One Color For All Lines lets you assign a separate
color to each line, overriding any color setting associated with the
line's style. Choosing this option displays the Color Selection dialog
box.

Choose a color from the Palette Colors list. You can customize the color with the Shade option. Choosing Custom Color displays the Custom Color dialog box. To create a new color, click in the color wheel and shading rectangle.

Choose Add to Palette to insert the color in the Palette list box in the Color Selection dialog box. Then type a name for the customized color in the Color Name text box.

Use the Red, Green, and Blue arrows to fine-tune a customized color. Click the up and down arrows to change red, green, or blue color numbers, then click the number to view the results in the example window.

After customizing lines, your changes are shown in the Lines section of the Customize Paragraph Border dialog box.

Spacing

Choosing Spacing at the Customize Paragraph Border dialog box displays the Border Spacing dialog box.

Choosing Automatic Spacing uses default 0.125-inch spacing for Outside Spacing (between box borders and adjacent text) and Inside Spacing (between box borders and enclosed text).

Deselecting Automatic Spacing and choosing Outside, Set All or Inside, Set All lets you enter precise measurements in the Outside Spacing and Inside Spacing boxes.

Shadow

Choosing Shadow in the Customize Paragraph Border dialog box displays the Shadow dialog box. A shadow gives a box a three-dimensional effect. Choose Shadow Type and a radio button to create a shadow. Notice that each radio button creates a shadow on two sides of the box. For example, Lower Right places a shadow along the right and bottom edges of the box.

Choosing Shadow Color displays the Color Selection dialog box, discussed earlier. Choose Shadow Width and type a number in the box to customize the thickness of the shadow. When you exit the Shadow dialog box, your changes are shown in the example box in the Customize Paragraph Border dialog box.

Corners

Choosing **C**orners in the Customize Paragraph Border dialog box displays the Border Corners dialog box. Choose **S**quare or **R**ounded to change the corner style. If you choose **R**ounded, you can customize the corners by typing a number in the Corner Radius box. Larger numbers create more rounded corners.

Fill

Choosing **F**ill from the Customize Paragraph Border dialog box displays the Fill Style and Color dialog box. Choosing Fill St**y**le displays the Fill Styles dialog box, discussed earlier. Choosing Foreground **C**olor or Background Co**l**or takes you to the Color Selection dialog box, discussed earlier. After choosing a fill style and foreground and background colors, your changes are reflected in the example windows in the Fill Style and Color dialog box.

Page Formatting

Choosing **L**ayout, **P**age displays the Page Format dialog box, shown in figure 4.8.

```
┌──────────────────────── Page Format ────────────────────────┐
│                                                              │
│   1. Page Numbering...  [None                             ]  │
│                                                              │
│  ┌─Center Page (Top to Bottom)─┐ ┌─F. Force Page──────────┐  │
│   2. ☐ Center Current Page         ○ Odd      ○ New         │
│   3. ☐ Center Pages                ○ Even     ● None        │
│                                                              │
│  ┌─Paper Sizes─────────────────────────────────────────┐    │
│   4. Paper Size/Type... [Letter (Portrait)           ]     │
│   5. Labels...          [                            ]     │
│   6. Subdivide Page...  [                            ]     │
│   7. Envelope...                                           │
│                                                              │
│   8. Double-sided Printing [None      ⬍]                   │
│   9. Suppress... (Page Numbering, Headers, etc.)          │
│   D. Delay Codes...                                        │
│   B. Page Borders...                                       │
│                                      [  OK  ]  [Cancel]    │
└──────────────────────────────────────────────────────────────┘
```

FIG. 4.8

The Page Format dialog box.

Most Page Format options work as they do in WordPerfect 5.1. The following paragraphs explain some minor differences and new features.

Page Numbering

Choosing Page Numbering displays the Page Numbering dialog box
(see fig. 4.9).

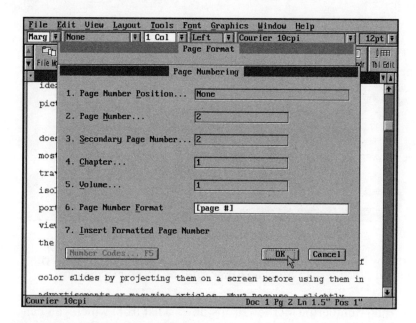

FIG. 4.9

The Page
Numbering
dialog box.

Page Number Position

Choosing Page Number Position displays the Page Number Position
dialog box. Notice that the options are the same as in WordPerfect 5.1
except for Font/Attribute/Color, which lets you choose a font and character attributes for page numbers. (In WordPerfect 5.1, you format page
numbers by applying font and character attributes directly to the ^B
page numbering code.) Choosing Font/Attribute/Color displays the
Font dialog box, where you can choose a font and apply attributes. The
Font dialog box is discussed in detail in Chapter 11.

Page Number

Returning to the Page Numbering dialog box and choosing the Page
Number option displays the Set Page Number dialog box (see fig. 4.10).

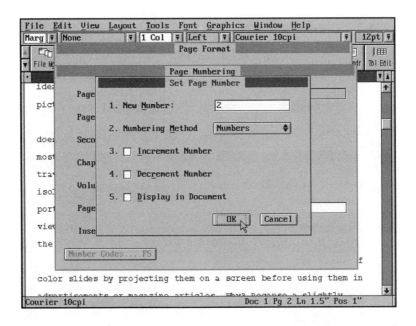

FIG. 4.10

The Set Page
Number dialog
box.

The New **N**umber option is located on the Format: Page Numbering
menu in WordPerfect 5.1. The other options listed are new in
WordPerfect 6.

Choosing Numbering **M**ethod drops down a list from which you can
choose **N**umbers, Lower **L**etters, Upper **L**etters, Lower **R**oman, or
Upper **R**oman. (The default is **N**umbers.)

Choosing **I**ncrement Number (the default) prints page numbers in ascending order. Choosing De**c**rement Number prints page numbers in
descending order.

Choosing **D**isplay in Document tells WordPerfect to display page numbers in the document screen. With this check box deselected, page
numbers aren't invisible in the editing screen.

Secondary Page Number

Returning to the Page Numbering dialog box and choosing **S**econdary
Page Number displays the Set Secondary Page Number dialog box,
which is exactly the same as the Set Page Number dialog box shown in
figure 4.10. If you specify a secondary page number, WordPerfect uses
that number as the first page number for page numbers you have inserted elsewhere on the page.

Chapter

Choosing Chapter from the Page Numbering dialog box displays the Set Chapter Number dialog box, which has exactly the same options as the Set Page Number dialog box, shown in figure 4.10. When you create a chapter number, WordPerfect inserts a chapter number code. This capability allows you to number pages in the format "Chapter 3, Page 2" with the Master Document feature. Master documents are discussed in detail in Chapter 9.

Volume

Choosing Volume displays the Set Volume Number dialog box, which has exactly the same options as the Set Page Number dialog box, shown in figure 4.10. When you create a volume number, WordPerfect inserts a volume number code. This capability allows you to number pages in the format "Volume 4, Chapter 3, Page 2" with the Master Document feature. Master documents are discussed in detail in Chapter 9.

Page Number Format

Choosing Page Number Format from the Page Numbering dialog box moves the cursor into the Page Number Format text box, which already includes the [page #] code. For example, you can format page numbers by typing introductory text and then inserting the page number code: type **Page No. [page #]** to print pages numbers in the format "Page No. 143."

Insert Formatted Page Number

Choose Insert Formatted Page Number when you want to insert a page number at the cursor position on the current page only. WordPerfect returns to the editing screen and inserts a page number formatted as specified with Page Number Format.

Number Codes

The Number Codes button displays the following options: **P**age Number, **S**econdary Page Number, **C**hapter Number, and **V**olume Number. Choose an option to insert the corresponding code in the Page Number Format box.

Center Page

The Center Page (Top to Bottom) option in the Page Format dialog box has changed slightly. You can now choose Center Current Page, the WordPerfect 5.1 default, or Center Pages to center all pages from the cursor forward.

Force Page

The Force Page area in the Page Format dialog box has two new options in WordPerfect 6: New and None. Choosing New works the same as inserting a hard page break, but prevents a soft page break just before the new page from inserting a blank page. Choosing None cancels the Force Page feature from the current page forward, or until you select the Force Page command again.

Paper Size/Type

Choosing Paper Size/Type in the Page Format dialog box displays the Paper Size/Type dialog box. This dialog box offers the same options as the Format: Paper Size/Type menu in WordPerfect 5.1. The only differences are that the names of the currently selected printer and .PRS printer file are displayed in the upper left corner; and the large letter A in the example box at lower left visually shows the landscape or portrait orientation of the selected paper type.

Labels, Subdivide Page, and Envelope

The Labels, Subdivide Page, and Envelope options in the Page Format dialog box are discussed in detail in Chapter 8.

Double-Sided Printing

Choosing Double-Sided Printing from the Page Format dialog box drops down a list of three options: None, Long Edge, and Short Edge. Choose Long Edge if you bind the document on the long edge of the page, or choose Short Edge if you bind the short edge of the paper.

Suppress

Choosing Suppress from the Page Format dialog box displays the Suppress (This Page Only) dialog box, which has exactly the same options as the Format: Suppress (this page only) menu in WordPerfect 5.1, with the exception of Watermark A and Watermark B. The Watermark feature is discussed at the end of this chapter.

Delay Codes

Choosing Delay Codes from the Page Format dialog box displays the Delay Codes dialog box, which has a single text box labeled Number of Pages to Delay Codes. The Delay Codes option, new in WordPerfect 6, lets you insert page formatting codes and then tell WordPerfect to ignore them for a specified number of pages. This capability is useful when you want to keep all formatting codes at the top of a document, but don't want them to take effect right away.

Page Borders

Creating lines around page borders in WordPerfect 5.1 is a tricky, time-consuming procedure. The Page Borders feature makes it much simpler. Choosing Page Borders from the Page Format dialog box displays the Create Page Border dialog box.

Choosing Border Style in the Create Page Border dialog box displays the Border Styles dialog box, discussed earlier. Choosing Fill Style displays the Fill Styles dialog box, discussed earlier. Choosing Customize displays the Customize Page Border dialog box, which is the same as the Customize Paragraph Border dialog box, discussed earlier.

Formatting Documents

Choosing Layout, Document displays the Document Format dialog box, shown in figure 4.11.

The WordPerfect 6 Document Format options will be familiar to WordPerfect 5.1 users, and are discussed in the following sections.

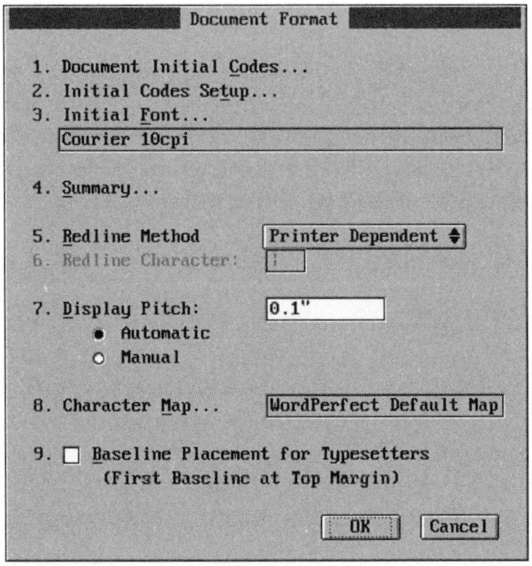

FIG. 4.11

The Document
Format dialog
box.

Document Initial Codes

Choosing Document Initial Codes from the Document Format dialog
box displays the Initial Codes dialog box, which works exactly the same
as the Initial Codes screen in WordPerfect 5.1, accessed with Format
(Shift+F8), Document, Initial Codes.

Initial Codes Setup

Choosing Initial Codes Setup from the Document Format dialog box
displays the same Initial Codes screen as choosing Setup (Shift+F1),
Initial Settings, Initial Codes in WordPerfect 5.1. Being able to change
document and default initial codes from the Document Format dialog
box is a convenience, reflecting the WordPerfect 6 programmers' atten-
tion to detail.

Initial Font

Choosing Initial Font from the Document Format dialog box displays
the Initial Font dialog box. The Initial Font dialog box includes the

printer and document base font options that were inconveniently located on the separate Select Printer: Initial Font and Document: Initial Font menus in WordPerfect 5.1.

Choosing **F**ont or **S**ize drops down lists from which you can choose an initial font and font size for the currently selected printer named at the top of the dialog box.

Choosing **C**urrent Document Only applies your font and size choices only to the on-screen document.

Choosing All **N**ew Documents makes your choices the default for all new documents in the future.

Summary

Choosing **S**ummary from the Document Format dialog box displays the Document Summary dialog box. Document Summaries are discussed in detail in Chapter 9.

Redline Method

Choosing **R**edline Method from the Document Format dialog box drops down a list from which you can choose **P**rinter Dependent, **L**eft, Alternating, or **R**ight. These options are on the Setup: Print Options menu in WordPerfect 5.1. Notice that the **R**ight option is new.

Display Pitch

The **D**isplay Pitch options in the Document Format dialog box are exactly the same as in WordPerfect 5.1, located on the Format: Document menu.

Character Map

Choosing Character **M**ap from the Document Format dialog box displays the Character Map dialog box, from which you can choose a WordPerfect character mapping. Character maps change the operation of the keyboard for typing in a foreign language. Separate character maps become available when you purchase and install a foreign language module.

Baseline Placement for Typesetters

The **B**aseline Placement for Typesetters option in the Document Format dialog box is exactly the same as in WordPerfect 5.1, located on the Format: Printer Functions menu.

Formatting Columns

The process of setting up newspaper and parallel columns is the same as in WordPerfect 5.1, except that three extremely useful new options have been added to the Text Columns feature: Balanced Newspaper, Line Spacing Between Rows, and Column Borders.

Choosing **L**ayout, **C**olumns displays the Text columns dialog box, shown in figure 4.12.

```
┌──────────────── Text Columns ────────────────┐
│                                               │
│  1. Column Type                               │
│       ● Newspaper                             │
│       ○ Balanced Newspaper                    │
│       ○ Parallel                              │
│       ○ Parallel with Block Protect           │
│                                               │
│  2. Number of Columns:          [2  ]         │
│                                               │
│  3. Distance Between Columns:   [0.5"]        │
│                                               │
│  4. Line Spacing Between Rows:  [1.0 ]        │
│                                               │
│  5. Column Borders...                         │
│                                               │
│  [Off]  [Custom Widths...]  [ OK ]  [Cancel]  │
└───────────────────────────────────────────────┘
```

FIG. 4.12

The Text Columns dialog box.

All of the options work the same as in WordPerfect 5.1 except for Newspaper, Balanced Newspaper, Line Spacing Between Rows, and Column Borders. The following sections describe the differences.

Balanced Newspaper

Choosing Balanced Newspaper tells WordPerfect to create columns of equal length on pages where the text does not fill the page.

Line Spacing Between Rows

Choosing Line Spacing Between Rows lets you set the amount of space WordPerfect automatically inserts between Parallel columns.

Column Borders

Choosing Column Borders displays the Create Column Border dialog box. The options in this dialog box work exactly the same as the options in the Paragraph Column Border dialog box, discussed earlier. The only difference is that if you choose Border Style, the Border Styles list contains two column-specific styles: Column Border (Between Only) and Column Border (Outside and Between).

Column Border (Between Only) draws a line between columns, and Column Border (Outside and Between) draws a line around each column.

Newspaper

Newspaper columns work a bit differently than they did in WordPerfect 5.1. First of all, columns are displayed in the editing screen side by side, by default. There is no longer an option to display columns vertically.

Also, pressing Ctrl+Enter after the last column at the right side of the page doesn't move the insertion point to the next page, as in WordPerfect 5.1; instead, it moves the insertion point down two lines and begins another row of columns. To begin a new page, you must first turn columns off: press Alt+F7 and choose Columns, Off, then press Ctrl+Enter (Hard Page).

Custom Widths

Choosing the Custom Widths button in the Text Columns dialog box displays the Text Columns dialog box, where you can adjust the width and spacing of columns individually and create borders for individual columns.

Formatting Tables, Envelopes, and Dates

Envelopes and Tables are discussed in detail in Chapter 8 and Chapter 15.

To insert the current date and time in a document, choose **L**ayout, **D**ate, and choose **T**ext, **C**ode, or **F**ormat.

Choosing **T**ext or **C**ode works exactly as in WordPerfect 5.1.

Choosing **F**ormat displays the Date Formats dialog box, which offers the same options as the Date Format and Setup: Initial Settings, Date Format menus in WordPerfect 5.1. However, the process of choosing a date format is easier in WordPerfect 6.

To select one of the standard formats, choose its radio button.

Follow these steps to customize a format:

1. Select the format's button and choose **E**dit. The Edit Date Format dialog box appears.

2. To insert a format from the Date Codes or Time Codes list boxes, double-click the desired format. With the keyboard, press F5 or Shift+F5, highlight a format, and press Enter.

Notice that the Date Preview box reflects your choices.

Other Formatting Options

Choosing **L**ayout, **O**ther displays the Other Format dialog box, shown in figure 4.13.

This dialog box serves the same purpose as the Format: Other menu in WordPerfect 5.1; it's a catch-all for functions that don't logically belong in any other formatting dialog box.

Block Protect

Block Protect works the same as in WordPerfect 5.1, by highlighting a block and pressing Shift+F8.

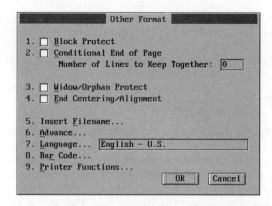

FIG. 4.13

The Other Format
dialog box.

In WordPerfect 6, you can protect a block by highlighting it and pressing Shift+F8 and choosing **O**ther, **B**lock Protect, OK.

Conditional End of Page

Conditional End of Page works the same as in WordPerfect 5.1, located on the Format: Other menu.

Widow/Orphan Protect

Widow/Orphan Protect works as in WordPerfect 5.1, located on the Format: Line menu.

End Centering/Alignment

End Centering/Alignment is new in WordPerfect 6. Choose this option when you want to type text that begins at the center of a line and extends to the right. First, choose **L**ayout, **L**ine, **J**ustification, **C**enter, OK. Then choose **L**ayout, **O**ther, End Centering/Alignment, OK and begin typing. The text begins at the center of the line and extends to the right.

Insert Filename

Insert Filename inserts a [Filename] code that prints the filename. This feature is new in WordPerfect 6.

If you have not yet saved a new on-screen document, no filename is displayed. After you save the file, the uppercased filename appears on-screen.

Advance

Advance has changed. Choosing **A**dvance displays the Advance dialog box. When you choose a radio button in the Horizontal or Vertical Position sections of the Advance dialog box, WordPerfect displays a text box where you can type the amount of the desired advance. WordPerfect 6 lets you enter both horizontal and vertical advance specifications without exiting the dialog box. This capability makes using Advance more convenient than in WordPerfect 5.1, where you had to create separate Advance codes to create the same effect.

Language

The Language feature has changed in WordPerfect 6; it is located on the Format: Other menu in WordPerfect 5.1. Choosing **L**anguage displays the Select Language dialog box, where you can choose a language from a list.

In order to choose a foreign language, you must first purchase a language module from WordPerfect Corporation. Foreign language modules include dictionaries, as in WordPerfect 5.1, but WordPerfect 6 language modules also convert program menus and dialog boxes to the foreign language.

To select a language that isn't listed, choose Other Language Code and type the code in the box. Language codes are supplied when you buy a language module from WordPerfect Corporation.

Bar Code

Choosing Ba**r** Code displays the POSTNET Bar Code dialog box. When you type a valid 9- or 11-digit ZIP code in the text box and press Enter, WordPerfect inserts the corresponding POSTNET bar code in the document screen. This function is useful with the labels feature, discussed in detail in Chapter 8.

Printer Functions

Choosing **P**rinter Functions displays the Printer Functions dialog box. This dialog box contains the same options as the WordPerfect 5.1 Format: Printer Functions menu, except for **B**inding Offset, located on the Setup: Print Options and Print menus in WordPerfect 5.1. The Binding Offset feature works as in WordPerfect 5.1.

Note that the **L**eading Adjustment feature now combines the WordPerfect 5.1 Primary [SRt] and Secondary [HRt] options. Typing an adjustment amount in the **L**eading Adjustment box adjusts both of these measurements in WordPerfect 6.

Formatting Margins

Choosing **L**ayout, **M**argins displays the Margin Format dialog box, shown in figure 4.14.

```
                    Margin Format
   ┌─Document Margins──────────────────────────┐
   │  1. Left Margin:              1"           │
   │  2. Right Margin:             1"           │
   │                                            │
   │  3. Top Margin:               1"           │
   │  4. Bottom Margin:            1"           │
   └────────────────────────────────────────────┘
   ┌─Paragraph Margins─────────────────────────┐
   │  5. Left Margin Adjustment:   0"           │
   │  6. Right Margin Adjustment:  0"           │
   │                                            │
   │  7. First Line Indent:        0"           │
   │  8. Paragraph Spacing:        1.0    ▲▼    │
   └────────────────────────────────────────────┘
                      OK      Cancel
```

FIG. 4.14

The Margin Format dialog box.

Notice that the Document Margins section includes line and page margin options, located separately on the Format: Line and Format: Page menus in WordPerfect 5.1.

The Paragraph Margins options in the Margin Format dialog box are new in WordPerfect 6. The following sections describe their uses.

Left and Right Margin Adjustment

Choosing Left Margin Adjustment and Right Margin Adjustment text boxes enable you to create precise margin indentations for selected paragraphs. If a paragraph isn't selected, these feature set margins from the cursor forward.

First Line Indent and Hanging Indent

To have WordPerfect automatically indent the first line of each paragraph in a selected text (or from the cursor forward), type a number greater than 0" in the First Line Indent box.

T I P   To create a hanging indent (where the first line of a paragraph extends into the left margin), type a negative number in the First Line Indent box.

Paragraph Spacing

WordPerfect 6 can automatically insert extra space when you press Enter at the end of a paragraph. You can apply this feature to selected text or from the cursor forward.

To specify the extra space you want to insert between paragraphs, choose Paragraph Spacing and type a number greater than 1.0 in the box. To decrease the space between paragraphs, type a number less than 1.0.

Justification

Choosing Layout, Justification displays a submenu with the following options: Left, Center, Right, Full, and Full, All Lines.

These options are the same as the justification options on the WordPerfect 5.1 Format: Line menu, except for Full, All Lines.

Choose Full, **A**ll Lines to justify all lines in a document, including short last lines at the end of paragraphs. This is a useful way to create a "designed" effect for display type, forcing justification of one or a few words across a line in order to spread the letters. It's much quicker than adjusting letter spacing with the Word/Letterspacing option in the Printer Functions dialog box.

Tabs

To set tabs, choose **L**ayout, **T**ab Set. WordPerfect displays the Tab Set dialog box, discussed earlier.

Alignment

Choosing **L**ayout, **A**lignment displays a secondary menu.

The following options work the same as in WordPerfect 5.1: **I**ndent (F4), **In**dent (Shift+F4), **B**ack Tab (Shift+Tab), **C**enter (Shift+F6), **F**lush Right (Alt+F6), **D**ecimal Tab (Ctrl+F6), and Hard **P**age (Ctrl+Enter).

Hanging Indent creates a 1-inch hanging indent for the current paragraph, beginning with the line that contains the cursor.

Headers, Footers, and Watermarks

You set up headers and footers in WordPerfect 6 essentially the same as in WordPerfect 5.1, except that WordPerfect 6 uses dialog boxes instead of menus.

The related Watermark feature is entirely new. A *watermark* is text or a graphics image printed as a light gray image over any other text and graphics on a page. You can use a watermark to print a company logo over the text of a price sheet, for example.

Creating Headers and Footers

Follow these steps to create a header in WordPerfect 6:

1. Choose **Layout**, **Header/Footer/Watermark**.

   WordPerfect displays the Header/Footer/Watermark dialog box, shown in figure 4.15.

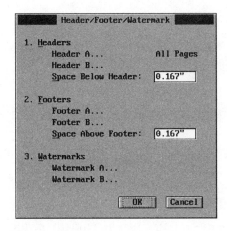

2. Choose **Headers**, then choosing Header **A**.

   WordPerfect displays the Header A dialog box. Notice that the header positioning options are the same as in WordPerfect 5.1.

3. Choose a header position, then choose **Create**.

   The header editing window appears, which in WordPerfect 6 looks the same as the document window, except that the status line displays the message Header A: Press Exit (F7) when done.

4. As in WordPerfect 5.1, type the header text, then press F7 or click on F7 in the status bar.

This action returns you to the Header/Footer/Watermark dialog box, where you can choose **Headers** again and select the **Space Below Header** option, which is new in WordPerfect 6. To add space below a header in WordPerfect 5.1, you press Enter to add lines or insert an Advance Down code at the end of the header text. The **Space Below Header** option makes it easier. Just type a number in the text box.

The process of creating footers is exactly the same as for creating headers, except that you choose a Footer A or Footer B in the Header/Footer/Watermark dialog box (refer to fig. 4.15).

Creating Watermarks

A watermark is a lightly shaded image printed on a page. When you create a watermark, WordPerfect overprints the watermark with the body text on the page.

Follow these steps to create a watermark:

1. Choose **Layout**, **Header/Footer/Watermark**, **Watermark**, then choose Watermark **A**.

   WordPerfect displays the Watermark A dialog box, which is exactly the same as the Header A dialog box, except for the box title.

2. Choose **Create**.

   WordPerfect displays the Watermark A editing screen, which in WordPerfect 6 looks exactly the same as the document window, except that the status line displays the message Watermark A.

3. Create the watermark.

   You can create watermarks with text or graphic images. In the Watermark A editing screen, position the text and/or image(s) where you want them to appear on the page. Using graphic images is discussed in Chapter 12.

4. When you're finished, press Exit (F7) to leave the Watermark A editing screen.

Other Layout Options

The **Footnote**, **Endnote**, and **Comment** options are discussed fully in Chapter 13. The **Styles** options are discussed in Chapter 7.

Editing Text

This chapter describes changes in the ways you can move, copy, and reference text in WordPerfect 6. You can still use the familiar WordPerfect function-key commands to access commands carried over from WordPerfect 5.1. Many of the options on the **E**dit menu work the same as in WordPerfect 5.1, but the WordPerfect 6 text-editing options include lots of improvements and new features, such as Undelete, Bookmark, and Hypertext.

Drag and Drop

WordPerfect 6 adds new mouse commands to speed text editing. To select text, drag the mouse pointer over the desired text, as in Word-Perfect 5.1. To move the highlighted block, click anywhere in the block and drag the text to a new location. Notice that as you drag with the mouse, the text cursor shows the position where the text will be drop-ped. To copy the highlighted block, hold down the Ctrl key when you release the mouse button. To leave the block selected after moving or copying it, hold down Ctrl and Alt while you release the mouse button.

Undo

Undo works a little differently than the WordPerfect 5.1 Restore com-mand. Choosing Edit, Undo (Ctrl+Z) reverses your most recent editing commands. If you type several words and want to delete them, you can press Ctrl+Z once instead of pressing Ctrl+Backspace several times. WordPerfect restores all the text you typed back to the last point where you used Backspace, Del, or one of the word-deletion functions.

To restore deleted text, choose **E**dit, **U**ndo or press Ctrl+Z. WordPerfect restores the text all the way back to the point where you began deleting. Undo restores deleted text whether you delete forward or backward, unlike WordPerfect 5.1 Undelete function, which can only restore text deleted forward.

Undo works only to one level of deleted text. Choosing **E**dit, **U**ndo (Ctrl+F5) twice cancels Undo and deletes the restored text again.

Undelete

Choosing **E**dit, **U**ndelete or pressing Esc displays the Undelete dialog box. Remember that in WordPerfect 6, F1 is the Help key and Esc is the Undelete key. To restore the WordPerfect 5.1 meanings of these keys, choose **F**ile, **S**etup (Shift+F1), **E**nvironment, and mark the **W**ordPerfect 5.1 Cursor Movement check box.

Undelete works just as in WordPerfect 5.1. To restore the deleted text, choose **R**estore. To view two levels of prior deletions, choose **P**revious, then choose **P**revious again.

Block Commands

Choosing **E**dit, **C**ut and Pas**t**e or pressing Ctrl+Del with a block of text highlighted deletes the highlighted text and stores it in a temporary area of memory called the Clipboard.

The deleted text remains intact in the Clipboard while you continue to edit and use Backspace and Del keys or Cu**t**, **C**opy, **P**aste, and **A**ppend functions from the **E**dit menu. Cut, Copy, Paste, and Append use an area of memory separate from the Clipboard.

To insert the text from the Clipboard, position the cursor where you want the insertion and choose **E**dit, **P**aste (Ctrl+V). WordPerfect inserts the text from the Clipboard.

Edit, **C**opy and Paste (Ctrl+Ins) works the same as Cut and Paste, except that the selected text is copied to the Clipboard, and the original text remains intact.

Move

You can select text in WordPerfect 6 by highlighting it with the mouse or with the Block (Alt+F4 or F12) or Move (Ctrl+F4) keys, just as in WordPerfect 5.1.

Pressing Ctrl+F4 (Move) displays the Move dialog box, which offers most of the same options as the Move menu in WordPerfect 5.1 (although the commands work a little differently). Notice also the new command: Delete and Append (see fig. 5.1).

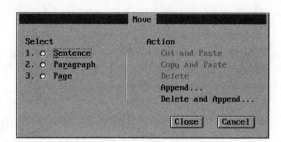

The Move dialog box.

When you choose Sentence, Paragraph, or Page, WordPerfect highlights the corresponding text and returns to the Move dialog box with the Action commands activated.

You can now choose an action command. If you choose Append or Delete and Append, the Append To dialog box appears.

Type the name of a file that you want to append the selected text to, then choose OK. WordPerfect appends the text to the named file and returns to the editing screen. If you choose Delete and Append, the selected text is deleted.

Move Block

If you select a block of text and then press Ctrl+F4 (Move), WordPerfect displays the Move Block dialog box, shown in figure 5.2.

Notice again that the options are the same as in the WordPerfect 5.1 Move menu, except that the Block Copy and Block Move commands are now called Cut and Paste and Copy and Paste. Notice the new command, Delete and Append, described in the preceding section.

Notice that Move isn't included on the Edit menu, and can only be activated by pressing Ctrl+F4.

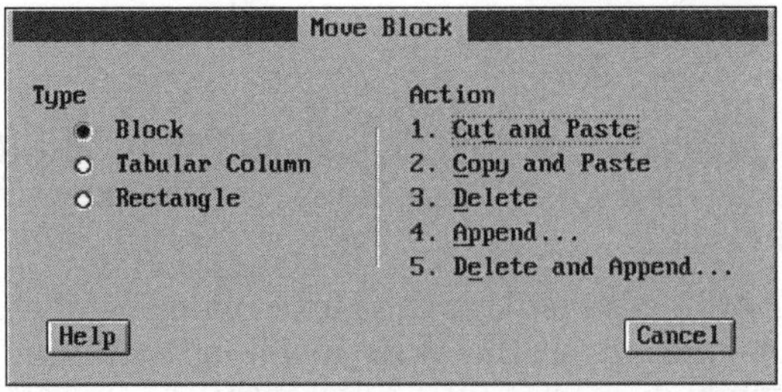

FIG. 5.2

The Move Block
dialog box.

Append

Choosing **Edit**, **A**ppend with a block of text selected displays a pull-
down menu with two options: To **F**ile and To **C**lipboard. Choosing To
File displays the Append To dialog box.

The **E**dit, **A**ppend, To **C**lipboard command is useful for "gathering"
blocks of text and inserting them at the same location in a file.

Choosing **E**dit, **B**lock or pressing F12 or Alt+F4 turns on the Block
function, which works exactly as in WordPerfect 5.1.

Select

Choosing **E**dit, **S**elect displays a secondary menu with the following
options: **S**entence, **P**aragraph, P**a**ge, **T**abular Column, and **R**ectangle.
Sentence, **P**aragraph, and P**a**ge work the same as the WordPerfect 5.1
Move command (Ctrl+F4). **T**abular Column highlights the tabular column containing the cursor, and **R**ectangle lets you highlight a rectangle
with the mouse or cursor movement keys.

Selecting Text with the Mouse

In WordPerfect 6, you can select text with the mouse. To select a word,
click the word once. To select a sentence, click the sentence three
times. To select a paragraph, click the paragraph four times.

Convert Case

The Convert Case command works the same as the Case Conversion command (Shift+F3) in WordPerfect 5.1, but has a new option: Initial caps, which capitalizes the first letters in all the words in the selected text.

Search

The Search command works essentially the same as in WordPerfect 5.1 but includes improved search options. Choosing Edit, Search (F2) displays the Search dialog box, shown in figure 5.3.

Notice that the WordPerfect 5.1 Backward Search, Case Sensitive Search, Find Whole Words Only, and Extended Search options have been conveniently assigned to a single dialog box in WordPerfect 6.

Choosing the Codes button or pressing F5 with the cursor in the Search For text box displays the Search Codes dialog box, shown in figure 5.4.

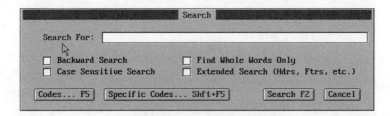

FIG. 5.3

The Search dialog box.

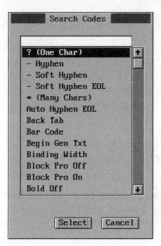

FIG. 5.4

The Search Codes dialog box.

To move quickly to a code in the list, press the first letter of its name, then use the arrow keys to highlight the code. Press Enter or double-click the code to insert it in the Search For text box.

Choosing Specific Codes or pressing Shift+F5 displays the Specific Codes dialog box, which works the same as the Search Codes dialog box shown in figure 5.4, except that it lists codes that require an argument. For example, choosing the [Bot Mar] code displays the Bottom Margin Search dialog box.

To enter an argument, type a number in the Search For text box and choose OK. WordPerfect inserts the code and its argument in the Search For text box: [Bot Mar:1"], for example.

Replace

Choosing Edit, Replace (Alt+F2) displays the Search and Replace dialog box, shown in figure 5.5.

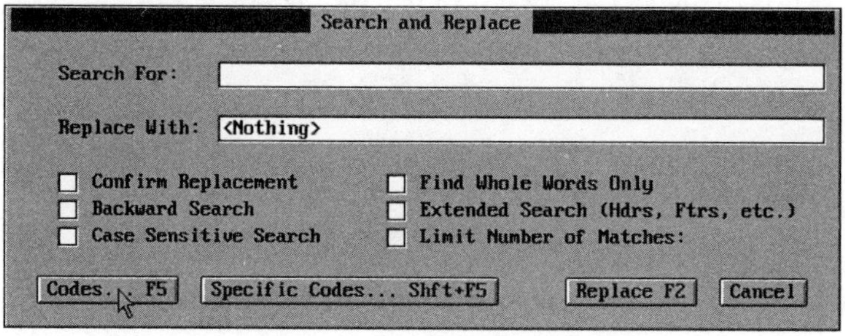

FIG. 5.5

The Search and Replace dialog box.

Notice the new Replace options in WordPerfect 6. They are the following:

- Choosing Find **W**hole Words Only tells WordPerfect to replace the search string only if it is a whole word and not contained within another word. For example, searching for *and* with Find **W**hole Words prevents replacement of the letters *and* in *sand, ampersand*, and *androgynous*.

- Choosing **L**imit Number of Matches displays a text box where you can enter the number of times you want WordPerfect to perform the replacement.

- The Codes and Specific Codes commands work the same as for Search, and are described earlier in the section titled "Search."

Bookmarks

The Bookmark feature places a hidden [Bookmark:] code in your document. You can then jump instantly to the bookmark code from anywhere in the document. This capability is very useful when you need to jump between several locations in one or more documents.

Choosing **E**dit, Boo**k**mark displays the Bookmark dialog box, shown in figure 5.6. Notice the Set **Q**uickMark (Ctrl+Q) and **F**ind QuickMark (Ctrl+F) buttons. These options are discussed in the following section.

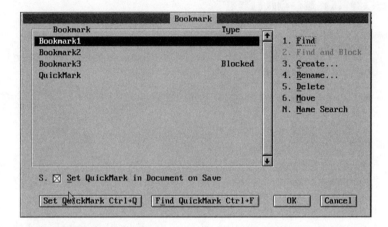

FIG. 5.6

The Bookmark dialog box.

Using QuickMark

You can use the QuickMark feature to quickly create a bookmark without using the Bookmark dialog box. In the document screen, press Ctrl+Q. (Or choose **E**dit, Boo**k**mark, Set **Q**uickMark.)

WordPerfect inserts a [Bookmark:QuickMark] code. You can now return instantly to the location of the QuickMark code from anywhere in the document by pressing Ctrl+F. (Or choose **E**dit, Boo**k**mark, **F**ind QuickMark.)

You can only create one QuickMark in a document, but you can create as many bookmarks in a document as you like. To learn how to create bookmarks, see the next section.

Setting a QuickMark Automatically on Save

Choosing **S**et QuickMark in Document on Save tells WordPerfect to insert a QuickMark at the cursor location when you save the on-screen document. To return to where you were working when you last saved the document, press Ctrl+F.

Creating Bookmarks

Follow these steps to create a bookmark:

1. Choose **E**dit, Bookmark, **C**reate. WordPerfect displays the Create Bookmark dialog box.

   Notice that WordPerfect automatically inserts the first 38 letters to the right of the cursor in the Bookmark Name text box. If there is no text to the right of the cursor, the BookMark Name text box remains empty.

2. Press Enter to accept the text in the Bookmark Name box, or type another name in the box. If you name the bookmark "Bookmark1," WordPerfect returns to the document and inserts a `[Bookmark:Bookmark1]` code.

3. To jump to a named bookmark, choose **E**dit, Bookmark and double-click the bookmark's name, or highlight the bookmark name and choose **F**ind.

WordPerfect returns to the document with the cursor positioned to the right of the bookmark code.

To mark selected text as a bookmark, follow these steps:

1. Highlight the text and choose **E**dit, Bookmark, **C**reate.

2. Type a name for the bookmark and press Enter.

WordPerfect displays `Blocked` in the Type column of the Bookmark list box. If you highlight a Blocked bookmark in the Bookmark list box, then choose Find and **B**lock, WordPerfect returns to the editing screen and finds and selects the bookmarked text. This capability is useful when you need to repeatedly copy and move text from several locations in a document. Choosing **M**ove in the Bookmark dialog box moves the high-lighted bookmark to the current cursor location in the document.

Hypertext

Hypertext is similar to Bookmark, but it's much more powerful. Hypertext inserts "buttons" in your document that, when clicked with the mouse, move instantly to a location you have linked with the hypertext button.

Hypertext buttons provide an excellent way to organize information in long documents. You can even create hypertext buttons that "jump" to other documents.

You can create hypertext buttons to run macros—for example, a button in a letterhead form that, when clicked, runs a macro that copies the name and address, opens a new document window, retrieves an invoice form, inserts the name and address, and moves the cursor to the invoice data area.

Setting Up a Hypertext Link

Choosing Tools, Hypertext displays the Hypertext dialog box, shown in figure 5.7.

Choosing Create Link displays the Create Hypertext Link dialog box, shown in figure 5.8.

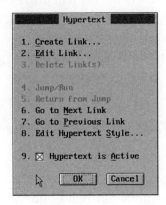

```
         Hypertext
  1.  Create Link...
  2.  Edit Link...
  3.  Delete Link(s)

  4.  Jump/Run
  5.  Return from Jump
  6.  Go to Next Link
  7.  Go to Previous Link
  8.  Edit Hypertext Style...

  9.  ⊠ Hypertext is Active

  ⩡      OK    Cancel
```

FIG. 5.7

The Hypertext dialog box.

```
┌─────────────────────────────────────────────────────────┐
│████████████████ Create Hypertext Link ████████████████  │
│ ┌─Hypertext Action──────────────────────────────────┐   │
│ │ 1. ● Go to Bookmark:        [_____]     │   │
│ │ 2. ○ Go to Other Document:  [_____]     │   │
│ │             Bookmark:       [_____]     │   │
│ │ 3. ○ Run Macro:             [_____]     │   │
│ └───────────────────────────────────────────────────┘   │
│ ┌─Hypertext Appearance──────────────────────────────┐   │
│ │ 4. ● Highlighted Text                              │   │
│ │ 5. ○ Button (Graphic)                              │   │
│ └───────────────────────────────────────────────────┘   │
│ [List Bookmarks... F5]              [  OK  ] [Cancel]    │
└─────────────────────────────────────────────────────────┘
```

FIG. 5.8

The Create
Hypertext Link
dialog box.

Creating a Simple Hypertext Button

Follow these steps to create a simple hypertext button that moves the
cursor to an existing bookmark:

1. Choose Tools, **H**ypertext to display the Hypertext dialog box.

2. Choose **C**reate Link to display the Create Hypertext Link dialog
   box.

3. Choose Go to **B**ookmark and type the bookmark's name.

4. If you cannot remember the names of all the bookmarks you have
   created, choose List Bookmarks or press F5.

5. Highlight a bookmark in the list and press Enter to insert the
   name in the Go to **B**ookmark text box.

6. Choose a Hypertext Appearance option.

For an explanation of the Hypertext Appearance options, see the next
section.

Choosing Hypertext Button Appearance Options

Notice in figure 5.8 that the Hypertext Appearance options let you create two button styles: **H**ighlighted Text or **B**utton (Graphic). Choosing
Highlighted Text with a block of text highlighted in your document
boldfaces and underlines the text and makes it a hypertext button (see
fig. 5.9).

If you choose **B**utton (Graphic), WordPerfect creates a graphic
hypertext button. You can then use graphics editing features to position, resize, and place text in the button. Graphics are discussed fully in
Chapter 12.

```
isolate the main subject from the background. (When taking
portrait pictures, don't crop closer than a head-and-shoulders
view, because eThis is a hypertext button.treme closeups of the
human face tend to repel the viewer.)
```

FIG. 5.9

A Highlighted
Text hypertext
button.

Turning On Hypertext

Choosing Hypertext is Active in the Hypertext dialog box turns on the
Hypertext feature. Choose Tools, Hypertext, and choose Hypertext is
Active or click the check box.

With the check box deselected, you can treat graphic hypertext buttons as graphic images. You can relocate buttons by dragging them
with the mouse.

With Hypertext is Active turned off, clicking a button once displays
graphic image handles you can drag with the mouse to resize the button. Double-clicking a graphic button opens the Edit Graphics Box dialog box, where you can change the size and position of the button and
create text to be displayed in the button. The WordPerfect 6 Graphics
features are discussed in Chapter 12.

Creating a Hypertext Button That Jumps to Another Document

Follow these steps to create a hypertext button that jumps to a bookmark located in another document:

1. Choose Tools, Hypertext to display the Hypertext dialog box.

2. Choose Create Link to display the Create Hypertext Link dialog
   box.

3. Choose Go to Other Document and type the document path and
   name in the text box.

4. Press Enter or Tab to move to the Bookmark box, then type the
   name of the bookmark located in the other document. Notice that
   List Bookmarks (F5) cannot list bookmarks located in other
   documents.

5. Choose a Hypertext Appearance option.

The Hypertext Appearance options are explained in the section "Choosing Hypertext Button Appearance Options," earlier in this chapter.

Creating a Hypertext Button That Runs a Macro

Follow these steps to create a hypertext button that runs a macro:

1. Choose Tools, Hypertext to display the Hypertext dialog box.

2. Choose Create Link to display the Create Hypertext Link dialog box.

3. Choose Run Macro and type the macro's name in the text box. Notice that with Run Macro selected, the List Bookmarks box becomes List Macros.

4. Choose List Macros or press F5 to display a list of macros.

5. Highlight a macro name and press Enter to insert its name in the text box.

6. Choose a Hypertext Appearance option.

The Hypertext Appearance options are explained in the section "Choosing Hypertext Button Appearance Options," earlier in this chapter.

Editing and Deleting Hypertext Links

Follow these steps to edit an existing hypertext link:

1. Choose Tools, Hypertext to display the Hypertext dialog box.

2. Choose Edit Link to display the Edit Hypertext Link dialog box.

WordPerfect displays the Edit Hypertext Link dialog box, which is exactly the same as the Create Hypertext Link dialog box, discussed earlier.

Follow these steps to delete a hypertext link:

1. Choose Tools, Hypertext to display the Hypertext dialog box.

2. Choose Delete Link to display the Delete Hypertext Link dialog box.

The Delete Hypertext Link dialog box is exactly the same as the Create Hypertext Link dialog box, discussed earlier.

Performing a Hypertext Jump

The quickest way to run a hypertext button is to click it with the mouse. In order for a hypertext button to work, the Hypertext is Active option in the Hypertext dialog box must be turned on. To turn on this option, choose Tools, Hypertext, Hypertext is Active, OK.

You can also perform a hypertext jump with the keyboard. Follow these steps:

1. Move the cursor to the first character of a text hypertext button, or to the immediate left of a graphics hypertext button.

2. Choose Tools, Hypertext to display the Hypertext dialog box.

3. Make sure that the Hypertext is Active check box is selected.

4. Choose Tools, Hypertext, Jump/Run.

WordPerfect returns to the document window and performs the hypertext jump.

Returning from a Hypertext Jump

You can "jump backwards" through any number of your most recent hypertext jumps. After performing one or more hypertext jumps, choose Tools, Hypertext, Return from Jump.

WordPerfect returns to the previous cursor position before your most recent hypertext jump. When you reach the cursor position where you make your first hypertext jump, WordPerfect removes the underlining from the R in Return from Jump in the Hypertext dialog box, and the command becomes unavailable.

Moving to the Next and Previous Hypertext Buttons

WordPerfect can take you to the next and previous hypertext buttons after and before the current cursor position. Choosing Tools, Hypertext, Go to Next takes you to the next hypertext button in the document after the cursor. Choosing Tools, Hypertext, Go to Previous moves the cursor to the previous hypertext button above the cursor.

Editing a Hypertext Style

When you create a text hypertext button with text selected, Word-Perfect boldfaces and underlines the selected text and marks it as a hypertext button. This process is described earlier in the section "Choosing Hypertext Button Appearance Options."

You can change the boldface and underline enhancements WordPerfect uses to format text hypertext buttons. Follow these steps:

1. Choose **Tools**, **Hypertext**, Edit Hypertext **S**tyle. WordPerfect displays the Hypertext Style dialog box.

2. Use function keys or the menu bar to change the appearance of Hypertext buttons.

3. Press F7 (Exit) to accept the new style and return to the Hypertext dialog box.

You can, for example, choose 24-point Times Roman Bold Italic for hypertext buttons. When you create a text hypertext button, WordPerfect formats the button's text with the new hypertext style.

Using the Speller, Thesaurus, and Grammatik

WordPerfect 6 not only provides many improvements to the Speller and Thesaurus but also adds an important writing tool: Grammatik. This powerful new module can check your documents for common grammar errors and readability.

Speller

The WordPerfect 6 spell checker enables you to create document-specific dictionaries and to check spelling from the cursor forward. These and many other improvements add convenience and efficiency to an already powerful feature.

98

Checking Spelling

To check spelling, follow these steps:

1. Choose **T**ools, **W**riting Tools, and **S**peller; or press Ctrl+F2.

    WordPerfect displays the Speller dialog box (see fig. 6.1).

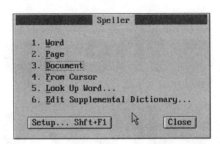

FIG. 6.1

The Speller
dialog box.

Notice one of two new options, **F**rom Cursor. WordPerfect 5.1 could check only the entire document. WordPerfect 6 checks the entire document by default, but **F**rom Cursor checks from the cursor forward.

The other new option, **E**dit Supplemental Dictionary, is described in the section "Creating and Editing Supplemental Dictionaries" later in this chapter.

2. Choose an option from the Speller dialog box.

3. When the Speller finishes checking, press Enter to return to the document window.

The following Speller options are available:

■ *Word.* If the word is misspelled, WordPerfect displays the Word Not Found dialog box (see fig. 6.2).

If the word is spelled correctly, WordPerfect returns to the Speller dialog box.

Notice in figure 6.2 that the options in the Word Not Found dialog box are the same as in WordPerfect 5.1, except that you can choose options with mnemonic keys as well as numbers in WordPerfect 6.

■ *Page.* This option checks the current page, as in WordPerfect 5.1, and displays the Word Not Found dialog box when a misspelled word is encountered.

■ *Document.* This option starts a spell-check from the top of the document.

Unlike WordPerfect 5.1, WordPerfect 6 checks case as well as spelling. When the program finds a word that it thinks should or should not be capitalized, the Capitalization Difference dialog box is displayed.

Choose **D**isable Case Checking to turn off this feature for the rest of the spell-check session. The remaining options are the same as for WordPerfect 5.1's number checking.

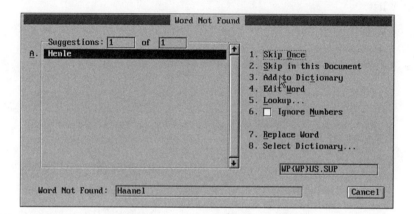

FIG. 6.2

The Word Not Found dialog box.

Counting Words

Notice in figure 6.1 that the word count option is no longer part of the speller. To count words, choose **T**ools, **W**riting Tools, **D**ocument Information. WordPerfect analyzes your document and displays the Document Information box (see fig. 6.3).

Creating and Editing Supplemental Dictionaries

To create or edit a supplemental dictionary, follow these steps:

1. Choose **T**ools, **W**riting Tools, **S**peller, **E**dit Supplemental Dictionary; or press Ctrl+F2 and choose **E**dit Supplemental Dictionary.

WordPerfect displays the Edit Supplemental Dictionary dialog box. In WordPerfect 6, you can create a document-specific supplemental dictionary.

2. To create a document-specific dictionary, highlight Document Specific and choose Create New Sup. Then type a name for the new dictionary and choose OK.

   To edit an existing dictionary, highlight its name and choose Edit.

   WordPerfect displays the Edit Supplemental Dictionary dialog box, with words you have already entered displayed in the Word list.

3. Edit the list and choose Close to return to the Speller dialog box.

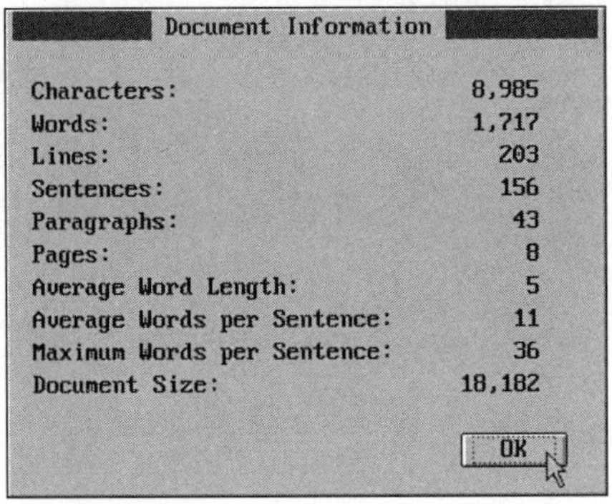

FIG. 6.3

The Document Information dialog box.

```
┌─────────── Document Information ───────────┐
│                                            │
│   Characters:                    8,985     │
│   Words:                         1,717     │
│   Lines:                           203     │
│   Sentences:                       156     │
│   Paragraphs:                       43     │
│   Pages:                             8     │
│   Average Word Length:               5     │
│   Average Words per Sentence:       11     │
│   Maximum Words per Sentence:       36     │
│   Document Size:                18,182     │
│                                            │
│                          [   OK   ]        │
└────────────────────────────────────────────┘
```

The Edit Supplemental Dictionary dialog box offers the following options:

- *Edit.* This option displays the highlighted word. Edit the word and choose OK.

- *Add.* This option displays a dialog box with these choices:

Word/Phrase to **S**kip	Type a word that WordPerfect should automatically skip during a spell-check. Then choose OK.
Word/Phrase with **R**eplacement	Type a word that WordPerfect should automatically replace during a spell-check. Then press Tab, type the replacement word, and choose OK.

| Word/Phrase with Alternates | Type a word for which WordPerfect should display alternatives during a spell-check. Press Tab and type alternative words, pressing Enter after each; then choose OK. |

■ *Delete.* Highlight a word and choose **Delete** to remove it from the list.

Customizing the Speller

WordPerfect 6 includes several new Speller setup options. To use these options, follow these steps:

1. Choose **Tools, Writing** Tools, **S**peller, Setup (Shift+F1).

   WordPerfect displays the Speller Setup dialog box, as shown in figure 6.4.

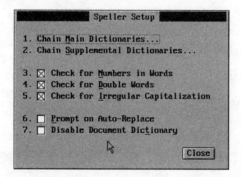

FIG. 6.4

The Speller Setup dialog box.

2. Choose options and then choose Close to return to the Speller dialog box.

WordPerfect provides these Speller Setup options:

■ *Chain Main Dictionaries.* This option displays a list of additional dictionaries that WordPerfect should use during a spell-check. You can purchase foreign language dictionaries from WordPerfect Corporation. Specialized legal and medical dictionaries are sold by other vendors. (Call WordPerfect Corporation for information.) Choose a dictionary and choose **A**dd Chain, Close.

- *Chain Supplemental Dictionaries.* This option works the same as Chain **Main** Dictionaries, except that supplemental dictionaries are listed instead of main dictionaries.

- *Check for Numbers in Words.* This option turns number checking on or off permanently. In WordPerfect 5.1, you can turn off number checking for only the current spell-check session.

- *Check for Double Words.* This option turns double-word checking on or off permanently. In WordPerfect 5.1, you cannot turn off double-word checking.

- *Check for Irregular Capitalization.* This option turns case checking on or off permanently. In WordPerfect 5.1, you can turn off case checking for only the current spell-check session.

- *Prompt on Auto-Replace.* You can enter in a supplemental dictionary any words that WordPerfect should automatically replace during a spell-check. (See the section "Creating and Editing Supplemental Dictionaries" earlier in this chapter.) **Prompt on Auto-Replace** tells WordPerfect whether to replace such words without prompting or whether to let you accept or cancel individual replacements.

- *Disable Document Dictionary.* WordPerfect 6 enables you to create document-specific supplemental Speller dictionaries. (See the earlier section "Creating and Editing Supplemental Dictionaries.") Disable Document Dictionary tells WordPerfect to ignore the document-specific dictionary for the on-screen document until you cancel this option.

Using WordPerfect 5.1 Supplemental Dictionaries

You can use supplemental dictionaries that you've created with WordPerfect 5.1. Follow these steps:

1. Choose **Tools**, **Writing Tools**; or press Alt+F1. Then choose **Speller**, **Edit Supplemental Dictionary**, **Create New Sup**.

2. At the Filename prompt, type the name of the existing WordPerfect 5.1 supplemental dictionary, then choose OK, Close, Close to return to the document screen.

WordPerfect adds the supplemental dictionary and makes it available for spell-checking in WordPerfect 6.

Thesaurus

With minor exceptions, the Thesaurus works the same in WordPerfect 6 and WordPerfect 5.1. To find synonyms, follow these steps:

1. Place the cursor on a word and choose **T**ools, **W**riting Tools (Alt+F1), **T**hesaurus.

   WordPerfect displays the Thesaurus dialog box (see fig. 6.5). Notice that synonyms are not wrapped to the next box to the right, as in WordPerfect 5.1. You must scroll down to view synonyms that don't fit in the box.

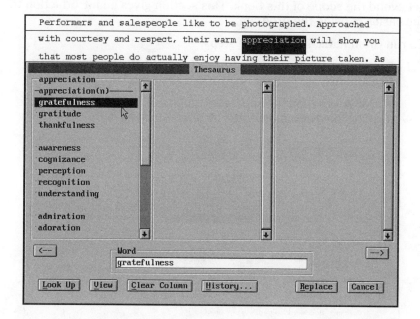

FIG. 6.5

The Thesaurus dialog box.

2. Highlight a synonym and choose **R**eplace, or choose Cancel to return to the document without replacing.

The following options are in the Thesaurus dialog box:

- *Look Up.* This option works the same as in WordPerfect 5.1, where it was called Look Up Word.

- *View.* This option works the same as in WordPerfect 5.1, where it was called View Doc.

- *Clear Column.* This option works the same as in WordPerfect 5.1.

■ *History.* This option, new in WordPerfect 6, displays a list of words you've looked up during the current Thesaurus session. To redisplay synonyms for a word on the list, highlight the word and choose Select. WordPerfect returns to the Thesaurus dialog box and displays the synonyms.

Grammatik

Grammatik is a powerful tool for checking grammar and readability. Because of Grammatik's extensive features, a complete description of it is beyond the scope of this book. This section gives an introduction to the basics of using the program.

To run Grammatik, follow these steps:

1. From an open document, choose **Tools**, **Writing Tools** (Alt+F1), **Grammatik**.

   WordPerfect runs the separate Grammatik program module and displays the Grammatik opening menu (see fig. 6.6).

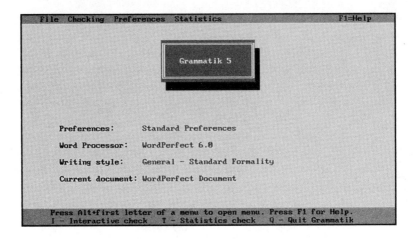

FIG. 6.6

The Grammatik opening menu.

2. Choose I - Interactive Check to run a full grammar check on the document.

   Or choose T - Statistics Check to display a readability summary for the document.

3. When you finish with Grammatik, choose Q - Quit Grammatik from the opening menu.

The following sections briefly describe the Interactive Check and Statistics Check options for checking grammar and readability.

Checking Grammar Interactively

Follow these steps to check grammar interactively:

1. Choose I - Interactive Check from the Grammatik opening menu.

   Grammatik begins checking the current document. When it finds the first problem in grammar or readability, Grammatik pauses and waits for you to edit or ignore the error (see fig. 6.7).

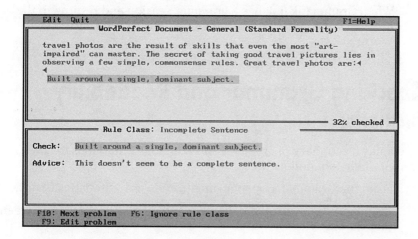

   FIG. 6.7

   The Grammatik grammar-checking screen.

   Don't be surprised if Grammatik identifies problems that aren't really problems at all. For example, it may stop at a name and an address or tell you that paragraphs should contain more than one sentence. When identifying possible writing errors, Grammatik assumes that too much caution is better than too little. You can tell Grammatik to ignore certain types of errors. For instance, Grammatik checks spelling as well as grammar and readability, but you can turn off spell-checking. Customizing Grammatik is beyond the scope of this book. For instructions, refer to the WordPerfect *User's Guide*.

2. Choose one of the following options when Grammatik finds an error:

   F10: Next Problem   This tells Grammatik to skip the current error and go to the next problem.

F9: Edit Problem	This moves you into the document, where you can edit the text. Press Esc to leave the editing window and check your changes for grammar and readability.
F6: Ignore Rule Class	This tells Grammatik to stop checking this type of problem for the rest of the current session.
F5: Ignore Phrase	This tells Grammatik to ignore phrases that use the same wording as the current problem.

3. When Grammatik finishes a grammar session and returns to the opening menu, choose Q - Quit Grammatik to return to WordPerfect.

Checking Grammar and Readability Statistics

To display a summary of grammar and readability statistics for the current document, follow these steps:

1. From the Grammatik opening menu, choose T - Statistics Check.

   Grammatik analyzes the document and displays a statistics screen (see fig. 6.8).

```
                                                    <F1: Help>

    Statistics for C:\WP60\WP)WPC{.GMK

  ┌ Readability Statistics ──────────────────────────────────────
    Flesch Reading Ease:  52        Flesch-Kincaid Grade Level: 9
    Gunning's Fog Index:  12

  ┌ Paragraph Statistics ────────────────────────────────────────
    Number of paragraphs: 50        Average length:    2.8 sentences

  ┌ Sentence Statistics ─────────────────────────────────────────
    Number of sentences:  141       Short (< 12 words):    92
    Average length:       11.5 words  Long  (> 30 words):    6
    End with `?`:         6
    End with `!`:         3

  ┌ Word Statistics ─────────────────────────────────────────────
    Number of words:      1672      Average length:       5.16 letters
                                    Syllables per word:   1.69

         <Enter: Next Screen>                <Esc: Done>
```

2. Press Enter to display interpretations of the readability statistics for the current document, as shown in figure 6.9.

3. Press Esc to return to the Grammatik opening menu.

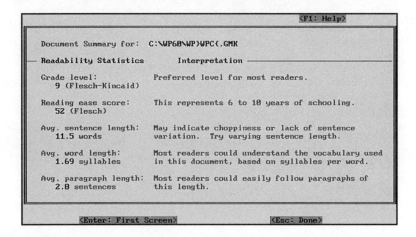

```
                                            <F1: Help>

   Document Summary for:  C:\WP60\WP}WPC{.GMK

 ─ Readability Statistics      Interpretation ──────────────────

   Grade level:             Preferred level for most readers.
     9 (Flesch-Kincaid)

   Reading ease score:      This represents 6 to 10 years of schooling.
     52 (Flesch)

   Avg. sentence length:    May indicate choppiness or lack of sentence
     11.5 words             variation.  Try varying sentence length.

   Avg. word length:        Most readers could understand the vocabulary used
     1.69 syllables         in this document, based on syllables per word.

   Avg. paragraph length:   Most readers could easily follow paragraphs of
     2.8 sentences          this length.


           <Enter: First Screen>              <Esc: Done>
```

FIG. 6.9

The readability statistics interpretation screen.

Customizing Grammatik

Grammatik offers dozens of customization options that go beyond the scope of this book. To customize the way Grammatik works, at the Grammatik opening screen, choose options from the **F**ile, **C**hecking, **P**references, and **S**tatistics menus. For specific information, consult the WordPerfect *User's Guide* or press F1 (Help) to display Grammatik's detailed, on-line help screens.

Using Styles

The Styles feature has been significantly enhanced in Word-Perfect 6, with a new paragraph style type, a new Shared Library feature for network users, and more convenient handling of style libraries.

Styles have a much more important role in WordPerfect 6. (As one WordPerfect programmer put it, they have "invaded the product.") WordPerfect now uses styles to perform tasks handled by individual commands in WordPerfect 5.1, such as formatting graphics boxes.

You cannot use styles created in WordPerfect 5.1. You must manually re-create your styles in WordPerfect 6. If you try to retrieve a style created in WordPerfect 5.1, WordPerfect 6 displays the message: Unknown major file version.

Creating Styles

If you have used styles in WordPerfect 5.1, you will find the process of creating and managing styles similar in WordPerfect 6, except that WordPerfect now uses dialog boxes instead of menus.

The following are the types of styles you can create:

- *Paragraph Style.* This style type is new in WordPerfect 6. When you type text with a paragraph style turned on, pressing Enter at the end of a paragraph turns the style off.

■ *Character Style.* This style is the same as the paired style type in WordPerfect 5.1.

■ *Open Style.* This style is the same as the open style type in WordPerfect 5.1.

Creating a Paragraph Style

Follow these steps to create a new paragraph style:

1. Choose **L**ayout, St**y**les; or press Alt+F8. WordPerfect displays the Style List dialog box, shown in figure 7.1.

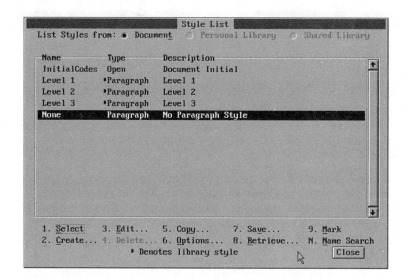

FIG. 7.1

The Style List
dialog box.

2. Choose **C**reate. WordPerfect displays the Create Style dialog box, shown in figure 7.2.

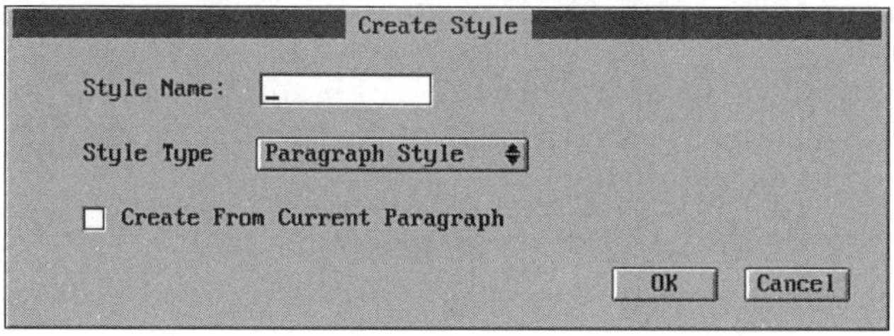

FIG. 7.2

The Create Style
dialog box.

3. Type a name in the Style **N**ame text box.

4. Choose **P**aragraph Style from the Style **T**ype drop-down list.

5. If you choose the **C**reate from Current Paragraph check box, WordPerfect automatically copies the formatting of the paragraph that contains the cursor into the style you named in step 3.

6. Choose OK. WordPerfect displays the Edit Style dialog box, shown in figure 7.3.

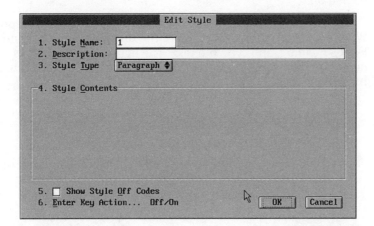

FIG. 7.3

The Edit Style dialog box.

7. Type an optional description for the style in the **D**escription text box. WordPerfect lists style descriptions in the Style List dialog box. Descriptions provide useful reminders of what styles do.

8. You can change the style type without returning to the Create Style dialog box. Choose a type from the Style **T**ype drop-down list box.

9. Choose Style **C**ontents. WordPerfect moves the cursor into the Style Contents box and changes the dialog box options.

10. In the Style Contents box, insert the formatting codes you want WordPerfect to apply to characters, paragraphs, or to insert as open codes.

    You can choose formatting options by pressing the function keys indicated at the top of the dialog box, or by choosing formatting commands from the menu bar. For example, you can change the font by pressing Ctrl+F8 or by choosing F**o**nt, **F**ont.

If a menu option isn't available from the Style Contents box, attempting to choose it from a menu does nothing.

You can type text in the Style Contents box. When you apply the style, WordPerfect inserts the text at the cursor.

11. Press F7 (Exit) to leave the Style Contents box.

12. Choose the Show Style **O**ff Codes check box to tell WordPerfect to insert a comment box in the document text when the style is turned on.

   Figure 7.4 shows formatting codes that change the font to Bodoni-WP Bold, create a left indent, mark the text for a table of contents level 3 heading, and type the text. The figure also shows a comment box for a style that inserts a hard return when the style is turned off.

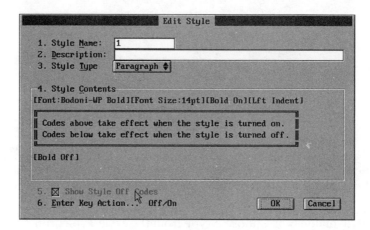

FIG. 7.4

The Edit Style dialog box showing a comment code.

13. Choose **E**nter Key Action to display the Enter Key Action dialog box, shown in figure 7.5. Then choose OK twice to return to the Style List dialog box.

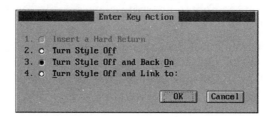

FIG. 7.5

The Enter Key Action dialog box.

This dialog box tells WordPerfect what you want it to do when the Enter key is pressed with the style turned on. The options are:

■ *Insert a Hard Return.* WordPerfect inserts a hard return when you press Enter with the style turned on.

■ *Turn Style Off.* WordPerfect turns the style off when you press Enter with the style turned on.

■ *Turn Style Off and Back* **On**. WordPerfect turns the style on and off again when you press Enter with the style turned on.

■ *Turn Style Off and Link To turns the style off and automatically switches to another style.* This option is useful for switching from a heading style to a body text style, for example. When you choose this option, WordPerfect drops down a list of all the existing styles. To choose a style to link to, double-click it or highlight it in the list and press Enter. You can also type the name of a non-existent style you will create in the future, then press Enter.

Creating a Character Style

Character styles in WordPerfect 6 are called "paired styles" in WordPerfect 5.1. A character style includes codes that turn character formatting on and off—for example, boldface, underline, and italic.

The basic steps for creating styles are discussed near the beginning of this chapter under "Creating a Paragraph Style." The example used in that section is for creating a paragraph style. Creating a character style is a little bit different. Follow these steps:

1. Press Alt+F8 (Styles) and choose **C**reate.

2. Choose Style **N**ame and type a name for the style, then choose **C**haracter Style, OK.

   WordPerfect displays the Edit Style dialog box, shown in figure 7.4. When you move the cursor into the Style **C**ontents area of the Edit Style dialog box, only two options appear: Font and Based on Style (see fig. 7.6). The Font dialog box contains the only formatting options that can be applied to characters. Based on Style is discussed later in this section.

   Figure 7.6 shows codes for character enhancements selected with the Font command (Ctrl+F8). (Fonts are discussed in detail in Chapter 11.)

   Notice in figure 7.6 that the codes turn the character enhancements on but don't turn them off. The next steps create the corresponding "style off" codes.

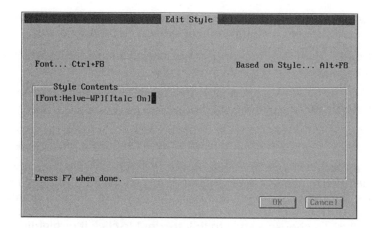

FIG. 7.6

The Edit Style
dialog box with
codes entered for
a character style.

3. Press F7 (Exit) and choose the Show Style **O**ff codes check box,
then choose Style **C**ontents again to resume editing the style.

It's a good idea to select the Show Style **O**ff codes check box before you begin creating the style in the Style Contents dialog box.
However, this example shows the Style Contents box without the
comment in figure 7.6.

4. You can now press the down arrow to position the cursor below
the comment box.

5. Press Ctrl+F8 (Font) and deselect the large, bold, and small caps
character enhancements in the Font dialog box.

WordPerfect enters the appropriate off codes, as shown in figure 7.7.

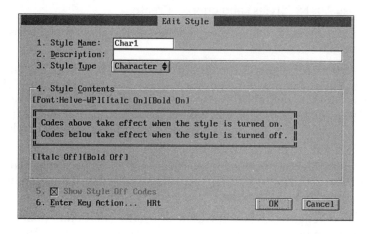

FIG. 7.7

The Edit Style
dialog box
showing charac-
ter formatting off
codes.

Creating an Open Style

Open styles insert codes such as fonts and margin settings that require no closing codes. Open styles remain in effect until you choose a different font, margin setting, and so on.

Follow these steps to create an open style:

1. Press Alt+F8 and choose **C**reate.

2. In the Create Style dialog box, type a name in the Style **N**ame text box.

3. Choose the **O**pen style type from the Style **T**ype drop-down list.

4. Choose OK.

5. In the Edit Style dialog box, type an optional description for the style in the **D**escription text box.

6. Choose Style **C**ontents.

   WordPerfect moves the cursor into the Style Contents box and changes the dialog box options, as shown in figure 7.8.

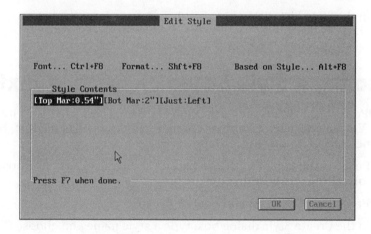

The Edit Style dialog box with the cursor in the Style Contents box, showing options for open styles.

7. In the Style Contents box, insert the formatting codes you want WordPerfect to apply to characters, paragraphs, or to insert as open codes. Figure 7.8 shows a font code entered for a boldface italic font.

   You can choose formatting options by pressing the function keys indicated at the top of the dialog box, or by choosing formatting commands from the menu bar. For example, you can change the font by pressing Ctrl+F8 or by choosing **F**ont, **F**ont.

If a menu option isn't available from the Style Contents box, attempting to choose it does nothing.

You can type text in the Style Contents box. When you apply the style, WordPerfect inserts the text at the cursor.

8. Press F7 (Exit) to leave the Style Contents box.

Notice that the Show Style Off Codes and Enter Key Action options aren't available for open styles because open styles don't have Off codes and aren't turned off by pressing the Enter key.

9. Choose OK to return to the Style List dialog box.

Basing a Style on an Existing Style

You can save time while creating styles by choosing the Based on Style option. Begin defining a style as described in the previous sections, then follow these steps:

1. With the cursor in the Style Contents box of the Edit Style dialog box, press Alt+F8 (Based on Style).

2. In the Style List dialog box, highlight a style from the list and choose Select.

Creating a Style Based on Existing Text

WordPerfect can "read" the formatting of existing text and insert it in a style. You can base paragraph or character styles on existing text, but not open styles. Follow these steps:

1. Position the cursor in the paragraph or on the character whose formatting you want to copy.

2. Press Alt+F8 (Styles) and choose Create.

3. In the Create Style dialog box, type a style name and choose the paragraph or character style type.

4. Mark the Create From Current Paragraph (or Create From Current Character) check box and choose OK.

WordPerfect displays the Edit Style dialog box, with formatting codes inserted in the Style Contents box for the paragraph or character that contains the cursor.

5. You can now edit the style contents, as described in the section "Editing a Style," or accept the style contents and choose OK to return to the Style List dialog box.

Working with Styles

Almost all of WordPerfect's features work at least a little bit differently in WordPerfect 6—including styles. You will find that the steps for working with styles are familiar, but subtly different from WordPerfect 5.1. Learning about the changes takes very little time and is described in this section.

Editing a Style

To edit a style, choose Alt+F8 (Style), highlight a style name in the Style List dialog box, and choose Edit on the Style List dialog box. The steps for editing a style are the same as for creating a style. Follow the steps in the previous section on creating a style.

Selecting a Style

To turn on a paragraph, character, or open style, choose Alt+F8 (Style) and double-click a style name in the Style List dialog box. With the keyboard, highlight a style and choose Select or press Enter.

You can turn off a paragraph style anywhere in a paragraph by choosing another paragraph style or by choosing None in the Style List dialog box.

Deleting a Style

Follow these steps to delete a style:

1. Press Alt+F8 (Style), highlight a style name in the Style List dialog box, and choose Delete. WordPerfect displays the Delete Style dialog box.

   You can delete a style from the Style List dialog box but retain in all documents formatted with the style all formatting codes created with the style. Or you can delete the style from the Style List dialog box and also remove from all documents formatted with the style all formatting codes created with the style.

2. Choose Including Codes to remove codes, or choose Leaving Codes to retain formatting created with the style.

WordPerfect deletes the style and returns to the Style List dialog box.

Copying a Style

Follow these steps to copy a style:

1. Press Alt+F8 (Style), highlight a style name in the Style List dialog box, and choose Copy. WordPerfect displays the Copy Styles dialog box.

2. Choose Document, Personal Library, or Shared Library.

Choosing Document copies the style into the document style library. For a discussion of style libraries, see "Working with Style Libraries" later in this chapter.

Choosing Personal Library copies the style into the currently selected personal library.

Choosing Shared Library copies the style into the currently selected personal library. This option is useful when you want to share a style with other users on a network.

Choosing Style Options

Follow these steps to set style options:

1. Press Alt+F8 (Style), highlight a style name in the Style List dialog box, and choose Options.

   WordPerfect displays the Style Options dialog box, shown in figure 7.9.

   You can link a personal and a shared style library to the on-screen document. When you do so, WordPerfect automatically lists the styles from those libraries in the Style list dialog box when you edit the document.

2. To link libraries to a document, choose Libraries Assigned to Document and type the name of the Personal and/or a Shared library you want to link.

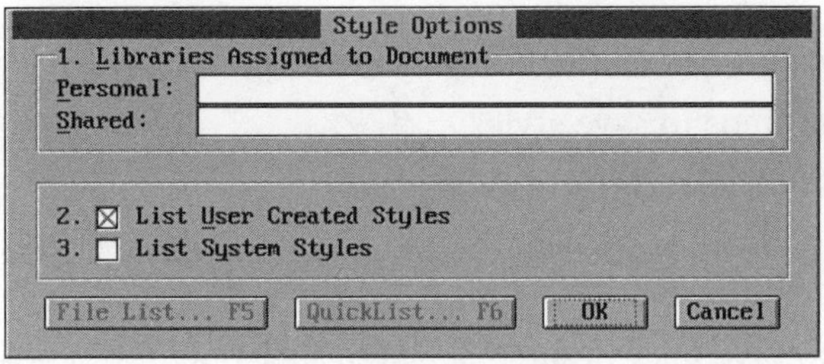

FIG. 7.9

The Style Options
dialog box.

WordPerfect comes with over 50 predefined "system" styles that
are used to set formatting options for such features as headers
and footers, graphics boxes, outline headings, and watermarks. By
default, only six system styles are displayed in the Style List dialog box: Heading 1 through Heading 5, and None. When you use all
the listed system heading styles in a document, WordPerfect automatically lists the next two system heading styles in the Style List
dialog box. For example, after you select Heading 5, WordPerfect
displays Headings 6 and 7.

A significant advantage in using the system heading styles is that
they're automatically marked for inclusion in a table of contents.
You don't need to mark headings manually for a table of contents
when you use these system styles.

Unlike user-created styles, system styles can be edited but cannot
be deleted.

3. To display user-created styles, choose the List User Created
   Styles check box.

4. To list all the system styles, choose List System Styles.

5. Choose OK to return to the Style List dialog box.

Saving Styles

When you exit WordPerfect, any new or edited styles you have created
are automatically saved. You don't need to use the Save command on
the Style List dialog box to save new or changed styles. However, if you
abandon the on-screen document without saving it, WordPerfect dis-
cards any styles you have created for the document and haven't copied
into a personal or shared library. To avoid losing your work, remember
to save the current document or copy styles into a library!

The Save option on the Style List dialog box lets you save styles in a separate file so you can share them with other users.

Follow these steps to save styles:

1. Press Alt+F8 (Style) and choose Save.

2. In the Save Styles dialog box, choose Filename and type a filename.

3. Choose Save User Created Styles to save only the styles you have created; or choose Save WP System Styles to save the system styles as well.

   You may want to save the system files if you have edited them and want to share the edited styles with other users.

4. Choose OK to return to the Style List dialog box.

Retrieving Styles

WordPerfect automatically retrieves system styles and any styles you have created. You use the Retrieve command only to retrieve styles that you or another WordPerfect user has saved with the Save command, as described in the previous section.

Follow these steps to retrieve a styles file:

1. Press Alt+F8 (Styles) and choose Retrieve.

2. In the Retrieve Styles dialog box, choose Filename and type a filename.

3. Choose Retrieve User Created Styles to save only the styles you have created; or choose Retrieve WP System Styles to save the system styles as well.

4. Choose OK to return to the Style List dialog box.

Marking Styles

You use the Mark option in the Style List dialog box to mark a group of styles you want to delete, copy, or save. To mark a style, highlight it in the list box, then choose Mark. When you choose Delete, Copy, or Save, WordPerfect applies those functions only to the marked styles.

Working with Style Libraries

WordPerfect 6 lets you attach styles to a document, a personal library, or a shared library, or any combination of the three. In the Style List dialog box, a bullet next to the style type indicates that the style belongs to a library. If you edit the style, the bullet disappears and the link to the library is broken, but you can save the style in a library again, as described in this section.

A *library* is simply a collection of styles. Saving styles in personal libraries can help you group styles according to their intended use: contract styles, report styles, invoice styles, desktop publishing styles, and so on.

WordPerfect lets you save styles in two types of libraries: personal and shared. These two kinds of libraries work exactly the same; only the name is different. Whether you display a personal or a shared library in the Style List dialog box, the options remain the same. Having two names is a convenient tool for saving certain styles for your own, personal use and making other styles available for use by other users on a network.

Another advantage of style libraries is that they enable WordPerfect 6 to work faster with documents that contain many styles. When you choose a style in WordPerfect 5.1, all the styles from the current library are added to the hidden prefix of the document, greatly slowing down normal editing operations. Storing styles in personal and shared libraries means that WordPerfect can attach fewer styles to the document prefix, with less loss of speed.

As you may have noticed, when you first display the Style List dialog box, the Personal **L**ibrary and **Sh**ared Library radio buttons are grayed and unavailable. To display the styles in personal or shared libraries, you must first link a personal and/or shared library to the document on-screen. These libraries don't have to contain styles, but you must attach them to the on-screen document. Follow these steps:

1. From the document screen, press Alt+F8 (Style) and choose **O**ptions.

2. If you haven't created any personal or shared libraries yet, and you want to begin saving styles in a personal library, type a name for the personal library in the Personal text box.

   If you want to begin saving styles in a shared library, type a name for a shared library in the Shared text box.

   If you want to save styles from the document in a personal and shared library, type a name in each box.

If you have already linked the current document with a personal and/or shared library, WordPerfect automatically inserts the names of the style libraries in the text boxes.

Notice that the Personal and Shared text boxes don't have drop-down lists from which you can choose the names of existing libraries. You must remember the names of any style libraries you create.

3. Choose OK to return to the Style List dialog box.

WordPerfect attaches the named style libraries to the current document. You can only attach one personal and one shared library to a document at the same time. To copy a style from one library to another, use the Options command to attach the desired personal or shared library, then choose Copy to copy styles from the document styles library into the personal and/or shared libraries.

4. You can now choose Personal Library or Shared Library to display the corresponding library dialog box.

The options at the bottom of the dialog box are exactly the same as when Document or Shared Library is selected. To find out how these options work, see the previous sections of this chapter.

If you press Alt+F8 (Styles) twice from the document screen, Word-Perfect returns to the library where you were working the last time you displayed the Style List dialog box.

Linking Styles

WordPerfect can automatically start a second style when you press Enter to close a style. You can link paragraph or character styles.

This technique is very useful for typing repetitive text. For example, suppose that you want to create a series of paragraphs with the alternating headings Question: and Answer:. Linked styles can type the Question and Answer headings with extra space inserted between sets of questions and answers. Moreover, you can link the Answer style to the Question style to create a loop. Pressing Enter to close one style automatically starts the other style.

You may decide to link character styles if, for example, you want an italic style to begin automatically when you turn off a boldface style.

Follow these steps to link styles:

1. Create two or more styles you want to link.

   Figure 7.10 shows the codes entered for a `Question:` style, as discussed in the example.

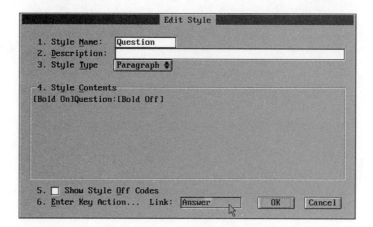

FIG. 7.10

The Edit Style dialog box with text and formatting codes entered for a questionnaire.

2. To link the styles, press Alt+F8 (Styles), highlight the first style you want to link, and choose Edit.

3. In the Edit Style dialog box, choose Enter Key Action.

   WordPerfect displays the Enter Key Action dialog box, where you tell WordPerfect what to do when you press Enter with the style turned on.

4. Choose **T**urn Style Off and Link To, and choose from the drop-down list the name of a style to link to. Choose OK to return to the Edit Style dialog box.

For the example, item number 6 in the Edit Style dialog box (Enter Key Action) now displays `Link: Answer`.

When you choose the Question style in the example, WordPerfect inserts the Question heading. When you press Enter at the end of the Question text, WordPerfect creates an Answer heading. When you press Enter at the end of the Answer text, WordPerfect inserts extra space and creates another Question heading. To break the loop and stop using the Question and Answer styles, press Alt+F8 (Styles) and choose a different style.

Envelopes, Labels, and Subdivided Pages

WordPerfect 6 improves on WordPerfect 5.1 by making many features easier to use—even when adding an entire new program module is required. An excellent example is the new Envelopes feature. Printing an envelope from the address of an on-screen letter requires a complicated macro in WordPerfect 5.1. WordPerfect 6 handles this task with easy-to-use dialog box options.

Printing labels can also be a frustrating task in WordPerfect 5.1. The Labels feature in WordPerfect 6 is much easier to use.

Desktop publishers will be delighted with the new Subdivided Pages option, which makes using different column formats on the same page much easier.

Envelopes

WordPerfect 6 can "read" the address from a letter displayed on-screen and print the address on an envelope. You don't need to select the address. Regardless of the cursor location, WordPerfect searches for a flush-left address and prints it on an envelope.

Printing an Envelope

To print an envelope, follow these steps:

1. Make sure that a document with a name and address is displayed on-screen.

2. Choose **L**ayout, En**v**elope. WordPerfect displays the Envelope dialog box with the address inserted in the **M**ailing Address box (see fig. 8.1).

FIG. 8.1

The Envelope dialog box displaying an address.

3. If the Envelope Size text box doesn't display an envelope definition, choose **E**nvelope Size and select a definition from the drop-down list.

If no envelope definitions are available for your printer, you need to create a definition. See the section "Creating an Envelope Paper Definition" later in this chapter.

4. If you want to omit the return address, choose the **O**mit Return Address check box. (To find out how to create a return address, see step 6.)

5. If you want to use the same return address each time you create an envelope, choose **S**ave Return Address as Default.

6. To create a return address, choose **R**eturn Address, type the return address, and press F7 (Exit).

7. To edit the mailing address or to type a mailing address if the on-screen document doesn't contain one, choose **M**ailing Address, type the address, and press F7 (Exit).

   WordPerfect can automatically read the ZIP code from the address and print the corresponding POSTNET bar code above the address on the envelope. Bar codes are used by the U.S. Postal Service to handle mass mailings at reduced postage rates.

8. To include a bar code, press Shift+F1 (Setup), choose **C**reate Bar Code, and then choose OK.

   If a ZIP code does not exist in the on-screen document, type a 9- or 11-digit ZIP code in the POSTNET **B**ar Code text box.

   Alternatively, to turn off the printing of bar codes, press Shift+F1 (Setup), choose **R**emove Bar Code Option, and choose OK.

9. Choose **P**rint to print the envelope, or choose **I**nsert to tell WordPerfect to insert the envelope on a separate page at the end of the document, separated from the rest of the document by hard page code.

If you choose **I**nsert, WordPerfect prompts you to load an envelope in the printer when it reaches the envelope page. For further information on selecting a paper size and type, see "Creating an Envelope Paper Definition" later in this chapter.

Remember that an envelope paper definition inserted at the end of a document changes the paper size and type settings for the document from that point forward. To insert text after the envelope definition, you may need to change the paper definition.

T I P If your document contains more than one address and you choose
Layout and then choose Envelope, WordPerfect may insert the
wrong address in the Mailing Address text box. To insert the correct
address, select the address before you create the envelope.
WordPerfect inserts the address in the Envelope dialog box.

Changing the Position of the Address

To change the positions where WordPerfect prints mailing and return
addresses with the Envelope feature, follow these steps:

1. Choose Layout, Envelope, and then press Shift+F1 (Setup).
   WordPerfect displays the Envelope Setup dialog box (see fig. 8.2).

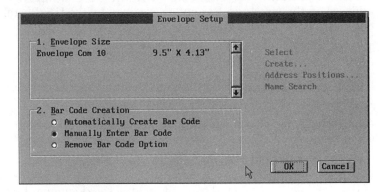

The Envelope
Setup dialog
box.

2. In the Envelope Size list, highlight an envelope definition and
   choose Address Positions. WordPerfect displays the Envelope
   Address Positions dialog box (see fig. 8.3).

3. In the Return Address and Mailing Address text boxes, type
   horizontal and vertical positions for the addresses.

4. To check the results of your settings, choose OK, OK, and Insert.
   WordPerfect inserts the envelope on the last page of the document and places the cursor at the end of the address.

5. Press Shift+F7 (Print) and choose Print Preview to view the
   envelope. Press Esc to return to the document screen.

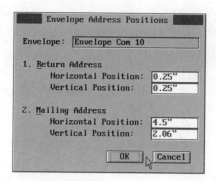

FIG. 8.3

The Envelope
Address Positions
dialog box.

To keep bar codes from printing, press Shift+F1 (Setup) from the Envelope dialog box and choose either **D**o Not Create Bar Code or **R**emove Bar Code Option.

Choosing **D**o Not Create Bar Code turns the bar code feature off for this document only. Choosing **R**emove Bar Code Option removes the bar code option from the Envelope dialog box until you choose **C**reate Bar Code to turn it back on again.

Creating an Envelope Paper Definition

For most printers, WordPerfect sets up one or more envelope definitions when you install the program. If no envelope definitions are listed in the Envelope dialog box, you can create one. Follow these steps:

1. From the document screen, choose **L**ayout, En**v**elope, Setup (Shift+F1).

2. Choose Envelope **S**ize and then choose **C**reate.

3. In the Paper Size/Type dialog box, choose **C**reate. WordPerfect displays the Create Paper Size/Type dialog box.

   Choosing paper size/type options is described in detail in Chapter 10. The following steps give abbreviated instructions for creating an envelope paper type.

4. In the Paper **N**ame box, type a name for the new envelope size/ type.

5. Choose Paper **T**ype and then choose Envelope from the drop-down list.

6. Choose Paper **L**ocation and then choose Continuous or Manual Feed from the Paper Location dialog box; choose **S**elect.

7. If you want WordPerfect to prompt you to load an envelope in your printer, activate the **P**rompt to Load check box.

8. Choose **O**rientation and then choose a portrait or landscape font from the Paper Orientation dialog box. Choose OK.

   Because the envelope address printing position is set, you can leave the A**d**just Text options at the default 0" settings.

9. Choose OK, Close to return to the Envelope Setup dialog box.

10. Highlight the new definition in the **E**nvelope Size box, and then choose **S**elect, OK to return to the Envelope dialog box.

WordPerfect inserts the new envelope definition in the **E**nvelope Size drop-down list box.

Choosing Fonts for Envelope Addresses

If you print an envelope without specifying fonts and without inserting the envelope text in your document, WordPerfect uses the font you specified in Initial Codes (see Chapter 4).

You may want to print the return address so it looks the same as the return address printed on your letterhead. Follow these steps to specify fonts for the mailing and return addresses:

1. In the Envelope dialog box, choose **R**eturn Address or **M**ailing Address.

2. Choose **F**ont, F**o**nt, choose a font and any character enhancements, then choose OK.

For complete instructions for using the Font dialog box, see Chapter 11.

Creating Envelopes during a Merge

WordPerfect can print envelopes automatically when you merge-print letters. To learn how to use this feature, see Chapter 14.

WordPerfect can print POSTNET bar codes on envelopes for mass mailings during a merge. This feature, which uses the new POSTNET merge code, is described in Chapter 14.

Creating POSTNET Bar Codes for Window Envelopes

WordPerfect can insert a POSTNET bar code anywhere in a document. Follow these steps:

1. Position the cursor where you want to insert a bar code.

2. Choose **L**ayout, **O**ther, Ba**r** Code. WordPerfect displays the POSTNET Bar Code dialog box.

3. Type the ZIP Code and choose OK.

WordPerfect inserts the bar code at the cursor.

> Use this shortcut to insert bar codes. Select a ZIP Code in your document. Then choose **L**ayout, **O**ther, Ba**r** Code. WordPerfect displays the POSTNET Bar Code dialog box with the ZIP Code automatically inserted. Choose OK. WordPerfect inserts the bar code at the cursor position, to the left of the ZIP Code. Press Backspace to delete the bar code. Move the cursor to where you want to insert the bar code. Press Esc, 1 to undelete the bar code and insert it at the cursor.
>
> **T I P**

Labels

The Labels feature has been improved in WordPerfect 6. For example, you can now choose a label paper size/type and then type label text on-screen. In Full Page mode, WordPerfect displays the labels in columns, just as they appear when printed.

Also, label definitions are no longer stored in individual printer files, so any label definitions you create are available for use with any printer. Another improvement is that when you use the Print dialog box to print a page of labels, WordPerfect knows to print the entire physical page of labels and not just one label (a logical page) as in WordPerfect 5.1.

Labels are separated on-screen in Text and Graphics modes by a line that indicates the width of the label, instead of a line extending all the way across the screen, as in WordPerfect 5.1. This line lets you know when you're approaching the end of a line when you're typing labels on-screen.

Creating Labels

To print labels, you must first choose one of the preset label definitions supplied with WordPerfect for your printer. If WordPerfect doesn't include a label definition for your printer, you can create your own. See "Creating Label Definitions" later in this chapter.

Follow these steps to choose a preset label definition:

1. Select the printer you want to use to print labels. (Printer selection is described in Chapter 10.)

2. Choose **Layout, Page.**

3. From the Page Format dialog box, choose **Labels.** WordPerfect displays the Labels dialog box, shown in figure 8.4.

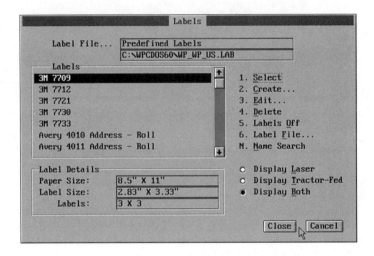

The Labels dialog box.

The options for creating label definitions on the Labels dialog box are discussed in detail under "Creating Label Definitions," later in this chapter. For now, continue with step 4.

4. Choose the type of predefined labels you want to display in the Labels list box: Display **L**aser, Display **T**ractor-Fed, or Display **B**oth.

5. Choose a predefined label definition from the **L**abels list.

   Notice in figure 8.4 that information about the highlighted definition is displayed in the Label Details information box.

6. Choose **S**elect. WordPerfect displays the Labels Printer Info dialog box, shown in figure 8.5.

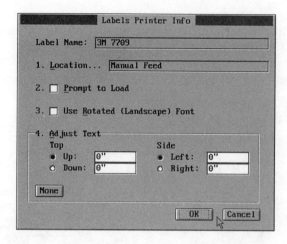

FIG. 8.5

The Labels Printer Info dialog box.

The Labels Printer Info dialog box lets you change options for the label definition.

Choosing **Location** displays the Paper Location dialog box.

7. Choose a paper location, then choose **S**elect to return to the Labels Printer Info dialog box.

8. Choose **P**rompt to Load if you want WordPerfect to prompt you to load each page in the printer.

9. Choose Use **R**otated (Landscape) Font if you want to print labels in Landscape mode.

10. Choose **A**djust Text and enter numbers in the **T**op and **S**ide boxes to change the position where WordPerfect begins printing label text.

11. Choose OK to return to the Page Format dialog box, then choose OK to return to the document screen.

You can now type labels in the editing screen or create a document file for merge-printing labels. (WordPerfect 6 uses the term *document file* instead of the WordPerfect 5.1 term *primary file*.)

Creating Label Definitions

If preset label definitions aren't available for your printer, or if you aren't happy with the way the supplied definitions work, you can create your own label definitions. Or, you can edit a supplied definition. Follow these steps to create or edit a definition:

1. Choose **L**ayout, **P**age, **L**abels, **C**reate (or highlight a label definition and choose **E**dit). WordPerfect displays the Create Label dialog box, shown in figure 8.6.

```
┌──────────────────── Create Label ────────────────────┐

    Label Description:  [3M 7709                        ]

    Label Paper Size... [8.5" X 11"                     ]

   ┌─ Label Size ──────────┐  ┌─ Distance Between Labels ─┐
     Width:    [2.83"]          Column: [0"]
     Height:   [3.33"]          Row:    [0"]

   ┌─ Number of Labels ────┐  ┌─ Label Margins ──────────┐
     Columns:  [3]              Left:   [0"]
     Rows:     [3]              Right:  [0"]
                                Top:    [0"]
   ┌─ Top Left Corner ─────┐    Bottom: [0"]
     Top:      [0.5"]
     Left:     [0"]          ┌─ Label Type ──────────────┐
                               ● Laser
     Printer Info...           ○ Tractor-Fed
                               ○ Both

   [Help]                        [  OK  ]  [Cancel]
└───────────────────────────────────────────────────────┘
```

FIG. 8.6

The Create Label
dialog box.

If you choose **E**dit, the Edit Label dialog box appears. It's exactly
the same as the Create Label dialog box, except that the Label
Description box holds the name of the definition you choose in
step 1.

2. If you're creating a label definition from scratch, type a name for
   the label in the Label **D**escription box.

   If you're editing an existing definition and want to save it under a
   new name, type the name in the Label **D**escription box.

3. Choose options for Label **S**ize, **N**umber of Labels, Printer **I**nfo, Top
   Left **C**orner, Distance **B**etween Labels, Label **M**argins, and Label
   Type.

   Except for Printer Info and Label Type, these options are the same
   as those listed on the Format: Labels menu in WordPerfect 5.1.

   Choosing Printer **I**nfo displays the Labels Printer Info dialog box,
   discussed earlier.

4. Choose **L**aser, **T**ractor-Fed, or **B**oth to make the label definition
   available with one or either type of printer selected.

5. Choose OK, **S**elect, and make any changes to the Labels Printer Info dialog box.

6. Choose OK twice to return to the document screen with the label definition selected.

You can now type labels in the editing screen, as described in the following section, or create a document file for merge-printing labels, as described in Chapter 14.

You can use Page mode or Print Preview to view your labels before printing.

Typing Labels

Use the following commands to perform the indicated functions while typing labels:

- *Ctrl+Enter (Hard Page)*. Ends one label and moves to the next.

- *Layout, **P**age, **C**enter Current Page, or Center **P**ages*. To center label text vertically for the current label or all labels.

- *PgDn and PgUp*. Move between labels.

- *Ctrl+Home, Label Number*. Moves to specified label number.

Subdivided Pages

The Subdivide Page feature makes it easy to divide a page evenly into columns and rows. This capability is very useful when you want to lay out several copies of a document on the same page—for example, an invitation or memo form. Figure 8.7 shows an example of a page divided using the Subdivide Page feature.

In WordPerfect 5.1, creating subdivided pages requires that you use the Labels feature. For example, to print four copies of a memo form on the same page, you create a label definition that prints four labels on a page. You then copy the memo text into each of the four labels.

The Subdivide Page feature in WordPerfect 6 can divide the page quickly and automatically into the number of rows and columns you specify. You can then move between subdivided pages using the same cursor-movement keys you use to move between normal document pages. WordPerfect numbers the subdivided pages separately.

FIG. 8.7

A subdivided page shown in Print Preview mode.

WordPerfect displays subdivided pages in Text and Graphics modes vertically on-screen. In Page mode and in Print Preview, subdivided pages are displayed as they will be printed, in rows and columns.

Follow these steps to create subdivided pages:

1. Choose **Layout**, **P**age, Subdivide P**a**ge. WordPerfect displays the Subdivide Page dialog box, shown in figure 8.8.

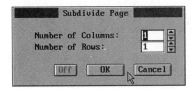

FIG. 8.8

The Subdivide Page dialog box.

2. In the Number of Columns and Number of Rows boxes, type the number of columns and rows, then choose OK twice to return to the document screen.

WordPerfect divides the pages in the document until you turn subdivided pages off by choosing **Layout**, **P**age, Subdivide P**a**ge, Off, and OK.

Working with Files

If you're already familiar with WordPerfect 5.1, you will have no trouble using WordPerfect 6 to open and manage files. You can use the same function keys to open, retrieve, and save files, and work with List Files (called File Manager in WordPerfect 6).

WordPerfect 6 refines these features and adds some entirely new commands that enable you to work with document files quickly and efficiently. Foremost among these commands are the QuickFinder and QuickList commands.

WordPerfect 6 offers no radically different document management tools, although Document Information is new. You can use Document Summary, Long Document Names, and Compare Documents, as in WordPerfect 5.1; however, these options work through dialog boxes instead of menus.

WordPerfect 6 includes WordPerfect Shell, a program module formerly sold separately by WordPerfect Corporation. Because a full description of Shell is beyond the scope of this book, this chapter gives some general information about the Shell.

Using the File Manager

You can use File Manager and Quick List to find, view, and open files. Follow these steps to start File Manager:

1. Choose File, File Manager; or press F5.

   WordPerfect displays the Specify File Manager List dialog box, shown in figure 9.1.

2. Type a directory specification in the Directory box (as explained in the next section).

Specifying a Directory

You can use wildcards to specify a directory. Notice in figure 9.1 that WordPerfect has already entered the wildcards *.*, indicating all files in the current directory.

Pressing F5 twice from the document screen displays the File Manager dialog box with all the files in the current directory listed.

You can also use the question mark (?) wildcard, which represents a character. For example, typing **c:\wp60\sm???.let** displays the files SMITH.LET, SMALL.LET, and SMILY.LET.

The asterisk (*) wildcard represents any number of characters in a filename. For example, typing **c:\wp60*.let** displays all files with the LET extension.

The following sections describe options in the Specify File Manager List dialog box.

Using Directory Tree

If you choose Directory Tree (F8) from the Specify File Manager List dialog box, WordPerfect displays the Directory Tree dialog box. This dialog box graphically shows the directory structure of the current disk, with the currently selected directory highlighted (see fig. 9.2).

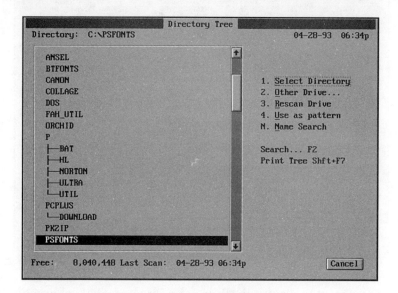

```
                       Directory Tree
Directory:  C:\PSFONTS                      04-28-93  06:34p

 AMSEL                              ↑
 BTFONTS
 CANON                                   1. Select Directory
 COLLAGE                                 2. Other Drive...
 DOS                                     3. Rescan Drive
 FAH_UTIL                                4. Use as pattern
 ORCHID                                  N. Name Search
 P
 ├─BAT                                   Search... F2
 ├─HL                                    Print Tree Shft+F7
 ├─NORTON
 ├─ULTRA
 └─UTIL
 PCPLUS
 └─DOWNLOAD
 PKZIP
 PSFONTS                            ↓

Free:   8,040,448 Last Scan:   04-28-93 06:34p       [Cancel]
```

FIG. 9.2

The Directory
Tree dialog box.

You can use the Directory Tree dialog box to display the files in a different directory or disk drive. Follow these steps:

1. At the Directory Tree dialog box, highlight the desired directory.

2. Choose **S**elect Directory.

   WordPerfect displays the File Manager dialog box with the files in the directory you highlighted in step 1 (see fig. 9.3).

3. If you want to list the files on another drive, choose **O**ther Drive to display the Other Drive dialog box. Then highlight the drive letter and choose Select.

4. If you want to tell WordPerfect to read and redisplay the directory tree, choose **R**escan Drive at the Directory Tree dialog box.

   You must use **R**escan Drive after you create, rename, or delete a directory with File Manager or a DOS command. Notice in figure 9.2 that the date in the upper right corner of the Directory Tree dialog box indicates the last time the directory tree was scanned.

5. If you want to return to the Specify File Manager List dialog box with the highlighted directory inserted in the Directory box, choose **U**se as Pattern.

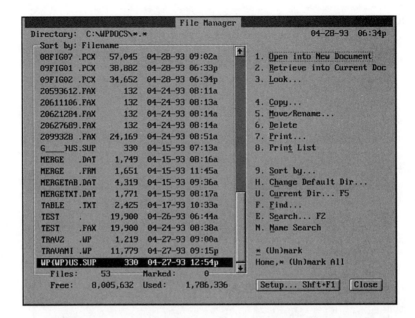

FIG. 9.3

The File Manager
dialog box.

6. If you want to display the Search for Directory dialog box, choose
   Search (F2). In that dialog box, type a directory name, choose
   Backward Search if desired, then choose Search (F2). WordPerfect
   highlights the directory name.

7. If you want to print a formatted copy of the tree listing, choose
   Print Tree (Shift+F7).

Using QuickList

QuickList is new in WordPerfect 6. It enables you to quickly display sets
of files by type; for example, letters, reports, shared styles, graphic
images, and so on. You can create your own file specifications, and you
can have QuickList display just one file, for example REPORT2.DOC.

To start QuickList from the document screen, choose File, File Manager; or press F5. Then choose QuickList (F6). WordPerfect displays the
QuickList dialog box, shown in figure 9.4.

Customizing QuickList File Types

Before you can use QuickList to display files by type, you must first tell
WordPerfect how to identify each type of file. Some people save all

letters with the extension LTR, for example, while others use the extension LET. Follow these steps to create a new QuickList file type:

1. From the QuickList dialog box, choose **C**reate.

   WordPerfect displays the Create QuickList Entry dialog box, shown in figure 9.5.

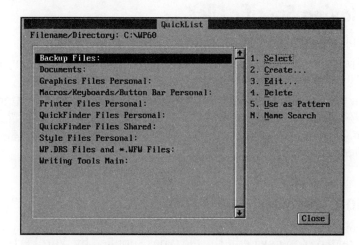

FIG. 9.4

The QuickList dialog box.

FIG. 9.5

The Create QuickList Entry dialog box.

2. In the Description box, type a description for the file specification.

   WordPerfect lists this description in the QuickList dialog box.

3. In the Filename/Directory box, type a file specification.

   You can use wildcards, as described earlier in this chapter in the section on Specifying a Directory. Or, you can type the directory path and name of a single file. Notice the Examples window in figure 9.5.

4. You can choose Directory Tree (F8) to insert a Filename/Directory using the Directory Tree dialog box, as described in the preceding section.

5. Choose OK to return to the QuickList dialog box.

Displaying Specific Files

To display specific files with QuickList, follow these steps:

1. From the document screen, choose **File**, **File Manager**; or press F5. Then choose QuickList (F6).

2. In the QuickList dialog box, highlight a QuickList file type (for example, Documents) and choose **Select**.

WordPerfect displays the File Manager dialog box with only files of the specified type displayed.

Editing QuickList File Types

You can change the file and path names for QuickList file types you have created. You must edit the file types supplied by WordPerfect before you can use them, since none of them includes a file specification. Follow these steps:

1. In the QuickList dialog box, highlight a file type from the list and choose **Edit**.

   WordPerfect displays the Edit QuickList Entry dialog box, which has exactly the same options as the Create QuickList Entry dialog, described earlier.

2. Make any desired changes in the **Description** and **Filename/Directory** boxes, then choose OK to return to the QuickList dialog box.

Deleting QuickList File Types

If you don't use some of the default file types WordPerfect displays in the QuickList dialog box, you may want to delete them. Just highlight a file type in the QuickList dialog box and choose **Delete**. Then choose **Yes** to confirm that you want to delete the file type.

Using Use as Pattern

Choosing Use as Pattern from the QuickList dialog box returns to the Specify File Manager List dialog box with the highlighted QuickList file type specification inserted in the Directory box. If you define a QuickList file type for reports, highlighting the Reports item in the list and choosing Use as Pattern returns to the previous dialog box and inserts the directory for the specified file type; for example, c:\wp60\reports.

Using Redo

Choosing Redo (F5) at the Specify File Manager List dialog box displays the File Manager dialog box with the same files displayed the last time you used File Manager.

Notice that pressing F5, F5 at the document screen works the same as in WordPerfect 5.1. You still cannot use Redo to redisplay floppy disk directories.

Using File Manager Options

The WordPerfect 6 File Manager is very similar to the List Files screen in WordPerfect 5.1 (refer to fig. 9.3).

Notice in figure 9.3 that WordPerfect 6 sorts the file list by filename extension by default. In WordPerfect 5.1, List Files sorts the list by filename.

Notice also in figure 9.3 that the following options are new or changed:

WordPerfect 6	WordPerfect 5.1
Print List	Press Shift+F7 at List Files screen
Sort by	Not available
Change Default Dir	Press F5 and type directory path
Current Dir (F5)	Press F5 (no options)
Search (F2)	Press F2 (not listed with options)
Home, * (Un)mark All Alt+F5	Alt+F5

Follow these steps to display the File Manager from the document screen:

1. Choose **F**ile, **F**ile Manager; or press F5.

   WordPerfect displays the Specify File Manager List dialog box.

2. Enter a file path in the Directory box and choose OK.

   WordPerfect displays the File Manager dialog box.

You can also use the following shortcuts:

- To quickly display all the files in the current directory, press F5, Enter.

- To redisplay the same files the last time you used File Manager during the current WordPerfect session, press F5 twice.

The following sections describe the options on the File Manager dialog box.

Open into New Document

Choosing **O**pen into New Document opens the highlighted file into a new document window. You can open up to nine files at once in WordPerfect 6, compared to just two in WordPerfect 5.1. To open several files at once, mark them before you choose **O**pen into New Document. To mark and unmark a filename, highlight it and press space bar or asterisk (*).

Retrieve into Current Doc

Choosing **R**etrieve into Current Doc retrieves the highlighted file into the current document at the cursor.

Look (Text Files)

Choosing **L**ook displays the highlighted file's document summary, if there is one. The **O**pen, **D**elete, and * Mark options are new in WordPerfect 6. These options are described in the following paragraphs. The remaining options work as they do in WordPerfect 5.1.

- *Open.* Choosing **O**pen opens the file in a new document window and returns to the document window.

- *Delete*. If you choose **Delete**, WordPerfect asks if you want to delete the file. Choose **Yes** to proceed, or choose **No** to cancel deletion and return to the dialog box.

- ** Mark*. Choosing *** Mark** returns to the File Manager, where the file's name appears in the list with an asterisk indicating that it is marked.

- *Look at Text*. Choosing **Look at Text** displays the text of the document in the Look at Document screen.

Several new options on the Look at Document screen in WordPerfect 6 are described in the following paragraphs:

- *Open*. This option opens the document in a new document window.

- *Delete*. This option deletes the file. WordPerfect prompts you to confirm the deletion.

- ** Mark*. This option marks the file and returns to the File Manager.

- *Look at Summary*. This option returns to the document summary.

- *Scroll*. This option scrolls the text down continuously until you choose **Scroll** again.

- *Block (Alt+F4)*. This option lets you select text.

- *Clipboard (Ctrl+F1)*. With text selected, this option displays the Clipboard dialog box. From the Clipboard dialog box, you can choose **Save Block to Clipboard** or **Append Block to Clipboard**. You can then retrieve the Clipboard into a document. You cannot move selected text into the Clipboard, nor can you paste text from the Clipboard into a document displayed in the Look at Document screen.

Look (Graphics and Sound Clips)

In WordPerfect 5.1, **Look** can only display text. In WordPerfect 6, **Look** can also display graphics and play back sound clips. To display a graphic image, press F5 (File Manager) and type a path and/or filename for a graphics file. Then highlight the file in File Manager and choose **Look**.

WordPerfect displays the file. If the file needs to be converted to WordPerfect 6 format, WordPerfect automatically loads ConvertPerfect and converts and displays the file.

Copy

To copy a file with the File Manager, highlight the filename and choose Copy. WordPerfect displays the Copy dialog box. Then type a name for the copy and choose OK. You can use Directory Tree (F8) or QuickList (F6), described earlier, to enter a filename for the copy.

Move/Rename

To move or rename a file, highlight a filename and choose Move/Rename. WordPerfect displays the Move/Rename dialog box. Type a new name and path for the file and choose OK. You can use Directory Tree (F8) or QuickList (F6), described earlier, to enter a filename.

Delete

To delete a file, highlight a filename and choose Delete. Then choose Yes to confirm that you want to delete the file, or choose No to cancel the deletion.

Print

To print a file with File Manager, highlight a filename and choose Print. In WordPerfect 5.1, choosing Print at the List Files screen simply prints the entire document. In WordPerfect 6, choosing Print displays the Print Multiple Page where you can choose various printing options. The Print Multiple Pages dialog box is described fully in Chapter 10.

Print List

The Print List option works the same as in WordPerfect 5.1. Choosing Print List prints a formatted directory listing of the files currently displayed in File Manager.

Sort By

Choosing Sort By displays the File Manager Setup dialog box, shown in figure 9.6.

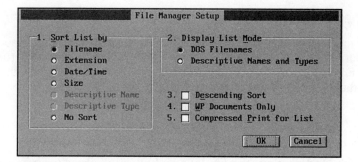

FIG. 9.6

The File Manager Setup dialog box.

The following paragraphs describe the options on the File Manager Setup dialog box:

■ *Sort List By*. Choose a sort criterion from this list, then choose OK to sort the File Manager list. WordPerfect uses the same sort criterion until you change it with Sort List. If you choose No Sort, the File Manager displays files in the same order as when you choose the DOS DIR command.

■ *Display List Mode*. Choose DOS Filenames to display only DOS filenames and no WordPerfect descriptive names or file types. Choose Descriptive Names and Types. WordPerfect changes the File Manager display to show descriptions and file types.

■ *Descending Sort*. This option sorts the directory in inverse alphabetic/numeric order.

■ *WP Documents Only*. WordPerfect can distinguish WordPerfect document files from program or graphics files, other program file formats, and other external file types. Choose this option to display only WordPerfect document files in File Manager.

■ *Compressed Print for List*. This option prints filenames in a smaller font when you choose Print List from File Manager, as described earlier.

Change Default Dir

Choosing Change Default Dir from the File Manager displays the Change Default Directory dialog box. To log on to a new directory, type the directory name or use Directory Tree (F8) or QuickList (F6) to insert a directory name in the box, as described earlier in this chapter.

If you type the name of a directory that doesn't exist, WordPerfect asks whether you want to create the directory. Choose Yes to create the directory and log on to it, or choose No to cancel the operation.

Current Dir

Choosing Current Dir (F5) from the File Manager displays the Specify File Manager List dialog box, where you can specify a new directory to list in File Manager. The Specify File Manager List dialog box is discussed earlier in the chapter.

Find

Choosing Find displays the Find dialog box. Find works exactly the same as in WordPerfect 5.1, except that you type the search pattern in a single-item dialog box instead of at the Word Pattern: prompt. Search patterns and operators work the same as in WordPerfect 5.1.

Notice the new Find option: Indexed Find. Choosing Indexed Find displays the QuickFinder File indexer dialog box. QuickFinder is described in detail later in this chapter.

Search

Choosing Search (F2) from the File Manager works the same as pressing F2 (Search) or Shift+F2 (Backward Search) in the WordPerfect 5.1 List Files screen. Choosing Search (F2) displays the Search for Filename dialog box.

Name Search

The Name Search option on the File Manager dialog box works exactly as it does in WordPerfect 5.1, except that choosing Name Search displays a Name Search text box where you type the search term. To locate a directory displayed in the File Manager list, type its name preceded by a backslash (\).

* (Un)mark and (Un)mark All

As in the WordPerfect 5.1 List Files screen, you can highlight a filename and press the asterisk key (*) to mark a file in the File Manager list. You can then choose Open, Copy, Move/Rename, Delete, Print, or Find to perform these operations on the marked files. To unmark a file, highlight its name and press asterisk (*) again.

To mark or unmark all the filenames displayed in File Manager, press Home, * or Alt+F5.

QuickFinder

QuickFinder is new in WordPerfect 6. QuickFinder indexes the text in WordPerfect document files so you can search files very quickly to locate files that contain specific text patterns. The following sections describe how to index and retrieve files with QuickFinder.

QuickFinder Indexes

QuickFinder creates an alphabetical list of every word in the files and directories you choose to index. You don't need to convert files created with WordPerfect 4.2, 5.0, or 5.1. You can create your own personal indexes or create shared indexes that can be accessed by other users on a network.

Follow these steps to create a QuickFinder index:

1. Choose File, File Manager; or press F5.

2. Choose Use QuickFinder (F4).

   WordPerfect displays the QuickFinder File Indexer dialog box, shown in figure 9.7.

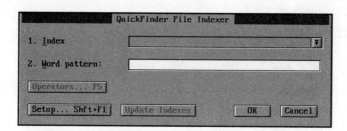

FIG. 9.7

The QuickFinder File Indexer dialog box.

3. Choose Setup (Shift+F1).

4. From the QuickFinder File Indexes Setup dialog box, choose Location of Files.

5. From the QuickFinder Index Files dialog box, choose Personal Path or Shared Path and type the directory where you want to store index files.

6. Choose OK to return to the QuickFinder File Indexes Setup dialog box.

7. Choose **C**reate Index Definition.

8. In the Create Index Definition dialog box, type an index description and press Enter. For example, you may type **EIR Reports**.

    WordPerfect automatically copies the first eight characters of the description into the Index Filename text box with spaces removed.

9. To accept the first eight characters of the index description name as the index filename, press Enter.

    Or, edit the Index Filename entry and press Enter.

10. Choose **A**dd.

11. In the Add QuickFinder Index Directory Pattern dialog box, type the directory or filename path for the files you want QuickFinder to index. You can also use File List (F5) or QuickList (F6) to insert a path name, as described earlier in this chapter.

12. If you want QuickFinder to index all the files in all the subdirectories of the specified directory, choose Include Subdirectories.

13. Choose OK to return to the Create Index Definition dialog box.

    WordPerfect inserts the directory path you typed in step 11 in the Directories and Files to Index list box.

14. Press F7 (Exit) to leave the Directories and Files to Index list box, and choose **O**ptions.

    WordPerfect displays the QuickFinder Index Options dialog box, shown in figure 9.8.

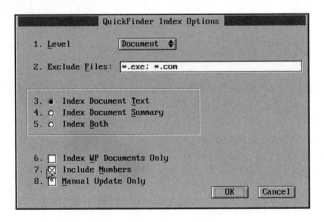

The following paragraphs describe the options on the QuickFinder Index Options dialog box:

- *Level.* Choosing this option displays a pop-up list with the options: **L**ine, **S**entence, **P**aragraph, **Pa**ge, **Se**ction, and **D**ocument. These options tell QuickFinder how much of each document to index. For example, if you choose **L**ine, QuickFinder indexes only the first line of each document.

- *Exclude Files.* This option tells QuickFinder which files to exclude from the index. QuickFinder ignores files with passwords, program files (EXE and COM filename extensions), index files (IDX filename extensions), and open files. Remember to remove passwords and close open files when you want those files included in an index. Type any file specifications for other file types you want to exclude (for example: *.ltr, *.not, and *.jot).

- *Index Document Text.* This option tells QuickFinder to index only each document's body text.

- *Index Document Summary.* This option tells QuickFinder to index only each document's document summary.

- *Index Both.* This option tells QuickFinder to index both body text and document summaries.

- *Index WP Documents Only.* This option tells QuickFinder to identify WordPerfect 4.2, 5.0, 5.1, and 6.0 documents and exclude all other document types.

- *Include Numbers.* This option tells QuickFinder to index numbers and words. You may want to turn this option off for documents that contain many numerical spreadsheets and tables, for example.

- *Manual Update Only.* If you choose **M**anual Update Only, the selected index isn't updated when you use the Update Indexes option on the QuickFinder File Indexer dialog box. You must regenerate the index, as described later in this chapter under "Updating and Regenerating Indexes."

15. Choose OK.

    WordPerfect returns to the Create Index Definition dialog box.

16. You can repeat the preceding steps to create other indexes, or choose OK to return to the QuickFinder File Indexes Setup dialog box.

17. Choose **G**enerate Marked Indexes.

WordPerfect displays an indexing status report screen.

WordPerfect generates the index and returns to the QuickFinder File Indexer dialog box.

You can now search for indexed text.

18. Choose Index, select an index type, then choose **W**ord Pattern. Type search text, and choose OK.

WordPerfect searches the indexed files and lists all files that contain the search string in the File Manager dialog box. You can now use **O**pen or **L**ook to locate the search text.

Indexes: Updating and Regenerating

To keep QuickFinder indexes current, you must update or regenerate the index after you make changes to the indexed files. Updating re-indexes only files that have changed, and regenerating re-indexes all the files in the index. Updating is somewhat faster, but regenerating creates an index that uses less disk space.

Follow these steps to update Quickfinder indexes:

1. Choose File, File Manager; or press F5.

2. Choose Use QuickFinder (F4).

3. Choose Update Indexes.

   QuickFinder updates the indexes and returns to the QuickFinder File Indexer dialog box.

4. Choose OK to return to the document window.

Update Indexes doesn't work with indexes that have been edited with Manual Update Only. (To learn how to choose Manual Update Only, see the preceding section.)

Follow these steps to regenerate an index:

1. Choose File, File Manager; or press F5.

2. Choose Use QuickFinder (F4).

3. Choose Setup (Shift+F1).

4. Highlight an index in the Index Description list.

5. Choose * (Un)mark to Regenerate to mark the file.

6. Repeat steps 4 and 5 to mark other indexes.

7. Choose **G**enerate Marked Indexes.

   WordPerfect regenerates the index and displays the indexing status report screen, then returns to the QuickFinder File Indexes Setup dialog box.

8. Choose Close, OK to return to the document window.

Index Editing

You edit an index to add or remove directories from the index. Follow these steps:

1. Choose File, File Manager; or press F5.

2. Choose Use QuickFinder (F4).

3. Choose Setup (Shift+F1).

4. In the QuickFinder File Indexes Setup dialog box, highlight an Index in the Index Description list box and choose **E**dit.

   WordPerfect displays the Edit Index Definition dialog box, with exactly the same options as the Create Index Definition dialog box, discussed earlier.

5. To remove a directory from the index, highlight it in the Directories and Files to Index list and choose **D**elete, then choose **Y**es to confirm the deletion.

6. To add a directory, choose Directories and Files to Index, then choose **A**dd.

   WordPerfect displays the Add QuickFinder Index Directory Pattern dialog box.

7. Type the name of the directory or filename pattern you want to add to the index.

   You can also insert a filename or directory with File List (F5) or QuickList (F6), as described earlier in this chapter.

8. To index files in subdirectories, choose Include Subdirectories.

9. Choose OK to return to the Edit Index Definition dialog box.

10. Press F7 (Exit), choose **O**ptions, and make any changes to the index as described in the section "QuickFinder Indexes" earlier in this chapter.

11. Choose OK and Close until you return to the document window.

QuickFinder Indexes: Deleting and Renaming

Follow these steps to delete or rename a QuickFinder index:

1. Choose **F**ile, **F**ile Manager; or press F5.

2. Choose Use QuickFinder (F4).

3. Choose Setup (Shift+F1).

4. Highlight an Index in the Index Description list box.

5. Choose **D**elete or **R**ename.

6. Choose **Y**es to confirm the deletion.

    Or, you can type a new name and choose OK.

7. Choose Close and OK until you return to the document window.

Index Search

After creating a QuickFinder index as described under "QuickFinder Indexes" earlier, you can use QuickFinder to quickly locate files containing search text. Follow these steps:

1. Choose **F**ile, **F**ile Manager; or press F5.

2. Choose Use QuickFinder (F4).

3. Choose Index and highlight the index you want to search.

4. Choose Word Pattern and type a word pattern to search for.

5. To use search operators, type the operators in the search text, or choose Operators (F5).

    WordPerfect displays the Word Pattern Operators dialog box.

6. Choose an operator and choose Insert.

    WordPerfect inserts the operator in the Word pattern text box.

7. Choose OK to begin the search.

Following are some examples of the use of operators:

Operator	Word Pattern	Finds
And (&)	dog & cat	Files containing the words *dog* and *cat*. The words can be anywhere in the document.

Operator	Word Pattern	Finds
Or (|)	dog | cat	Files that contain the words *dog* or *cat* or both words. The words can be anywhere in the document.
Not (-)	dog - cat	Files with the word *dog* but not *cat*.
Match character (?)	cat?	Files that contain *cats*.
Match character (?)	c?t	Files that contain *cat*, *cut*, *cot*, and so on.
Match multiple characters (*)	cat*	Files that contain *cat*, *cats*, *caterer*, *catapult*, and so on.

QuickFinder lists files containing the search term in the File Manager, where you can open or look at the text and locate the search term.

Methods for Saving QuickFinder Indexes

QuickFinder indexes are saved with the filename extension IDX. You can specify a directory for these files using either of two methods.

Method 1:

1. Choose Setup (Shift+F1), **L**ocation of Files.

2. Choose **Q**uickFinder Files. Type a file path in the **P**ersonal Path and/or **S**hared Path boxes, then choose OK, OK, Close.

Method 2:

1. Choose **F**ile, **F**ile Manager (F5), Use QuickFinder (F4), Setup (Shift+F1), Location of **F**iles.

2. Type a file path in the **P**ersonal Path and/or **S**hared Path boxes, then choose OK, Close, OK.

Opening, Retrieving, and Saving Files

The WordPerfect 6 Save and Retrieve commands contain no surprises for WordPerfect 5.1 users. However, WordPerfect 6 can open nine documents at once, each in its own window. To make the windowing feature easier to use, WordPerfect 6 has a new option—Open. This section describes the steps to open, retrieve, and save files.

Open and Retrieve

WordPerfect 6 introduces a new way to bring documents into the editing screen. The Open command, new in WordPerfect 6, automatically brings the file you specify into its own editing window. You can open up to nine documents in separate windows in WordPerfect 6.

The Retrieve command, familiar to users of WordPerfect 5.1, brings a file into a new document screen *or* inserts it into a displayed document at the cursor.

Opening a Document

Follow these steps to open a document in its own, separate editing window:

1. Choose **File**, **O**pen; or press Shift+F10.

   WordPerfect displays the Open Document dialog box, shown in figure 9.9.

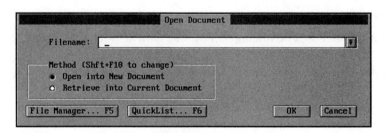

WordPerfect 6 uses Shift+F10 for the Open command. In WordPerfect 5.1, Shift+F10 was the Retrieve command. In WordPerfect 5.1, you cannot open a document in its own window in one step as in WordPerfect 6; you have to move to the second document screen with the Switch command (Shift+F3), then use Retrieve (Shift+F10) to bring a document into Doc 2.

2. Type a filename to open the named file.

   If you click the arrow at the right end of the **F**ilename box or press the down arrow with **F**ilename selected, WordPerfect displays the four files you last saved. To open one of these files, double-click its name or highlight the name and press Enter.

3. Choose **O**pen into New Document (the default) or **R**etrieve into Current Document.

   Retrieve into Current Document allows you to change your mind and bring the file into the current document instead of into a new document, without returning to the editing screen and choosing Retrieve.

   You can use File Manager (F5) or QuickList (F6) to insert a filename. File Manager and QuickList are described earlier in this chapter in the sections on File Manager and QuickList.

4. Choose OK.

WordPerfect retrieves the file into a new window, or into the current document at the cursor if you chose **R**etrieve into current document.

Retrieving a Document

Retrieve inserts a file in the current document window at the cursor. Follow these steps:

1. Place the cursor where you want to insert the document.

2. Choose File, **R**etrieve; or press Shift+F10, Shift+F10.

   WordPerfect displays the Retrieve Document dialog box, which contains exactly the same options as the Open Document dialog box, shown in figure 9.9.

3. Type a filename to retrieve.

   If you click the arrow at the right end of the **F**ilename box or press Down Arrow with **F**ilename selected, WordPerfect displays the four files you last edited. To retrieve one of these files, double-click its name or highlight the name and press Enter.

4. Choose **O**pen into New Document (the default) or **R**etrieve into Current Document.

You can press Shift+F10 to toggle between the **M**ethod options.

Open into New Document enables you to change your mind and bring the file into a new document window instead of the current document, without returning to the editing screen and choosing **F**ile, **O**pen or pressing Shift+F10.

You can use File Manager (F5) or QuickList (F6) to insert a filename. File Manager and QuickList are described earlier in this chapter in the sections "File Manager" and "Using QuickList."

5. Choose OK.

WordPerfect retrieves the file into the current window, or into a new window if you chose **O**pen into New Document.

Opening and Retrieving Files in Other Formats

WordPerfect can automatically translate files created with a number of other programs. Follow these steps:

1. Choose **F**ile, **O**pen; or choose **F**ile, **R**etrieve to display the Open Document or Retrieve Document dialog box.

2. Type the name of the file and choose OK.

   WordPerfect displays the File Format dialog box, with more than 50 file formats (see fig. 9.10).

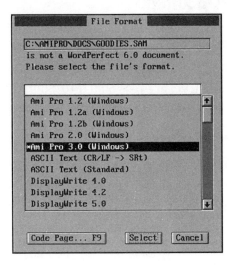

FIG. 9.10

The File Format dialog box.

3. If the correct file format is highlighted, choose Select.

   Or, move the highlight to the correct file format and choose Select.

WordPerfect converts the file and opens it in a new window or retrieves it into the current document, depending on whether you chose **O**pen or **R**etrieve in step 1.

If the correct format isn't listed, you may be able to use the source program to export the file in a format WordPerfect can read. Refer to that program's documentation.

Exiting and Closing

As in WordPerfect 5.1, you can exit WordPerfect 6 by pressing the F7 (Exit) key. In addition, WordPerfect 6 has two new commands for exiting the program: Close and Exit WP. All three commands are described in this section.

Closing a Document

Follow these steps to close the on-screen document without exiting WordPerfect:

1. With an open document in the editing window, choose **F**ile, **C**lose.

   WordPerfect closes the document and returns to the blank editing window.

   Or, if you have made changes to the document since it was last saved, WordPerfect displays the Document dialog box, shown in figure 9.11.

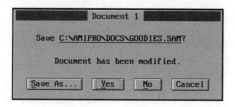

FIG. 9.11

The Document dialog box.

2. Choose **Y**es to save the document and return to the blank editing window.

Or, choose **No** to abandon the Close command and return to the document window.

Or, choose **S**ave As to display the Save Document dialog box, shown in figure 9.12.

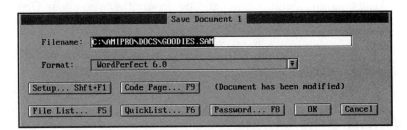

FIG. 9.12

The Save
Document dialog
box.

The Save Document dialog box lets you save the document under a new name and, optionally, in another word processing format.

3. To save the file under a new name, choose Filename and type the new name.

4. To save the file in another format, choose Format and highlight the desired format in the drop-down list.

5. Choose OK.

   If the filename already exists, WordPerfect prompts you to confirm the overwrite.

6. Choose **Yes** to overwrite the existing file, or choose **No** to cancel the operation and return to the Save Document dialog box where you can type a different filename.

WordPerfect drops down a list of word processor file formats. Highlight a format and press Enter.

The following paragraphs describe the remaining options on the Save Document dialog box:

■ *Setup (Shift+F1).* Choosing this option displays the Save Setup dialog box. The **F**ast Save option on the Save Setup dialog box works just as in WordPerfect 5.1. **D**efault Save Format lets you choose another word processor format that WordPerfect automatically uses to save files until you change the setting.

■ *Code Page (F9).* Choosing this option lets you choose a foreign language from the Code Page dialog box. If you choose a foreign language and choose **S**elect, WordPerfect translates hidden codes into the specified language. In order to use this option, you must first purchase the corresponding language model from WordPerfect Corporation.

- *File List (F5)*. Choosing this option displays the Select List dialog box. If you type a file or directory path in the Directory box and choose OK, WordPerfect displays the File List dialog box. To insert a filename in the Save Document dialog box, highlight the name and choose **S**elect. The remaining options on the File List dialog box let you display a new **D**irectory, use **F**ile Manager (F5), **U**se as Pattern a file spec displayed in the Dir box, or use **N**ame Search to locate a file in the list.

- *QuickList (F6)*. This option is described in detail earlier in this chapter, in the section "Using QuickList."

- *Password*. For detailed information on creating, editing, and deleting passwords, see the section titled "Using Passwords," later in this chapter.

Exiting a Document

WordPerfect 6 has two Exit options:

- File, Exit; or press F7
- File, Exit WP; or press Home, F7

Follow these steps to use Exit:

1. Choose **F**ile, **E**xit; or press F7.

   If you have made changes to a file in the document window since the last save, WordPerfect displays the Document dialog box.

2. Choose **S**ave As, **Y**es, **N**o, or Cancel.

   If you choose **N**o, WordPerfect displays the Exit dialog box.

3. Choose **Y**es to exit to DOS without saving the file.

   Or, choose **N**o to return to abandon your editing changes and return to a blank document screen.

   Or, choose Cancel to cancel the operation and return to the document.

Follow these steps to use Exit WP:

1. Choose **F**ile, E**x**it WP; or press Home, F7.

   If you have made changes to the on-screen file since the last save, WordPerfect displays the Exit WordPerfect dialog box with the Save check box marked and the Save and Exit button displayed (see fig. 9.13).

FIG. 9.13

The Exit
WordPerfect
dialog box.

2. Choose Save and Exit to have WordPerfect save the file without prompting you to confirm the file overwrite. WordPerfect returns to DOS.

Or, unmark the Save check box. WordPerfect changes the Save and Exit button to an Exit button.

3. Choose Exit to return to DOS without saving the on-screen file.

WordPerfect doesn't prompt you to confirm that you want to abandon your changes. If you have not made changes to an on-screen file since the last save, WordPerfect displays the Exit WordPerfect dialog box with the Exit button displayed.

If you choose **File, Exit** WP with no file displayed in the document window, and no changes made to the (Untitled) document, WordPerfect displays the Exit WordPerfect dialog box with no filename in the Filename box and the Save button unmarked. In that case, type a filename and mark the Save check box. WordPerfect changes the Exit button to Save and Exit. Choose Save and Exit to save the file and exit to DOS.

Choosing (Un)**mark** All toggles the Save check box on and off and toggles the Exit button to Save and Exit.

Exiting a Document with More than One Open Document

If you choose **File, Exit** with more than one document open, WordPerfect displays the Exit dialog box for the current document.

Choosing **Yes** displays the window with the next-higher number. For example, if you exit Document 2, WordPerfect displays Document 3. If you are working in Document 2 with only Documents 1 and 2 open, exiting Document 2 takes you to Document 1.

You can click on the dot in the upper left corner of the screen to exit the current document. This action is the same as choosing **File, Exit**.

Choosing File, Exit WP with more than one window open displays the Exit WordPerfect dialog box with all the open files listed, as shown in figure 9.14. You can now mark the Save check box for each file individually, or choose (Un)mark All to toggle all the check boxes on and off. Choosing Exit or Save and Exit closes the files with Save check boxes marked. With all the check boxes marked, WordPerfect saves each file and returns to DOS.

FIG. 9.14

The Exit WordPerfect dialog box when you have more than one window open.

Using Location of Files

You can tell WordPerfect which directory you use to store documents. WordPerfect then saves files in the specified directory without your having to type the directory path. Follow these steps:

1. Press Shift+F1 (Setup) and choose Location of Files, Documents.

2. Type a path to the directory where you save documents.

3. Press Enter and choose OK, Close to return to the document screen.

Using Passwords

As in WordPerfect 5.1, you can password-protect documents in WordPerfect 6. A protected file cannot be opened, retrieved, printed, copied, moved, or deleted unless you know the password.

Creating and Editing Passwords

Follow these steps to create or edit a password:

1. Choose File, Save As.

2. In the Save Document dialog box, choose Password (F8).

   WordPerfect displays the Password dialog box.

3. Type a password (23 characters maximum) or edit the existing password.

   WordPerfect doesn't display the password. This precaution is a simple way to keep others from learning the password.

   WordPerfect prompts you to re-enter the password.

4. Type the password again, then choose OK to return to the Save Document dialog box.

The next time you open the document, WordPerfect displays the Password dialog box. Type the password and choose OK to open the document.

Removing a Password

Follow these steps to remove a password:

1. With the document displayed, choose File, Save As.

2. Choose Password (F8).

3. Choose Remove (F6).

WordPerfect removes the password and returns to the Save Document dialog box.

How Secure Are WordPerfect Passwords?

WordPerfect passwords can be "cracked" by knowledgeable individuals using password-decoding software. Password-protected documents can also be deleted with the DOS Del and Erase commands.

When you assign a password, WordPerfect also protects backup and temporary buffer files created after you assign the password. Backup and temporary files created before you assign a password are not protected.

If you save a password-protected file in another word processor format, as described earlier in this chapter in the section "Opening, Retrieving, and Saving Files," the password is not retained.

Managing Documents

You will find the document management tools basically the same as in WordPerfect 5.1, except that Document Information is new. The options now work through dialog boxes instead of menus.

Getting Document Information

Document Information tells you the number of characters, words, lines, sentences, paragraphs, pages, and total bytes in the on-screen document. It also displays average word length, average words per sentence, and maximum words per sentence.

Follow these steps to display Document Information:

1. Choose **Tools**, **Writing** Tools, **Document** Information; or press Alt+F1 and choose **Document** Information.

   WordPerfect displays the Document Information box, shown in figure 9.15.

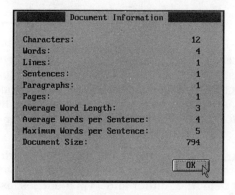

FIG. 9.15

The Document Information box.

2. Choose OK to return to the document window.

Using Document Summaries

Document Summary works as in WordPerfect 5.1. However, in WordPerfect 6 you can customize the Document Summary dialog box, and you can print summaries.

Follow these steps to create a Document Summary:

1. Choose **F**ile, S**u**mmary.

   WordPerfect displays the Document Summary dialog box, shown in figure 9.16.

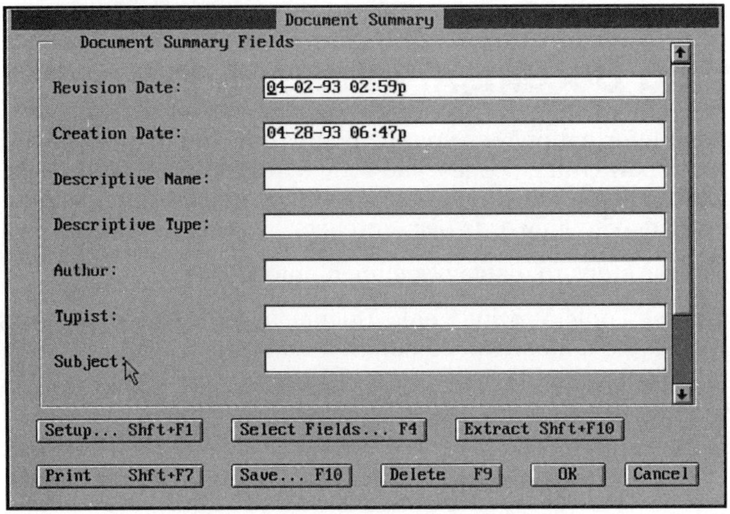

FIG. 9.16

The Document
Summary dialog
box.

```
┌──────────────────────── Document Summary ────────────────────────┐
│ ┌─ Document Summary Fields ─────────────────────────────────┐ ▲ │
│ │                                                            │   │
│ │  Revision Date:      │04-02-93 02:59p                   │  │   │
│ │                                                            │   │
│ │  Creation Date:      │04-28-93 06:47p                   │  │   │
│ │                                                            │   │
│ │  Descriptive Name:   │                                  │  │   │
│ │                                                            │   │
│ │  Descriptive Type:   │                                  │  │   │
│ │                                                            │   │
│ │  Author:             │                                  │  │   │
│ │                                                            │   │
│ │  Typist:             │                                  │  │   │
│ │                                                            │   │
│ │  Subject:            │                                  │  │ ▼ │
│ └────────────────────────────────────────────────────────────┘   │
│ ┌ Setup... Shft+F1 ┐  ┌ Select Fields... F4 ┐  ┌ Extract Shft+F10 ┐│
│ ┌ Print  Shft+F7 ┐ ┌ Save... F10 ┐ ┌ Delete  F9 ┐ ┌ OK ┐ ┌ Cancel ┐│
└───────────────────────────────────────────────────────────────────┘
```

You must scroll down to display the Account, Keywords, and Abstract fields. Also, Descriptive Type is called Document Type in WordPerfect 5.1. In WordPerfect 6, you can customize the Document Summary dialog box, adding and removing fields, as described below under Customizing the Document Summary Dialog Box.

2. Choose Extract (Shift+F10), **Y**es to have WordPerfect insert the 160 characters to the right of the cursor or after a RE: heading in the Subject field; the Author and Typist entries last saved with a summary during the current WordPerfect session; and the first 400 characters of the document in the Document Summary Abstract field.

3. Fill in any desired fields and choose OK to return to the document window.

Customizing the Document Summary Dialog Box

You can add and remove fields from the WordPerfect 6 Document Summary dialog box. Follow these steps:

1. Choose File, Summary, Select Fields (F4).

   WordPerfect displays the Select Summary Fields dialog box, shown in figure 9.17.

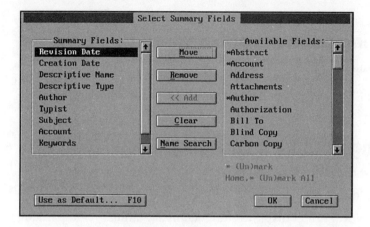

FIG. 9.17

The Select Summary Fields dialog box.

2. To remove a summary field, highlight it in the Summary Fields list and choose Remove.

   WordPerfect removes the field from the list. Notice that fields listed under Summary Fields are marked with an asterisk (*) in the Available Fields list.

3. To add a summary field, highlight it in the Available Fields list and choose Add or press the asterisk key (*).

   WordPerfect copies the field into the Summary Fields list.

4. To clear the Summary Fields list, choose Clear, Yes.

5. To use the customized Summary Fields as the default for all documents, check Use as default.

   Or, to use the customized Summary Fields for the current document only, leave the Use As Default check box blank.

6. Choose OK to return to the Document Summary dialog box.

Printing a Summary

You can send a copy of the Document Summary dialog box information to your printer. Choose File, Summary. Then choose Print (Shift+F7). WordPerfect prints the summary information.

Deleting a Summary

To delete a document summary, choose File, Summary, Delete (F9), Yes.

Saving a Document Summary

You can save document summary information in its own file. This works as in WordPerfect 5.1. From the Document Summary dialog box, press F10 (Save), choose Yes, type a filename, and choose OK.

Using Document Summary Setup Options

Follow these steps to change document summary options:

1. Choose File, Summary, Setup (Shift+F1).

   WordPerfect displays the Document Summary Setup dialog box.

2. Choose the summary setup options.

The following paragraphs describe the document summary setup options, which work the same as in WordPerfect 5.1:

- *Subject Search Text.* WordPerfect automatically looks for a RE: heading and inserts the first 160 characters to the right of RE: in the Subject field. To have WordPerfect search for a different heading, type the new heading in the Subject Search Text box.

- *Default Descriptive Type.* Type a document type in this box to have WordPerfect automatically enter the type in the Descriptive Type field when you create a summary.

- *Create Summary on Exit/Save.* Choose this check box to have WordPerfect display the Document Summary dialog box each time you exit or save a document until you create a summary for that document.

Using Master Documents

The Master Document feature works the same in WordPerfect 6 as in WordPerfect 5.1. The steps for formatting and printing a master document are the same and, therefore, are not described in detail here. Because the process uses dialog boxes instead of menus, the following steps for creating a subdocument link are provided for illustration:

1. Choose **F**ile, **M**aster Document; or press Alt+F5. Then choose **S**ubdocument.

2. In the Include Subdocument dialog box, type a filename and choose OK.

WordPerfect inserts a comment box with the name of the subdocument, just as in WordPerfect 5.1.

Using WordPerfect Shell

This section introduces you briefly to the WordPerfect Shell, a program module now included with WordPerfect 6. To run WordPerfect from Shell, you first run Shell from the DOS prompt, as described in the Shell User's Guide. You can then start WordPerfect by choosing it from a Shell menu.

Following are the basic capabilities of Shell:

- *Task Switching.* WordPerfect Shell enables you to switch from one program to another without exiting to DOS. You can load up to nine programs in memory at once (or up to 40 with a custom Shell installation). You can switch instantly to any program by choosing the program's hot key (mnemonic).

- *Data Transfer.* You can use the Shell Clipboard to copy and move data between programs.

- *Shell Macros.* A Shell macro can switch between programs and carry out commands in each program.

- *Shell Message Board (Electronic Mail).* With the Message Board, you can write notes to yourself and send electronic mail messages to other users on a network. You can create messages in the Shell Message editing screen, and you can attach files to messages.

- *Screen Saver.* The Shell includes a built-in screen saver utility that protects your computer's monitor from being damaged when the screen is inactive for an extended period.

Printing

To be able to use your printer with WordPerfect 6, you must first install a printer. You normally do this installation when you install WordPerfect, as described in Chapter 1. You can later install another printer or switch between printers from within WordPerfect, without exiting to DOS and running the Install program. This chapter describes the options for installing and editing printer definitions in WordPerfect. This chapter also gives you detailed instructions on using WordPerfect to print documents.

Selecting and Adding Printers

As in WordPerfect 5.1, you use the Select Printer function to select a new printer, add a printer from within WordPerfect, or edit an existing printer definition.

Selecting a Printer

The steps for selecting a printer are the same as in WordPerfect 5.1. However, you use dialog boxes instead of menus. Follow these steps:

1. Choose File, **P**rint/Fax; or press Shift+F7. WordPerfect displays the Print dialog box (see fig. 10.1).

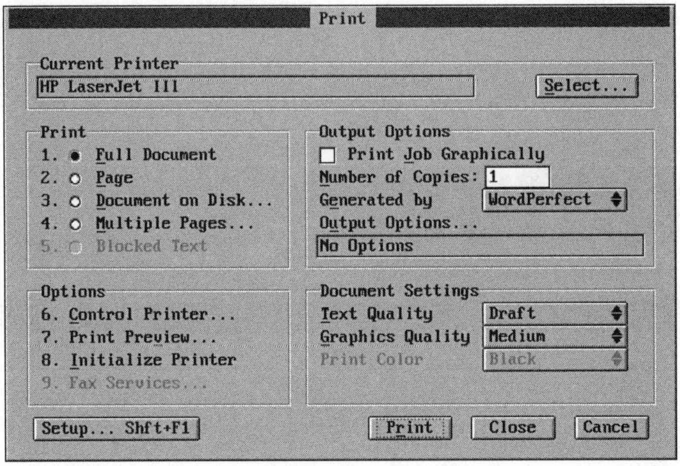

FIG. 10.1

The Print dialog box.

2. Choose **S**elect. WordPerfect displays the Select Printer dialog box.

3. Highlight a printer name and choose **S**elect. WordPerfect returns to the Print dialog box. The printer's name appears in the Current Printer box.

4. Choose Close to return to the document window.

The printer that you selected becomes the default until you choose another printer.

Adding a Printer

You can add a printer definition in WordPerfect without using the Install program. The process is the same as for WordPerfect 5.1, except that you use dialog boxes instead of menus. Follow these steps:

1. Choose File, **P**rint/Fax; or press Shift+F7.

2. Choose **S**elect.

3. Choose **A**dd Printer. WordPerfect displays the Add Printer dialog box.

If WordPerfect displays a `Printer Files Not Found` message or if
the printer that you want to add isn't on the list, choose **O**ther Dir,
type the name of another directory where .ALL printer files are
located, and choose OK. If you haven't installed other printer files in
another hard disk directory, exit WordPerfect and run the Installation program to install the printer files.

T I P

4. Highlight the printer you want to add; then choose **S**elect.
   WordPerfect displays the Printer Filename dialog box.

5. Choose OK, or type a new filename and then choose OK.
   WordPerfect displays the Information dialog box.

You can use File List (F5) or QuickList (F6) to insert a name. For
more information, see Chapter 9, "Working with Files."

T I P

6. Choose Close. WordPerfect displays the Edit Printer Setup dialog
   box (see fig. 10.2).

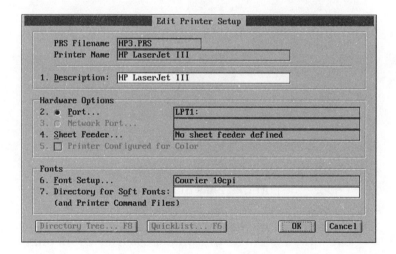

FIG. 10.2

The Edit Printer
Setup dialog
box.

7. Edit the printer setup as described in the next section; then choose
   OK, Close. Finally, choose Close to return to the document screen.

WordPerfect adds the printer to the list in the Select Printer dialog box.

Editing a Printer Setup

You edit a printer definition when you want to change the printer port, network port, sheet feeder, color configuration, font setup, or the directory where soft fonts are stored. To accomplish this edit, follow these steps:

1. Choose **File**, **Print/Fax**; or press Shift+F7.

2. Choose **Select**.

3. Highlight the name of a printer and choose **Edit**. WordPerfect displays the Edit Printer Setup dialog box (refer to fig. 10.2).

4. Edit the printer setup by choosing from the following options in the Edit Printer Setup dialog box. To return to the document window, choose OK, Close, Close.

   ■ *Description.* This option enables you to type a description for the printer.

   ■ *Port.* This option displays the Port dialog box (see fig. 10.3). In the Port dialog box, you can make the following choices:

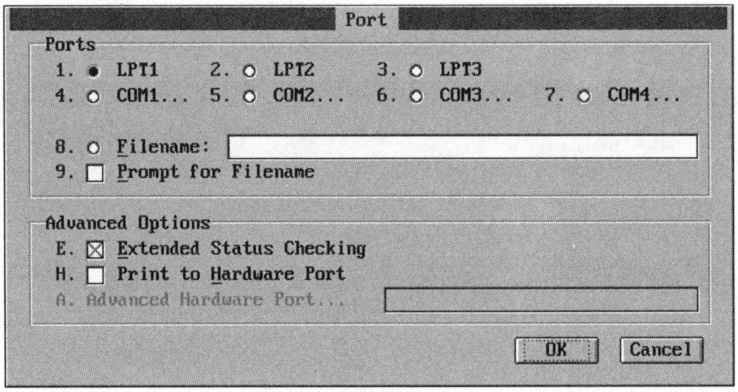

FIG. 10.3

The Port dialog box.

Choose the port that links the printer to the computer.

Choose **Filename** if you want to print to a file. Type the filename and choose OK. Remember to deselect this option when you want to use the printer again instead of printing to a file.

Choose **Prompt** for Filename if you want to type a new filename each time you print to a file.

Choose **Extended** Status Checking and Print to **Hardware** Port to set advanced printer configuration options. For more information about these options, see the WordPerfect 6 *User's Guide.*

■ *Network Port.* This option is only available if you have in-stalled WordPerfect 6 for use on a network. Choosing this option displays the Network Port dialog box.

In the Network Port dialog box, choose the options for Server, Queue, Server/Queue Name, and Suppress Top of Form. For complete information on setting up WordPerfect on a network, see WordPerfect's *User's Guide*.

■ *Sheet Feeder.* This option displays the Sheet Feeder dialog box. Choose a sheet feeder from the list, then choose OK. WordPerfect displays information about the feeder. Choose OK to return to the Edit Printer Setup dialog box.

■ *Printer Configured for Color.* This option tells WordPerfect that your printer can print in color.

■ *Font Setup.* This option displays the Font Setup dialog box. Setting up fonts is discussed in detail in Chapter 11.

■ *Directory for Soft Fonts.* This option enables you to type a directory path to tell WordPerfect where to find soft fonts.

Printing a Document

You can print a document in the document window or a document that is stored on disk.

Printing the On-Screen Document

Follow these steps to print the on-screen document:

1. Choose File, **P**rint/Fax; or press Shift+F7. WordPerfect displays the Print dialog box.

2. Choose Full Document, **P**rint to begin printing the full document. Alternatively, choose **P**age, **P**rint to begin printing just the current page.

Printing a Document on Disk

Follow these steps to print a document stored on disk:

1. Choose File, **P**rint/Fax, **D**ocument on Disk. WordPerfect displays the Document on Disk dialog box.

2. Type the filename of the document that you want to print; then choose OK. WordPerfect displays the Print Multiple Pages dialog box, which was described earlier in the section "Printing Multiple Pages."

T I P You can use File List (F5) or QuickList (F6) to insert a filename. These features are described in Chapter 9.

3. Fill in any desired options in the Print Multiple Pages dialog box. Choose OK to begin printing and return to the document screen.

Printing Multiple Pages

You can print several pages of the on-screen document. Follow these steps:

1. Choose **F**ile, **P**rint/Fax, **M**ultiple Pages. Choosing **M**ultiple Pages displays the Print Multiple Pages dialog box (see fig. 10.4).

```
                 Print Multiple Pages
    1. Page/Label Range:   (all)
    2. Secondary Page(s):
    3. Chapter(s):
    4. Volume(s):

    5. Odd/Even Pages  Both ▼

    6. ☐ Document Summary
    7. ☐ Print as Booklet
    8. ☐ Descending Order (Last Page First)

                            [  OK  ]   [ Cancel ]
```

FIG. 10.4

The Print Multiple Pages dialog box.

2. Choose from the following options in the Print Multiple Pages dialog box. Then choose OK to return to the Print dialog box.

■ *Page/Label Range*. Choose this option and type a page range in the same way that you would in WordPerfect 5.1.

Label refers to printing labels. WordPerfect 6 prints sheet labels differently than WordPerfect 5.1. For example, you no longer have to specify the page range 1-30 to print a sheet of 30 labels. When you specify a page number, WordPerfect 6 correctly interprets the command and prints all 30 labels on the physical page.

- *Secondary Pages.* Choose this option and type the range of secondary pages that you want to print. Secondary page numbering is described in Chapter 4.

- *Chapter(s).* Choose this option and type the range of chapters to be printed. WordPerfect 6 uses the following order of precedence: volume, chapter, pages. For example, if you choose Volume 3, WordPerfect prints only the chapters and pages from Volume 3. If you choose Chapter 44, WordPerfect prints only pages from Chapter 44. Chapter numbering is described in Chapter 4.

- *Volume(s).* Choose this option and type the range of volumes to be printed. Volume numbering is described in Chapter 4.

- *Odd/Even Pages.* Choose this option and a pop-up list appears. From this list you can choose **B**oth (the default), **O**dd, or **E**ven.

- *Document Summary.* Choose this option to print the document summary. To print all or part of the main document with the document summary, specify the page range in the **P**age/Label Range text box. To print only the summary, leave **P**age/Label Range blank.

- *Print as **B**ooklet.* Choose this option to have WordPerfect number printed pages in the correct booklet (signature) order. For information on formatting documents as booklets, see "Subdivided Pages" in Chapter 8.

- *Descending Order (Last Page First).* Choose this option to print backward. If your printer ejects paper face up, this option saves you from arranging pages in ascending order.

Printing Blocked Text

You can select text in a document and then print just the selected text. Follow these steps:

1. Select the text that you want to print.

2. Choose **F**ile, **P**rint/Fax; or press Shift+F7. WordPerfect displays the Print dialog box with the **B**locked Text radio button selected.

3. Choose P**r**int.

WordPerfect prints the selected text. The text prints in the same position on the page in which it appears in the document. To print the selected text at the top of its own page, move the cursor to the beginning of the text and enter a temporary hard page break (Ctrl+Enter). Follow steps 1-3 to print the block; then delete the page break.

Previewing Before Printing

Print Preview has changed a great deal in WordPerfect 6. You can scroll text horizontally, zoom in and out, and display thumbnail views. You still cannot edit text in Print Preview.

Viewing a Document

Follow these steps to display a document using Print Preview:

1. Choose **F**ile, Print Preview; or press Shift+F7 and choose Print Preview. WordPerfect displays the document in the Full Page Print Preview mode (see fig. 10.5).

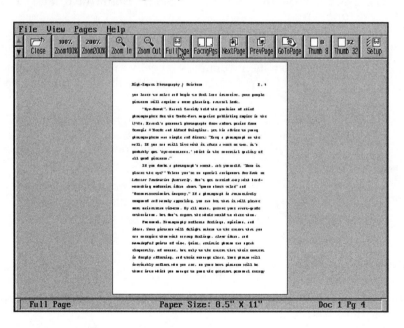

A document displayed in Full Page Print Preview mode.

2. Choose options from the Print Preview Button Bar or from the Print Preview menu bar.

To exit Print Preview, click the Close button, press F7 (Exit), or choose **F**ile, **C**lose.

Setting Print Preview Options

The WordPerfect 5.1 Setup: View Document options have migrated to the Print Preview File menu in WordPerfect 6. Follow these steps to set Print Preview options:

1. From the Print Preview screen, choose File, Setup. WordPerfect displays the Print Preview Options dialog box.

2. Choose View Text in Black & White and/or View Graphics in Black & White.

These options work the same as in WordPerfect 5.1. Notice, however, that the Bold Displayed with Color option is no longer available.

Setting Print Preview View Options

You can set most Print Preview view options with the Button Bar or with the View menu. The following options appear on the Button Bar from left to right:

Button Bar Option	Description
Button Bar Scroll Arrows	Click to scroll the Button Bar left or right.
Close	Exit Print Preview.
Zoom100%	Click to display a 100% view.
Zoom200%	Click to display a 200% view.
Zoom In	Click to Zoom in, in 25% increments.
Zoom Out	Click to Zoom out in 25% increments.
FullPage	The default. Click to view the full page.
FacingPgs	Click to view the facing page.
NextPage	Click to view the next page.
PrevPage	Click to view the previous page.
GoToPage	Click and type a number; then choose OK to go to the desired page.
Thumb 8	Click to display eight thumbnail-sized pages.

continues

Button Bar Option	Description
Thumb 32	Click to display 32 thumbnail-sized pages.
Setup	Click to view text and graphics in black-and-white.
BBar Edt	Click the down scroll arrow to display this option, then click to add, move, or delete buttons from the Button Bar, and to add menu items to the Print Preview Menu Bar.
BBar Opt	Click the down scroll arrow to display this option, then click to change the position of the Button Bar and the format of the buttons.

After changing the view, you can restore the display to its default, Full Page view. Choose View, Reset. You cannot choose this option with the Button Bar.

Changing the Button Bar Setup

As with the document window Button Bar, you can change the Preview Button Bar options. Follow these steps:

1. To toggle the Button Bar on and off with Print Preview displayed, choose View, Button Bar.

   WordPerfect turns off the Button Bar. You may want to hide the button bar to display a larger image of the document in Print Preview.

2. To edit the Button Bar, choose View, Button Bar Setup, Edit. WordPerfect displays the Edit Button Bar dialog box.

3. Use the dialog box to add, edit, remove, and move buttons.

Follow these steps to set Button Bar Options:

1. From Print Preview, choose View, Button Bar Setup, Options. WordPerfect displays the Button Bar Options dialog box.

2. Choose a Position option to move the Button Bar to a new location in the Print Preview window.

3. Choose a Style option to display Picture and Text (the default), Picture Only, or Text Only.

Changing the Button Bar style changes the size of the buttons, allowing documents to be displayed in larger sizes. Figure 10.6 shows Print Preview with text-only buttons displayed at the left side of the screen.

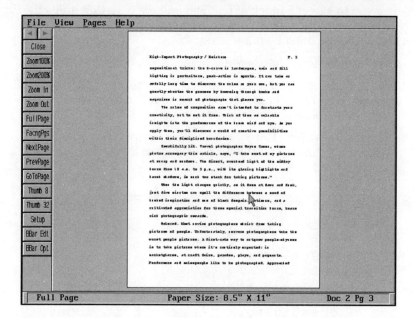

FIG. 10.6

Print Preview with text-only buttons on the left side of the screen.

Notice that with text-only buttons displayed on the left side of the screen, several more buttons are displayed: Setup, BBar Edt, and BBar Opt.

Zooming In

With the Zoom Area option, you can select part of a displayed document and enlarge it. Follow these steps:

1. From the Print Preview screen, choose View, Zoom Area. WordPerfect changes the mouse cursor to a magnifying glass.

2. Drag the magnifying glass cursor to select an area of the document; then release the mouse button.

WordPerfect fills the screen with the area you selected. You can zoom up to a maximum 400% view. Notice that the current zoom percentage is displayed in the status bar.

Selecting an Area

The Select Area option on the View menu of the Print Preview screen enables you to select a block of text and enlarge it so that it fills the screen. You can then choose Select Area again to display a different portion of the document. Follow these steps:

1. In Print Preview, choose View, Select Area.

2. When you click the mouse button, the cursor turns into a magnifying glass. Drag the cursor to select a block of text. When you release the mouse button, the selected block of text fills the screen.

3. Choose View, Select Area. WordPerfect displays a thumbnail-sized view of the current page with the selected text shown (see fig. 10.7).

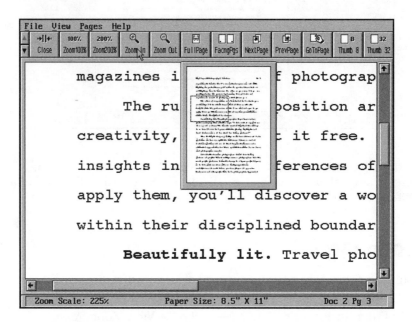

FIG. 10.7

The Select Area thumbnail page display.

4. Drag the selection rectangle to a new location to display that portion of the page.

Zooming Using the Mouse

You can zoom in Print Preview by clicking the left mouse button once to enlarge the displayed portion of the page by 25%.

You can also drag using the mouse to zoom in on a portion of the displayed text. Releasing the mouse button fills the screen with the selected text, up to a maximum zoom of 1000%.

You can press Escape in Print Preview to cancel the redrawing of the Print Preview screen.

Inserting Printer Commands

The Printer Commands function works essentially the same in WordPerfect 6 as in WordPerfect 5.1, except that it uses a dialog box.

Follow these steps to insert a printer command in an open document:

1. Choose **Layout, Other, Printer** Functions, **Printer** Commands. WordPerfect displays the Printer Commands dialog box (see fig. 10.8).

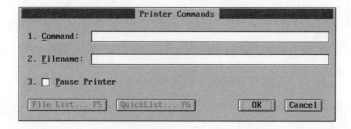

FIG. 10.8

The Printer
Commands
dialog box.

2. Type printer commands in the **Command** box, or type the name of a printer command file in the **Filename** box.

3. To pause the printer at the current location of the cursor when the document prints, mark the **Pause** Printer check box.

4. Choose OK until you return to the document window.

Controlling the Printer

Control Printer works exactly the same in WordPerfect 6 as in Word-Perfect 5.1 except for three new options.

Follow these steps to use Control Printer:

1. Start printing a document.

T I P   You don't have to print a document to display the Control Printer dialog box, but the options are not active unless a job is being processed.

2. From the Print dialog box, choose **C**ontrol Printer. WordPerfect displays the Control Printer dialog box (see fig. 10.9).

```
┌────────────────────────── Control Printer ──────────────────────────┐
│  ┌─ Current Job ──────────────────────────────────────────────────┐ │
│  │ Job Number: 2                      Page Number:  1              │ │
│  │ Status:     Printing               Current Copy: 1 of 1         │ │
│  │ Message:    None                                               │ │
│  │ Paper:      Letter (Portrait) 8.5" x 11"                       │ │
│  │ Location:   Continuous feed                                    │ │
│  │ Action:     None                                              │ │
│  │                                                               │ │
│  │ Percentage Processed:  0    [                              ]   │ │
│  └───────────────────────────────────────────────────────────────┘ │
│  ┌─ Job  Document              Destination ──────────┐  ↑          │
│  │  2   C:\...\TRAVEL2.WP       LPT 1                 │     1. Cancel Job │
│  │                                                   │     2. Rush Job  │
│  │                                                   │     3. * (Un)mark │
│  │                                                   │     4. (Un)mark All │
│  │                                                   │  ↓          │
│  └───────────────────────────────────────────────────┘            │
│  Text       Graphics     Copies   Priority    [ Stop ]   [ Go ]   │
│  Draft      Medium       1        Normal                          │
│                                   [Network... F8]   [Close]       │
└──────────────────────────────────────────────────────────────────┘
```

FIG. 10.9

The Control Printer dialog box.

Notice in figure 10.9 that all of the options are the same as in WordPerfect 5.1 except for Network, * (Un)mark, and (Un)mark All.

Notice also that WordPerfect 6 displays not only the current page number being processed, but the percentage processed as well.

You use * (Un)mark and (Un)mark All to mark documents in the print job list. To mark or unmark a single job, highlight it and press asterisk (*). To mark or unmark all jobs, choose (Un)mark All. After marking the job, you can choose **R**ush Job to move the job(s) to the top of the print queue, or choose **C**ancel Job to cancel the marked job(s). When you choose **R**ush or **C**ancel, WordPerfect prompts you to choose **Y**es or **N**o to proceed or abort the process.

Printing through a Network

The Network option in the Control Printer dialog box is new in WordPerfect 6. Choosing Network (F8) displays the network server queue so that you can check which jobs are printing, and in what order.

Setting the Print Quality

The Text Quality and the Graphics Quality options in the Print dialog box control print resolution. Higher resolution creates clearer type but takes longer to print.

You set these options exactly the same way as in WordPerfect 5.1. Choose Text Quality or Graphics Quality; then choose Do Not Print, Draft, Medium, or High.

Notice that the Document Settings area of the Print dialog box in WordPerfect 6 contains two new options: Print Color and Network Options.

The Print Color option is only available if you have installed a color printer. Choosing Print Color displays a pop-up list with two choices: Black and Full Color. Choose Black only if you need to print in black-and-white on a color printer.

The Network Options option is only available if you are running WordPerfect 6 on a Novell NetWare network. Choosing Network Options displays the Network Options dialog box. Choose Banner to print a banner that prints with the current document. A *banner* is a leading page that identifies the network user who printed the job. Form Number is for use primarily by network administrators. Consult the network documentation for further information.

Notice that only documents with a form setting of 0 (zero) are printed, unless you change the form number setting in Netware.

Choosing Output Options

Output options include such printer-specific items as output bins and a printer jogger. They also enable you to print multiple copies and choose between generating print jobs with WordPerfect, your printer, or a network.

Printing Reversed Text (Printing Graphically)

Choose the Print Job Graphically option in the Print dialog box when you have used graphics features that your printer doesn't normally support. For example, WordPerfect can't print reversed images (white text on a black background) with many printers, but it may be able to generate these images when Print Job Graphically is selected.

When you choose Print Job Graphically, WordPerfect looks for graphics fonts that most closely match the fonts you have used in your document.

Changing the Number of Copies

The Number of Copies option works exactly as it does in WordPerfect 5.1. To print more than one copy of a document, choose Number of Copies and type the number of copies you want. Then set any other options and start the print job.

Generating Print Jobs

Use Generated By to tell WordPerfect to control multiple-copy print jobs from WordPerfect, the Printer, or a Network.

If you choose WordPerfect, WordPerfect prints the number of copies specified under Number of Copies. Copies are collated in the printer bin.

If you choose Printer, WordPerfect sends one copy of the print job to the printer and tells the printer to make the desired number of extra copies. The copies are not collated. For example, if you want to print three copies of a two-page document, the printer creates three copies of page 1 and then three copies of page 2.

Choosing Network collates the copies in the printer bin.

Choosing Output Options

Choosing Output Options in the Print dialog box displays the Output Options dialog box. This option is available only with printers that have a sheet feeder, offset jogger, or multiple bins.

Some of the options in the Output Options dialog box may be grayed and unavailable. Depending on your printer, you can make the following choices:

- Choose **S**ort to have WordPerfect collate multiple copies of a document.

- Choose **G**roup to print multiple copies that are uncollated (prints copies of page 1, then copies of page 2, and so on).

- Choose **N**one to use WordPerfect's default printing method (collated or uncollated) for your printer.

- Choose **O**utput Bins to select a bin for the print job; then highlight the correct bin in the list.

- Choose Offset **J**ogger to separate copies of printed documents in the output bin, if your printer has this capability.

Initializing a Printer

Choosing **I**nitialize Printer from the Printer dialog box displays the Initialize Printer message box. You use Initialize Printer only to download soft fonts to your printer. For detailed information on using fonts in WordPerfect 6, see Chapter 11. To initialize a printer, choose Initialize Printer, **C**ontinue.

Using Fonts

WordPerfect 6 adds several new font features: a Font button on the Ribbon that you can click to choose fonts, and a FontInstaller utility that automates the process of installing Type 1, Intellifont, TrueType, and Bitstream Speedo fonts.

WordPerfect 6 comes with a number of fonts that you can scale and display on graphics monitors and print on supported graphics printers. This chapter describes the new font features.

Choosing a Font

The process of choosing a font in WordPerfect 6 is very similar to WordPerfect 5.1. Pressing Ctrl+F8 (Font) displays the Font dialog box, from which you choose options that are inconveniently located on five separate menus in WordPerfect 5.1: the Font Size, Appearance, Normal, Base Font, and Color menus.

Follow these steps to change the font:

1. Choose Font, Font; or press Ctrl+F8. WordPerfect displays the Font dialog box, shown in figure 11.1.

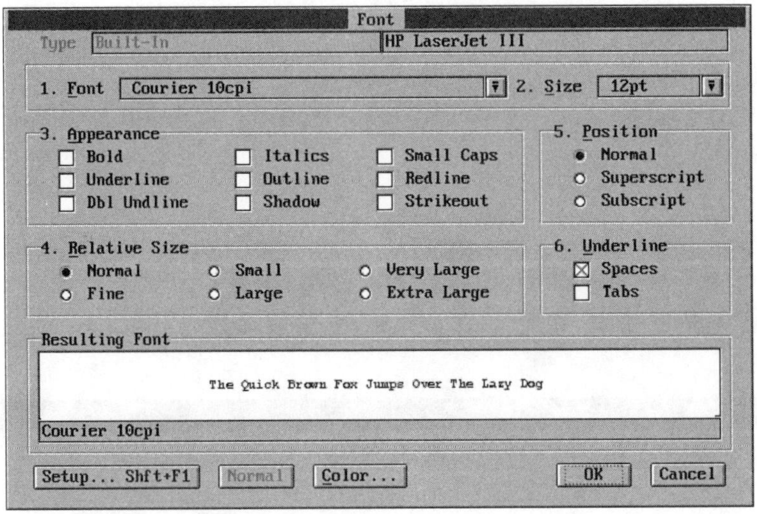

FIG. 11.1

The Font dialog box.

2. Choose options from the dialog box, then choose OK. Notice in figure 11.1 that the WordPerfect 5.1 Base Font list has become the Font list on the Font dialog box.

3. To change the base font, choose **Font**, highlight a font name, press Enter, choose **Size**, choose a size, and press Enter. If the font you choose is scalable, you can type an exact point size in the **Size** dialog. Notice in figure 11.1 that your changes are reflected in the Resulting Font window.

4. Choose **Appearance**. These character enhancement options are the same as on the WordPerfect 5.1 Font Appearance menu.

5. Choose a **Relative Size**.

Notice that these options are the same as on the WordPerfect 5.1 Font Size menu, except that **S**uperscript and Su**b**script are now located separately in the Position area, and that **N**ormal appears twice, in the Position and Relative Size areas. Choosing **N**ormal Position turns off superscript or subscript, and choosing **N**ormal Relative Size restores the font to the size currently displayed in the Size box. You can customize the percentages that WordPerfect 6 uses for relative font sizes. See the section "Setting Up Fonts" later in this chapter.

The Underline **S**paces and **T**abs options are located on the Format: Other menu in WordPerfect 5.1, and work the same way in Word-Perfect 6.

Setting Up Fonts

Notice that in WordPerfect 6, font setup is different from font installation, which is discussed in the section "Installing Soft Fonts with the WordPerfect Font Installer," later in this chapter.

Follow these steps to set up fonts:

1. Choose Font, Font; or press Ctrl+F8 to display the Font dialog box.

2. Choose Setup (Shift+F1).

WordPerfect displays the Font Setup dialog box, shown in figure 11.2.

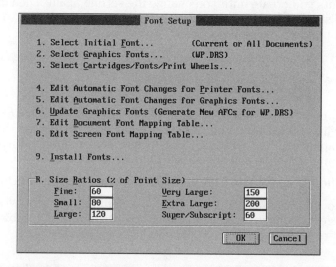

```
                    Font Setup
 1. Select Initial Font...        (Current or All Documents)
 2. Select Graphics Fonts...      (WP.DRS)
 3. Select Cartridges/Fonts/Print Wheels...

 4. Edit Automatic Font Changes for Printer Fonts...
 5. Edit Automatic Font Changes for Graphics Fonts...
 6. Update Graphics Fonts (Generate New AFCs for WP.DRS)
 7. Edit Document Font Mapping Table...
 8. Edit Screen Font Mapping Table...

 9. Install Fonts...

 R. Size Ratios (% of Point Size)
    Fine:  [60]     Very Large:      [150]
    Small: [80]     Extra Large:     [200]
    Large: [120]    Super/Subscript: [60]

                            [ OK ]   [Cancel]
```

FIG. 11.2

The Font Setup dialog box.

The sections that follow describe the options on the Font Setup dialog box.

Selecting an Initial Font

Choosing Select Initial Font from the Font Setup dialog box displays the Initial Font dialog box, shown in figure 11.3. Like WordPerfect 5.1, WordPerfect 6 lets you choose an initial base font for the printer, for a single document, and for all documents. The Initial Font dialog box lets you choose the font that WordPerfect 6 uses for the current document or for all documents until you change the setting again.

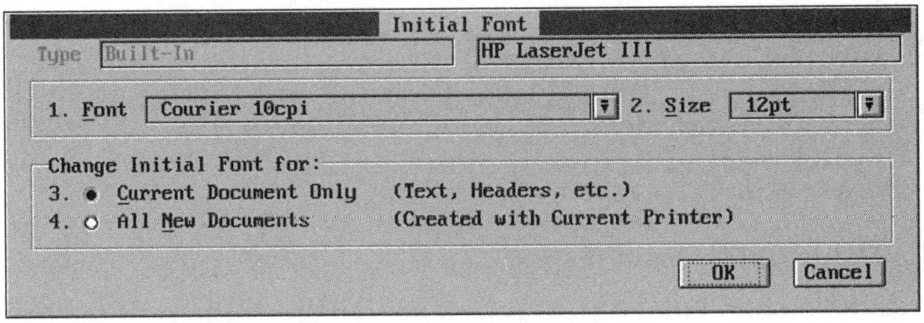

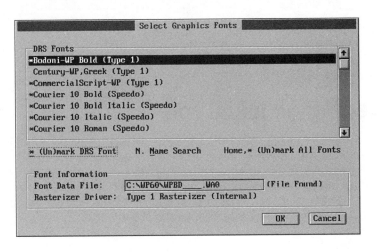

FIG. 11.3

The Initial Font dialog box.

Choose **C**urrent Document Only to set the initial font for the on-screen document, or choose All **N**ew Documents to set the initial font for all documents you create until you change the setting again. Then choose font and size from the **F**ont and **S**ize list boxes and choose OK to return to the Font Setup dialog box.

Selecting Graphics Fonts

The Graphics Fonts feature is new in WordPerfect 6. WordPerfect comes with graphic fonts that can be printed with any printer that supports graphic printing. Graphics fonts can be scaled and are displayed on-screen in the style and size they will be printed.

Follow these steps to add a graphic font to the list of available fonts:

1. Choose **G**raphics Fonts from the Font Setup dialog box. WordPerfect displays the Select Graphics Fonts dialog box, shown in figure 11.4.

FIG. 11.4

The Select Graphics Fonts dialog box.

2. In the DRS Fonts list, highlight a font and press asterisk (*) to mark it.

3. Choose OK to return to the Font Setup dialog box.

Selecting and Editing Cartridges/Fonts/ Print Wheels

Choosing **C**artridges/Fonts/Print Wheels displays the Select Cartridges/ Fonts/Print Wheels dialog box, shown in figure 11.5.

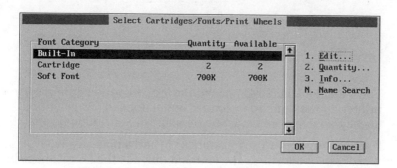

The Select Cartridges/ Fonts/Print Wheels dialog box.

This dialog box lets you tell WordPerfect which cartridges, fonts, or print wheels are available for use with the printer. To choose a soft font set, cartridge, or print wheel, highlight it in the Font Category list and choose OK.

You can edit a font definition. Follow these steps:

1. In the Select Cartridges/Fonts/Print Wheels dialog box, highlight the definition you want to edit and choose **E**dit.

   WordPerfect displays the Select Built-In Fonts, Select Cartridge, Select Print Wheel, or Select Fonts dialog box. All of these dialog boxes have the same options: * Present When Job Begins, **N**ame Search, and Home, * (Un)mark All. Figure 11.6 shows the Select Built-In Fonts dialog box.

   Marking a font with an asterisk (*) tells WordPerfect the font is available by default and doesn't need to be downloaded at the start of each print job. However, soft fonts marked with an asterisk need to be downloaded to the printer using the **I**nitialize Printer option on the Print dialog box. For further information, see Chapter 10.

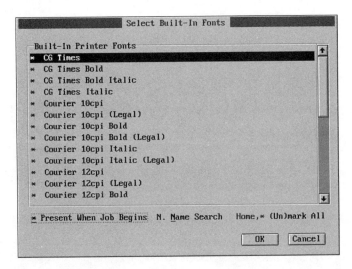

FIG. 11.6

The Select Built-In
Fonts dialog box.

The + Can be Loaded/Unloaded During Job option appears if your
printer allows fonts to be loaded and unloaded. If this option
doesn't appear, fonts must be present when printing begins.

If you mark a font with an asterisk (*) and a plus sign (+),
WordPerfect considers the font and unloads the font if space in
printer memory is needed to swap in another font. Fonts that are
swapped out are reloaded when the job is completed. Fonts
marked with a plus sign and an asterisk are considered to be ini-
tially present when WordPerfect is started.

If you have a print wheel you use most of the time, mark it with an
asterisk (*); otherwise, WordPerfect prompts you to insert the
print wheel every time you use it.

2. Highlight fonts in the list and mark or unmark them using
   * (asterisk). Use Home, * to mark or unmark all the fonts in the
   list at once. You can change the Quantity setting for the Font
   Category in the Select Cartridges/Fonts/Print Wheels dialog box.

3. Choose **Quantity**, type a number, and choose OK. Quantity indicates the number of cartridge slots, the amount of printer
   memory for soft fonts, or the number of print wheels. The default
   value depends on the installed printer. If you add memory to your
   printer or purchase new cartridges or soft fonts, you can change
   the Quantity value accordingly.

Don't change Quantity for soft fonts beyond your printer's actual memory. If you type a quantity larger than your printer memory and attempt to download soft fonts using the unavailable memory, your documents will not print properly.

4. If you choose Info, WordPerfect displays the Information dialog box, which provides information about installation and use as well as WordPerfect Corporation technical support for the selected font category.

5. Choose OK, OK to return to the Font Setup dialog box.

Editing Automatic Font Changes for Printer Fonts

Choosing Edit Automatic Font Changes for Printer Fonts displays the Edit Automatic Font Changes dialog box. Automatic font changes are font attributes that you select from the keyboard or with the Font dialog box without having to select a new font—for example, Bold (F6), Very Large Print, and so on. Choosing Edit from the Edit Automatic Font Changes dialog box displays the Edit Font Attribute dialog box, shown in figure 11.7.

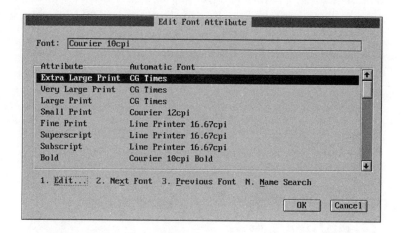

FIG. 11.7

The Edit Font Attribute dialog box.

Follow these steps to change the font that WordPerfect selects when you choose a font attribute:

1. Highlight an attribute and choose Edit.

If you first choose Next Font or Previous Font, WordPerfect switches the font name in the Font box to the next or previous font on the Select Font to Edit list in the Edit Automatic font Changes dialog box. WordPerfect displays the Select New Automatic Font Change dialog box, shown in figure 11.8.

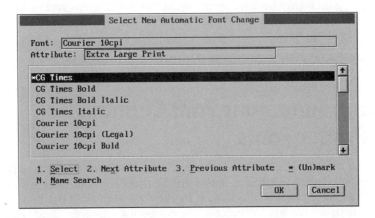

FIG. 11.8

The Select New Automatic Font Change dialog box.

Figure 11.8 shows the font that WordPerfect uses when you choose Extra Large Print when Courier 10cpi is the currently selected font. Notice in the figure that choosing Extra Large Print automatically switches the font to Courier 5cpi Dbl-High, which is marked with an asterisk (*).

2. To change the attribute, highlight a font in the list and mark it with an asterisk (*). You can only mark one font.

3. Choose Select to return to the Edit Font Attribute dialog box, or choose Select, OK, OK to return to the Font Setup dialog box. Or, choose Next Attribute or Previous Attribute to edit the next or previous attribute without returning to the Edit Font Attribute dialog box.

Editing Automatic Font Changes for Graphics Fonts

Choosing Edit Automatic Font Changes for Graphics Fonts displays the Edit Automatic Font Changes dialog box. This dialog box lets you change the font choices that WordPerfect uses to print attributes for fonts printed graphically. The process of changing font attributes for graphics fonts is essentially the same as for changing printer font attributes, as described in the previous section.

Updating Graphics Fonts

Choosing Update Graphic Fonts (Generate New AFCs for WP.DRS) from the Font Setup dialog box tells WordPerfect to update the printer driver files to incorporate your latest editing changes to graphics font attributes. When you choose this option, WordPerfect displays a progress report box while it updates the fonts, then returns to the Font Setup dialog box.

Editing the Document Font Mapping Table

Choosing Edit Document Font Mapping Table from the Font Setup dialog box displays the Document Font Mapping Table dialog box, shown in figure 11.9.

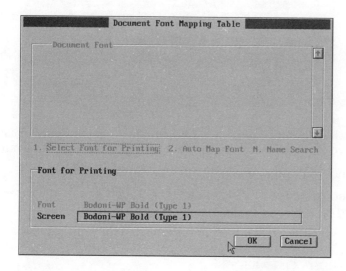

FIG. 11.9

The Document Font Mapping Table dialog box.

This dialog box lets you choose the printer font that corresponds to a font choice displayed in a document. For example, you can tell WordPerfect which printer font to use when it encounters a Times Roman font specification in a document. Follow these steps:

1. Highlight a font in the Document Font dialog box and then choose **S**elect Font for Printing. WordPerfect drops down a list of fonts available with the currently selected printer.

2. Highlight a font on the list and press Enter; then choose OK to return to the Font Setup dialog box.

Editing the Screen Font Mapping Table

Choosing Edit **S**creen Font Mapping Table from the Font Setup dialog box displays the Screen Font Mapping Table dialog box, shown in figure 11.10.

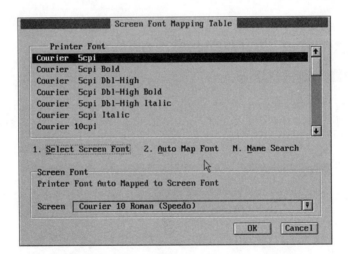

FIG. 11.10

The Screen Font Mapping Table dialog box.

This dialog box lets you assign the fonts that WordPerfect displays on-screen to a printer font from the Font dialog box. Follow these steps:

1. Choose **P**rinter Font and highlight a font from the list.

2. Choose **S**elect Screen Font and highlight a font on the Screen Font list.

3. Press Enter and choose OK to return to the Font Setup dialog box.

Installing Soft Fonts with the WordPerfect Font Installer

When you choose Install Fonts from the Font Setup dialog box, WordPerfect runs the WordPerfect Font Installer program and displays the Select Font Type menu, shown in figure 11.11.

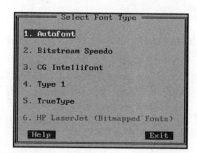

FIG. 11.11

The WordPerfect Font Installer program's Select Font Type dialog box.

You use the Font Installer to install soft fonts. WordPerfect 6 supports the six font types listed on the menu: **A**utofont, **B**itstream Speedo, **C**G Intellifont, **T**ype 1, **T**rueType, and **H**P LaserJet (Bitmapped Fonts). The HP LaserJet menu item is grayed and unavailable unless you have installed a LaserJet printer and selected it.

Follow these steps to install soft fonts:

1. From the Select Font Type menu, choose a font type. WordPerfect displays the Location of Files dialog box. For each font type, the Location of Files menu lists different options, because each soft font brand requires that files be stored in different directories. For example, the Location of Files dialog box for Bitstream Speedo soft fonts lists options for the location of .SPD/.TDF Files and the WP.DRS File.

2. Choose Location of Files options and type file paths, then choose OK. WordPerfect displays the Select Fonts for [Font Name] dialog box.

3. Highlight a font and press asterisk (*) to mark it for installation. You can also use (Un)mark All Printer Fonts (P) and (Un)mark All Graphic Fonts (G) to mark the corresponding fonts in the list. And you can choose **D**irectories for Files to list soft fonts stored in other directories.

4. After marking fonts, choose **I**nstall Marked Fonts. WordPerfect installs the fonts and returns to the Select Font Type dialog box.

5. Choose Exit to return to WordPerfect.

Changing Size Ratios for Relative Font Size Options

You can change the font size that WordPerfect chooses when you apply a relative font size (Fine, Small, Large, Very Large, and Extra Large). Follow these steps:

1. From the Font Setup dialog box, choose Size **R**atios.

2. Type a new percentage in the **F**ine, **S**mall, **L**arge, **V**ery Large, **E**xtra Large, and Su**p**er/Subscript boxes.

Resetting the Font to Normal

You can quickly reset the font to the initial font for all documents. Choose F**o**nt, F**o**nt, Normal, OK. Or, choose the initial font with the font button on the Ribbon. To learn how to set the initial font for all documents, see the section "Select Initial Font" earlier in this chapter.

Changing the Font in Document Text

You change the font of document text in WordPerfect 6 just as in WordPerfect 5.1, by inserting a font code before the text or by selecting the text and choosing a font. With WordPerfect 6, you can quickly change the font with the mouse, by clicking the Font button on the Ribbon.

You no longer have to choose fonts, character enhancements, and relative font sizes from separate menus, as in WordPerfect 5.1. WordPerfect 6 lets you select all these options from the Font dialog box. To display the Font dialog box, choose F**o**nt, F**o**nt; or press Ctrl+F8.

Special Features

PART

III

OUTLINE

Using Graphics

You can use the WordPerfect 6 Graphics features to create boxes for text and figures. The most important change in WordPerfect 6 is that graphics boxes are now based on style instead of options codes. You now can move boxes without having to remember to move the corresponding option code. You can set a single style for all the graphics boxes in a document and then change the formatting for all boxes by simply editing the style.

The options for positioning and formatting graphics boxes have greatly expanded. WordPerfect can now wrap text around the contours of a graphic image. You can create boxes with rounded corners, wrap text around just one or both sides of a box, and place captions on any side of a box and rotate the captions. You can create borders, fills, and gradients to use with paragraphs, pages, and columns.

Creating a Graphics Box

Using WordPerfect 6, you can create a graphics box in one of two ways:

- You can retrieve an image, chart, or drawing into a document directly. WordPerfect automatically formats the imported figure as a box.

- You can create a box style and then insert text or artwork in the box.

Importing an Image Directly

Follow these steps to retrieve an image in WordPerfect graphics format (WPG) or another supported graphics format:

1. Position the cursor where you want to place the image.

2. Choose **Graphics**, **R**etrieve Image. WordPerfect displays the Retrieve Image File dialog box.

3. Type the file name of an image and choose OK.

You can use File List (F5) or QuickList (F6) to insert a filename, as described in Chapter 9, or you can insert an image you have previously copied to the Clipboard (Ctrl+F1).

Using the default Figure Box style, WordPerfect imports the image into a figure box. If the image is not in the WordPerfect 6 image file format, WordPerfect automatically converts the image with ConvertPerfect.

Creating a Graphics Box Style

In WordPerfect 5.1, you can create Figure, Table, Text, User, and Equation Boxes. WordPerfect 6 adds three new box types: Button Box, Watermark Image Box, and Inline Equation Box.

Although the box types have different style options for borders, fills, corner styles, line color, and so on, you can place any kind of text or image in any type of box. The different names are offered so that you can number different box types in separate lists with WordPerfect's Automatic Box Numbering feature. Style options replace the WordPerfect 5.1 graphics options.

Follow these steps to create a graphics box style:

1. Move the cursor to where you want to insert a graphics box.

2. Choose **Graphics**, Graphics **B**oxes (Alt+F9), **C**reate. WordPerfect displays the Create Graphics Box dialog box (see fig. 12.1).

3. Choose Based on Box Style. WordPerfect displays the Graphics Box Styles dialog box (see fig. 12.2).

4. Highlight a style in the list and choose **S**elect.

   The options for working with styles are discussed in detail in Chapter 7.

5. Choose other options (discussed in the sections that follow) from the Create Graphics Box dialog box. Choose OK. WordPerfect creates a box and displays it in the document window.

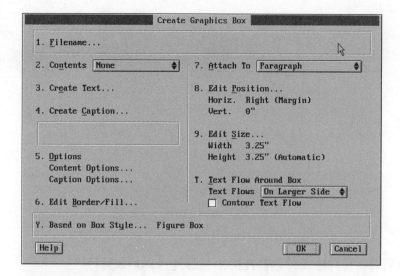

FIG. 12.1

The Create
Graphics Box
dialog box.

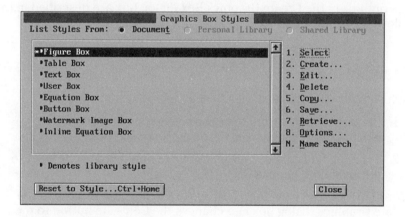

FIG. 12.2

The Graphics
Box Styles dialog
box.

After editing box settings, you can selectively reset them to their defaults. Follow these steps:

1. From the Create Graphics Box dialog box, choose Based on Box Style and then choose Reset to Style (Ctrl+Home). WordPerfect displays the Reset Box Values to Box Style Values dialog box (see fig. 12.3).

2. Choose any options you want to reset to the defaults; then choose OK.

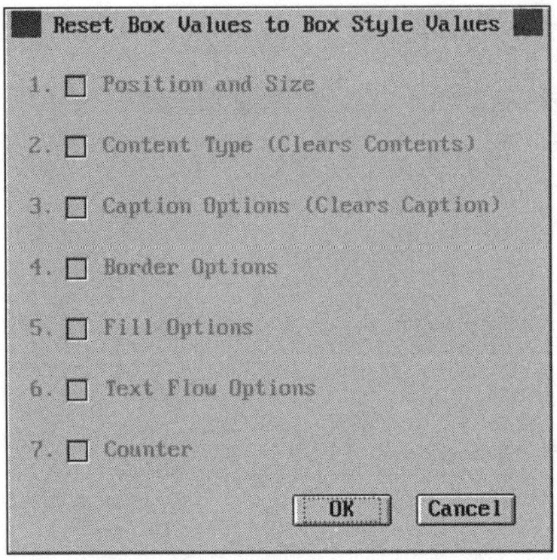

FIG. 12.3

The Reset Box
Values to Box
Style Values
dialog box.

Using the Graphics Box Options

The options in the Create Graphics Box dialog box are described in the following sections.

Filename

Follow these steps to retrieve a file into a graphics box:

1. Choose Filename from the Create Graphics Box dialog box. WordPerfect displays the Retrieve File dialog box.

2. Type the filename of a graphics image or a text file you want to retrieve; then choose OK.

WordPerfect inserts the text or image in the box and returns to the Create Graphics dialog box and changes the Contents button to the corresponding file type. You can use File List (F5) or QuickList (F6) to insert a filename, as described in Chapter 9. You can also use Clipboard (Ctrl+F1) to insert text or graphics into the graphics box from the Clipboard. Using the Clipboard is described in Chapter 5.

Contents

Choosing Contents from the Create Graphics Box dialog box displays a pop-up list of contents types: Image, Image on Disk, Text Equation, and None.

Create Text (Create Equation, Image Editor)

When you choose Create Text from the Edit Graphics Box dialog box, WordPerfect displays a text entry screen in the document window. As in WordPerfect 5.1, you can change the font and margins in the graphics box text editor. You can also define columns, create tables, use block operations, rotate text, retrieve documents, and create graphics boxes containing images or text.

If you choose the Equation Box style, option number 3 becomes Create Equation. Choosing this option takes you into the WordPerfect Equation Editor. When you exit the Equation Editor, WordPerfect returns to the Create Graphics Box dialog box.

If you choose the Watermark Image Box style, option number 3 becomes Image Editor. Choosing this option takes you into the WordPerfect 6 graphics Image Editor, which has changed quite a bit from the Image Editor in WordPerfect 5.1. Using the Image Editor is described later in this chapter under "Using the Image Editor."

Create a Caption

You can create a caption for any type of graphics box. Choosing Create Caption displays the caption editor in the document window (see fig. 12.4).

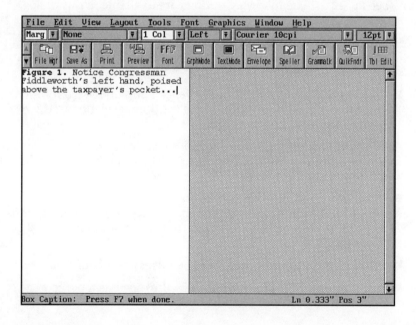

FIG. 12.4

The caption editor.

As in WordPerfect 5.1, you can change the font and margins in the caption editor. When you press F7 (Exit) to leave the caption editor, WordPerfect inserts the first 27 letters of the caption in the Create Caption text box and changes its name to Edit Caption.

WordPerfect 6 offers improved options for positioning captions. These options are described later in the chapter under "Caption Options."

Content Options

Choosing **O**ptions, Co**n**tent Options from the Create Graphics Box dialog box displays the Content Options dialog box. Use this dialog box to quickly position text or an image in a graphics box. You can also set items such as margins and justification for graphics box text using the graphics box text editor (see the previous section, "Create Text").

Choosing **P**reserve Image Width/Height Ratio preserves the shape of an image when you insert it in a box. With this option turned off, WordPerfect fits an image in a box, even if its width/height ratio changes.

Caption Options

Choosing **O**ptions, **C**aption Options displays the Caption Options dialog box (see fig. 12.5). The following options are available in this dialog box:

- *Side of Box*. This option reveals a pop-up list from which you can choose a caption position relative to a side of the box: **B**ottom, **T**op, **L**eft, or **R**ight.

- *Relation to Border*. This option reveals a pop-up list from which you can choose the position of the caption in relation to the box border: **O**utside, **I**nside, or **O**n.

- *Position*. This option reveals a pop-up list from which you can choose how you want WordPerfect to align the caption in relation to the graphic box: **C**enter, **L**eft, or **R**ight.

- *Offset from Position*. This option enables you to offset the caption from the left or right side of the box (for horizontal captions) or up or down from the top or bottom of the box (for vertical captions).

- *Offset, Set*. This option specifies the offset in units of measure.

- *Offset, Percent*. This option specifies the offset as a percentage of the width or height of the box.

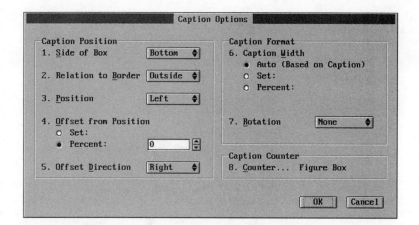

FIG. 12.5

The Caption
Options dialog
box.

- *Offset Direction*. This option tells WordPerfect to calculate the caption offset left or right from the right or left edge of the box (for horizontal captions) or up or down from the bottom or top of the box (for vertical captions).

- *Caption Width, Auto*. This option sets the caption width based on the caption's contents.

- *Caption Width, Set*. This option enables you to specify a caption width in units of measure.

- *Caption Width, Percent*. This option enables you to specify a caption width as a percent of the box width.

- *Rotation*. This option reveals a pop-up list from which you can choose a degree of rotation for the caption: None, 90°, 180°, or 170°.

- *Counter*. This option displays the Counters dialog box. Counters are described in detail in Chapter 13.

Border/Fill

Choosing Edit **B**order/Fill from the Create Graphics Box dialog box displays the Edit Graphics Box Border/Fill dialog box (see fig. 12.6). You use this dialog box to choose a box border style and line, color, spacing, shadow, corner, and fill options. Notice that the line and spacing options are located in the graphics box options menus in Word-Perfect 5.1. Notice also that WordPerfect 6 offers a variety of fill styles.

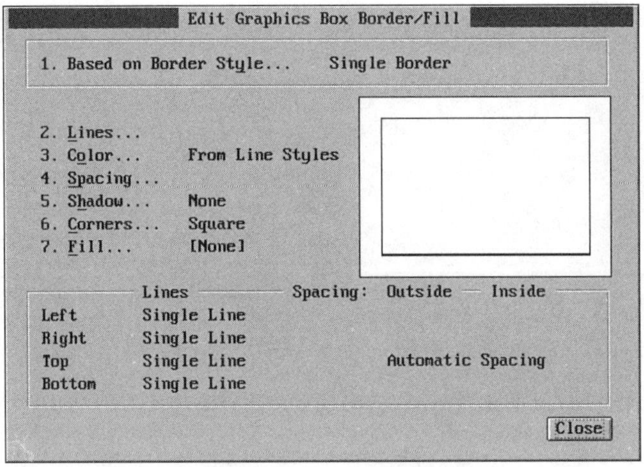

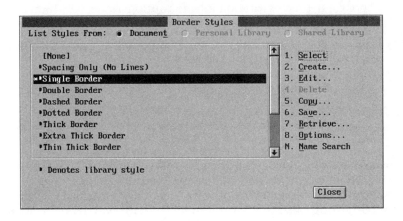

FIG. 12.6

The Edit Graphics Box Border/ Fill dialog box.

The following list describes the options on the Edit Graphics Box Border/Fill dialog box:

■ *Based on Border Style.* This option displays the Border Styles dialog box (see fig. 12.7). The steps for choosing and editing styles are discussed in Chapter 7. Notice in figure 12.7 that scrolling to the end of the styles list displays options for column and button borders.

Choose a border style and then choose Close to return to the Edit Graphics Box Border/Fill dialog box. Your choices are reflected in the sample window in the dialog box.

FIG. 12.7

The Border Styles dialog box.

■ *Lines.* This option displays the Border Line Styles dialog box. Choosing Select **A**ll displays the Line Styles dialog box. This dialog box contains the same style options as the Border Styles dialog box, except for the column border styles. Choosing Select All sets all the border options to the style you select in the Line Styles dialog box.

In the Border Line Styles dialog box, choose Left Line, Right Line, Top Line, or Bottom Line to display the Line Styles dialog box and choose a style for an individual box line.

- *Color.* This option displays the Border Line Color dialog box. Choosing Use Color From Each Line Style enables you to choose a separate color for each box line. You must set individual line colors using the Based on Border Style option in the Edit Graphics Box Border/Fill dialog box.

  In the Border Line Color dialog box, choosing Choose One Color For All Lines displays the Color Selection dialog box. Choosing colors is discussed in Chapter 4 under "Paragraph Borders."

- *Spacing.* This option displays the Border Spacing dialog box. In the Border Spacing dialog box, choosing Automatic Spacing uses WordPerfect's default 0.167" spacing for all box borders. Deselecting Automatic Spacing and choosing Outside, Set All displays a text entry box where you can type a number for outside box spacing. Choosing Inside, Set All displays a text entry box where you can type a number for inside box spacing. The remaining options in the Border Spacing dialog box are the same as in the Word-Perfect 5.1 graphics box option menus.

- *Shadow.* This option displays the Shadow dialog box. Choose Shadow Type and select an option in order to place the shadow. Choosing Shadow Color displays the Color Selection dialog box, discussed in Chapter 4 under "Paragraph Borders." Choose Shadow Width and type a number to change the shadow width. Your changes are reflected in the sample box when you return to the Edit Graphics box Border/Fill dialog box.

- *Corners.* This option displays the Border Corners dialog box. Choose Square or Rounded corners. If you choose rounded corners, you can also choose Corner Radius and type a number to make larger or smaller rounded corners.

- *Fill.* This option displays the Fill Style and Color dialog box. Choosing Fill Style displays the Fill Styles dialog box. Choosing and editing styles is discussed in Chapter 7.

  Laser-printed text may be difficult to read when printed over a fill pattern darker than 10%. For typeset text, legibility becomes difficult above 20% fill. Higher fill percentages are primarily useful when creating empty boxes for decorative purposes (such as a thin horizontal box as part of newsletter column headings).

Choosing a fill style returns to the Fill Style and Color dialog box. The chosen fill style is displayed in the Foreground Color and Current Fill text boxes.

Choosing Foreground Color or Background Color displays the Color Selection dialog box. In this dialog box, you can change the fill foreground and background to a color other than gray. Choosing colors is discussed in Chapter 4 in the section "Paragraph Borders."

Figure 12.8 shows the sample area of the Edit Graphics Box Border/Fill dialog box with options selected for a shadow box with rounded corners and a 10% fill pattern.

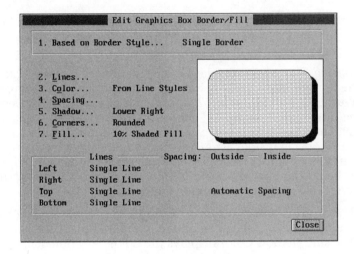

FIG. 12.8

A shadow box with rounded corners and a 10% gray fill.

Attach To

Choosing Attach To in the Create Graphics Box dialog box reveals a pop-up list with the same options that are available for attaching boxes in WordPerfect 5.1: Paragraph, Page, and Character Position.

A new option, Fixed Page Position, anchors a box to the text that surrounds it. If you add or delete text before the box, the box remains in the same position on the same page.

Edit Position

With Fixed Page Position selected, choosing Edit Position displays the Fixed Page Position dialog box. Choose Distance From Left of Page and Distance From Top of Page to position the box on the page.

With Paragraph position selected, choosing Edit **P**osition displays the Paragraph Box Position dialog box. Choosing **H**orizontal Position reveals a pop-up list from which you can choose **S**et, **L**eft, **R**ight, Centered, or **F**ull. These options are the same options as in WordPerfect 5.1, except for **S**et. Choosing **S**et displays a text box where you can type a number to specify how far the box should be offset from the left margin.

If you set the horizontal position to **L**eft, **R**ight, Centered, or **F**ull, you can choose **O**ffset from Position. Choose **L**eft or **R**ight to display a text box where you can type a number indicating how far to offset the box from the left or right margin. **D**istance from Top of Paragraph works as it does in WordPerfect 5.1. A new option, **A**llow Box to Overlap Other Boxes, enables you to place a paragraph-anchored box so it overlaps other boxes on the page.

With Page Position selected, choosing Edit **P**osition displays the Page Box Position dialog box. The options in this dialog box look similar to those in WordPerfect 5.1, but some have changed.

Choosing **H**orizontal Position reveals a pop-up list from which you can choose **S**et, **L**eft, **R**ight, Centered, or **F**ull. Choosing Position **R**elative To reveals a pop-up list from which you can choose **M**argins, **C**olumns, or C**o**lumn. The **M**argins option works the same as in WordPerfect 5.1, but two options for positioning page-anchored boxes relative to columns are now available.

Choosing **C**olumns displays two text boxes where you can type numbers indicating which columns you want to position a box relative to. Choosing C**o**lumn displays just one text box where you can type a number indicating which column to set the box relative to. Choosing Vertical Position reveals a pop-up list from which you can choose **S**et, **T**op, **B**ottom, **C**entered, or **F**ull.

Choosing Off**s**et from Position reveals a pop-up list from which you can choose **N**one, **U**p, or **D**own. Choosing **U**p or **D**own displays a text box. You can type a number in this text box to indicate how far to offset the box from the vertical position. Choosing Allow Box to **M**ove Page to Page with Text moves the box to the next page if you insert a sufficient amount of text above the box code.

Choosing **A**llow Box to Overlap Paragraph Boxes enables you to create a page-anchored box that overlaps any existing paragraph-anchored boxes. Choosing **F**ull Page creates a box around the page.

Choosing Edit **P**osition with the Character box position selected displays the Character Box Position dialog box. Choose a box position relative to the text baseline: **T**op, **B**ottom, **C**enter, or Content B**a**seline. Choose Box Changes Text Line Height to avoid overprinting a large box onto a previous line.

214

Edit Size

Choosing Edit **S**ize displays the Graphics Box Size dialog box, regardless of the box anchor type.

Text Flow Around Box

WordPerfect 6 provides new options for the way text flows relative to graphics boxes. Choosing Text **F**lows reveals a pop-up list from which you can choose **O**n Larger Side (the default), On **L**eft Side, On **R**ight Side, On **B**oth Sides, on **N**either Side, or **T**hrough Box. Choose an option indicating how you want text to flow relative to the box. Choosing Contour Text Flow wraps the text around the contours of a graphics figure.

Editing a Graphics Box

Follow these steps to edit a graphics box:

1. Choose **G**raphics, Graphics **B**oxes, **E**dit. WordPerfect displays the Select Box To Edit dialog box (see fig. 12.9). You can also double-click a graphics box in the document window to display the Edit Graphics Box dialog box.

```
┌──────────── Select Box To Edit ──────────────┐
│                                             ▖ │
│  1. ● Document Box Number:  [2          ]     │
│                                               │
│  2. ○ Counter Number                          │
│              Counter  [ Figure Box      ][▼]  │
│              Number:  [2          ]           │
│                                               │
│  3. ○ Next Box                                │
│                                               │
│  4. ○ Previous Box                            │
│                                               │
│                          [Edit Box] [Cancel]  │
└───────────────────────────────────────────────┘
```

FIG. 12.9

The Select Box To Edit dialog box.

2. Choose Document Box Number and type a number, choose **C**ounter Number and type a counter and number, or choose **N**ext Box or **P**revious Box. Then choose Edit Box.

3. Choose editing options as previously explained in the section "Creating a Graphics Box."

Using the Image Editor

The WordPerfect 6 graphics Image Editor can crop, rotate, scale, and adjust color and fill patterns for images. With the Image Editor, you can crop images, adjust brightness and contrast, change height and width, reverse the image, convert color images to black-and-white, and flip images horizontally and vertically.

You can also choose different methods for creating image dot patterns: ordered dithering, error diffusion, or halftoning. You may find that one type works better than the others for printing or photocopying a specific image.

Follow these steps to use the graphics Image Editor:

1. Choose **G**raphics, Graphics **B**oxes, **E**dit. WordPerfect displays the Select Box To Edit dialog box. You can also double-click this dialog box to display the Edit Graphics Box dialog box.

2. Choose Document Box **N**umber and type a number, choose **C**ounter Number and type a counter and number, or choose **N**ext Box or **P**revious Box. Then choose Edit Box. WordPerfect displays the Edit Graphics Box dialog box.

3. Choose Image **E**ditor. WordPerfect displays the Image Editor (see fig. 12.10).

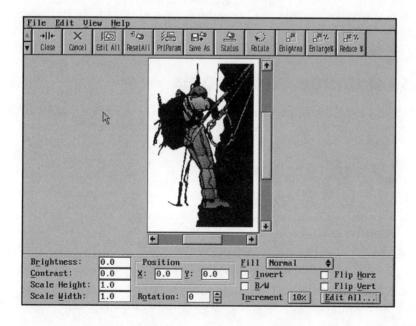

FIG. 12.10

The Image Editor.

NOTE The Image Editor option is available only for creating and editing graphics images.

The following sections describe the Image Editor options.

Using WordPerfect Presentations

If you have installed the WordPerfect Presentations program, you can use it with images you create using WordPerfect. From the Image Editor, choose File, WP Presentations. For further instructions, see the WordPerfect Presentations *User's Guide*.

Adjusting Screen Options

To display images on a larger scale, you can turn off the Button Bar and also turn off the Status Box at the bottom of the screen. Choose View, Status Box and/or View, Button Bar. Choose View, Button Bar Setup, and then choose Edit or Options to edit or change options for the Button Bar.

If you select Options and choose to display pictures-only buttons, you see 17 buttons instead of the 12 buttons displayed in the default text-and-pictures mode. You can choose all button options from the menu bar and Status Box.

Using Image Editor Tools

All the options available through the menu bar, Button Bar, and status bar can be selected by choosing Edit All. Choosing Edit All displays the Edit All dialog box (see fig. 12.11).

The following list describes the options in the Edit All dialog box. Remember that you can also choose these items from the menu bar, Button Bar, or Status Box.

- *Flip Horizontal and Flip Vertical.* These options are the same as in WordPerfect 5.1.

- *Invert Color.* This option changes the colors of the displayed image to their complementary colors.

- *Show Background.* This option turns off and on any background colors or gradients that are saved with the image.

- *Black and White.* This option converts a color image to black-and-white.

- *B/W Threshold.* This option changes the grays in a black-and-white image. Try various numbers to see the effect. Changing the B/W Threshold can help save images that otherwise print poorly, especially on photocopying machines. The range of values is 1-255.

- *Brightness.* This option changes the saturation of the colors in an image. With black-and-white images, Brightness lightens or darkens the image. The range of value is from –1 (all black) to +1 (all white). With the Status Box displayed at the bottom of the Image Editor, you can change the brightness by pressing the comma (,) and period (.) keys.

- *Contrast.* This option changes the contrast of color and black-and-white images. With the Status Box displayed at the bottom of the Image Editor screen, you can adjust the contrast by pressing the < (less than) and > (greater than) keys. The range of values is from –1 (low contrast) to +1 (high contrast).

- *Position.* These options are the same as in WordPerfect 5.1.

- *Fill.* Choosing **T**ransparent allows document text and box lines behind an image to show through the image. Choosing **W**hite converts a color image to white with black lines.

- *Print Parameters.* Choosing Print Parameters displays the Image Print Parameters dialog box (see fig. 12.12).

The Print Parameters dialog box enables you to change factors that affect the resolution of an image. When an image prints or photocopies poorly, you may be able to achieve improved results by changing the Dither **M**ethod, Dither **S**ource, and/or Halftone **O**ptions. Choose **O**rdered Dither to use ordered patterns of pixels to simulate colors or grays.

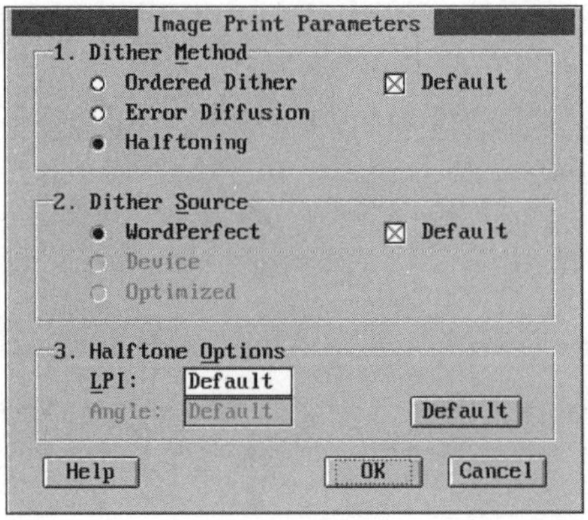

FIG. 12.12

The Image Print Parameters dialog box.

Choose **Error Diffusion** to use random dots to create smoother transitions in color and grayscale images. Choose **Halftoning** to use evenly spaced dots of variable diameter to give the illusion of varied shades of gray or hues of color. When you choose **Halftoning**, you can set the dot pattern to control the resolution. Choose LPI and type a number of lines per inch to change the resolution. Choose **WordPerfect** as the Dither Source to have WordPerfect convert a vector image to bitmap format before sending it to the printer. Choose **Device** to print an image on a PostScript printer and have the printer convert the vector image to bitmap format. Choose **Optimized** if you set the default dithering to Optimized in your printer file. If you don't do this, **Optimized** is grayed and unavailable. The **Angle** halftone option is grayed unless you select a PostScript printer. Change this setting to experiment with its effect on printed images.

Cropping an Image

You crop a graphics image by moving it within its graphics box. Follow these steps:

1. With the image displayed in the graphics Image Editor, type **n** or choose **In**crement to set the amount of movement.

2. Use the arrow keys to move the image within the box, or drag the horizontal and vertical scroll bars.

To restore the original image position, choose **Edit**, **Position**, Re**s**et Size and Position.

Scaling an Image

To change the size of a graphics image in the Image Editor, press PgUp and PgDn to enlarge or reduce the image.

To scale an area of an image, follow these steps:

1. In the Image Editor, choose **E**dit, **P**osition, Enlarge **A**rea.
2. Drag the magnifying glass cursor and enclose the area you want to enlarge.
3. Release the mouse button to fill the box with the selected area.

To scale the height and width of an image, follow these steps:

1. With the status bar displayed in the Image Editor, choose Scale **W**idth and type a number to scale the width.
2. Choose Scale Hei**g**ht and type a number to scale the height.

Rotating an Image

Follow these steps to rotate an image in the Image Editor:

With the status bar displayed in the Image Editor, choose **R**otation and type a number to specify the amount of rotation. Alternatively, click the arrow symbols to increment and decrement the amount.

You can also click the Rotate button and drag one of the rotation axes to rotate the figure, or choose **E**dit, **P**osition, **R**otate. Then use the + and – keys to rotate the axes, and press Enter to rotate the figure.

Flipping an Image

To flip an image horizontally or vertically with the status bar displayed in the Image Editor, choose Flip **H**orz or Flip **V**ert.

To save an image, choose **F**ile, Save **A**s. Type a filename, and choose OK.

T I P

220

Moving and Sizing a Graphics Box

In WordPerfect 6, you can move or size graphics boxes with the mouse in Graphics or Page mode. To move a box, just drag it to the new location. To resize the box, click it once and drag the handles.

For very precise box placement or when in Text mode, you move a graphics box by changing the position settings in the Edit Graphics Box dialog box. For details, see "Edit Position" earlier in this chapter. The instructions given in that section are for creating a box. The steps to edit a box are the same, except that you double-click the box to display the Edit Graphics Box dialog box. With the keyboard, choose **G**raphics, Graphics **B**oxes, **E**dit. Then choose Document Box **N**umber, **C**ounter Number, or Ne**x**t Box or **P**revious Box, and **E**dit Box.

Creating Graphics Lines

Only a few minor aspects of creating graphics lines have changed in WordPerfect 6. Follow these steps to create a graphics line:

1. Choose **G**raphics, Graphics Lines (Alt+F9), **C**reate. WordPerfect displays the Create Graphics Line dialog box (see fig. 12.13).

2. Choose line options; then choose OK.

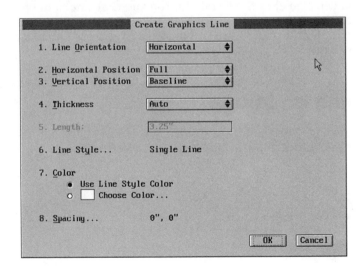

FIG. 12.13

The Create Graphics Line dialog box.

Notice in figure 12.13 that the options are the same as in WordPerfect 5.1, except for Line Style, Color, and Spacing. These options are discussed in the following list:

- *Line Style.* This option displays the Line Styles dialog box, which contains the same options as the Border Styles dialog box. Selecting and editing styles is discussed in detail in Chapter 7, "Using Styles."

- *Use Line Style Color.* This option tells WordPerfect to use the color of the currently selected line style.

- *Chooses Color.* This option displays the Color Selection dialog box. Selecting colors is discussed in Chapter 4 in the section "Paragraph Borders."

- *Spacing.* For a horizontal line, this option displays the Horizontal Graphics Line Spacing dialog box.

  This new option enables you to set the spacing above and below a line. Type numbers in the Space Above Line and Space Below Line boxes; then choose OK to return to the Create Graphics Line dialog box.

  For a vertical line, choosing Spacing in the Create Graphics Line dialog box displays the Vertical Graphics Line Spacing dialog box. Type a number in the Spacing box to set the amount of spacing on both sides of the line.

Deleting a Graphics Line

To delete a graphics line, click the line and press Del. Alternatively, turn on Reveal Codes (Alt+F3) and delete the line's hidden code.

Moving a Baseline Graphics Line

When you drag a horizontal line with Vertical Position set to Baseline, the position of the line indicated in the Create Graphics Line dialog box from Baseline changes to a specific measurement. The line no longer moves with the text to which you first attached it. To change the vertical position back to baseline, use the Edit Graphics Line dialog box as previously described in the section "Creating Graphics Lines."

Using Line Draw

To use Line Draw, choose **G**raphics, Line **D**raw and draw the line using the same controls as in WordPerfect 5.1.

Using Reference Tools

This chapter discusses changes in the following WordPerfect features: comments, compare documents, counters, cross-reference, footnotes and endnotes, generate, hidden text, index, list, redline/strikeout, table of authorities, and table of contents. Except for minor enhancements, these features work much the same as in WordPerfect 5.1.

Using Comments

As in WordPerfect 5.1, comments are not printed unless you convert them to text. You can hide comments for undistracted editing and to allow you to see the final, printed position of elements on the page.

Creating a Comment

The steps for creating a comment are essentially the same as in WordPerfect 5.1, except that WordPerfect 6 uses dialog boxes instead of menus. Follow these steps:

1. Choose **Layout, Comment, Create**. WordPerfect displays the Notes editing screen.

   Or

   Press Ctrl+F7. WordPerfect displays the Notes dialog box, shown in figure 13.1.

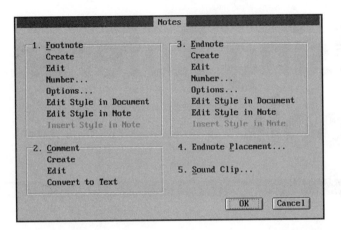

2. Choose **Comment, Create**. WordPerfect returns to the editing window and displays the following message in the status line: Comment: Press Exit (F7) when done.

3. Type the comment and press Exit (F7) to return to the document window.

In WordPerfect 6, you can choose set margins and use fonts and character enhancements in comments; in WordPerfect 5.1, you can only apply character enhancements. You can also insert date codes, graphic images, and use the speller and thesaurus in the comment editing window.

WordPerfect displays the comment in a double-lined box. If you press F7 (Exit) from an empty comment editing window, no comment box is created.

Editing a Comment

Follow these steps to edit a comment:

1. Position the cursor just after the comment.

2. Choose **Layout, Comment, Edit**, then edit the comment and press F7 (Exit) to return to the editing screen.

Hiding a Comment

To hide comments in WordPerfect 5.1, you have to use the Setup: Edit-Screen Options menu. In WordPerfect 6, you can simply switch to Page mode, or you can turn off the comments display for all view modes by following these steps:

1. Choose View, Screen Setup, and deselect the Display Comments check box.

2. Choose OK to return to the document window.

Converting a Comment to Text

Comments don't print unless you first convert them to text. You can only convert one comment at time. Follow these steps:

1. Position the cursor just after the comment.

2. Choose Layout, Comment, Convert to Text.

WordPerfect removes the comment box and inserts its text in the document. WordPerfect converts only the first document above the cursor.

Converting Text to a Comment

You can select text and copy or move it into a comment. Follow these steps:

1. Select the text you want to convert, then choose Layout, Comment, Create. WordPerfect inserts the text in the comment editing screen.

2. Press F7 (Exit) to return to your document.

Comparing Documents

Compare Documents (Document Compare in WordPerfect 5.1) includes some helpful enhancements. To compare two documents, follow these steps:

1. Open the newer version of a document and choose File, Compare Documents, Add Markings. WordPerfect displays the Compare Documents dialog box, shown in figure 13.2.

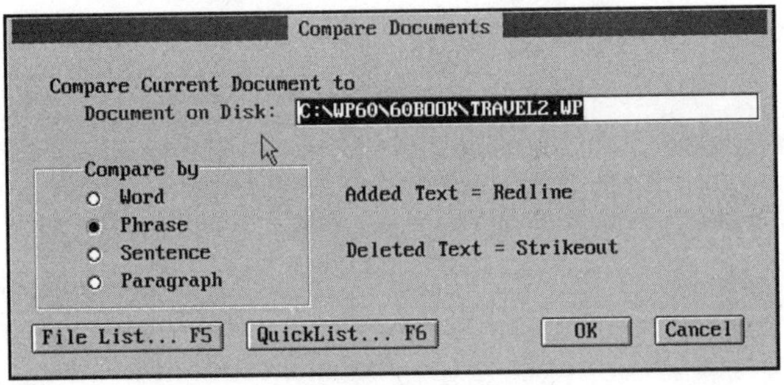
Compare Documents
Compare Current Document to
Document on Disk: C:\WP60\60BOOK\TRAVEL2.WP
Compare by
Word
Phrase
Sentence
Paragraph
Added Text = Redline
Deleted Text = Strikeout
File List... F5
QuickList... F6
OK
Cancel

FIG. 13.2

The Compare Documents dialog box.

2. Type on disk the path and name of a document you want to compare to the on-screen document.

3. Choose Compare by **W**ord, **P**hrase, **S**entence, or P**a**ragraph. This feature, new in WordPerfect 6, tells WordPerfect whether to mark paragraphs, sentences, phrases, or words where differences occur.

4. Choose OK to begin comparing documents.

As in WordPerfect 5.1, added text is marked with Redline, and deleted text is marked with Strikeout. Text that has moved is preceded with the message `THE FOLLOWING TEXT WAS MOVED` and followed by the message `THE PRECEDING TEXT WAS MOVED`.

As in WordPerfect 5.1, you can remove redline and strikeout from the newer version of the file, cancelling most editing changes made since the earlier version was created. Heavily edited documents may not exactly resemble the original version after markings are removed. Follow these steps to remove markings:

1. Choose **F**ile, Compare **D**ocuments, **R**emove Markings. WordPerfect displays the Remove Markings dialog box.

2. To restore the document as closely as possible to its original condition, choose **R**emove Redline Markings and Strikeout Text. Or, choose Remove **S**trikeout Text Only to retain markings for text that was added.

3. Choose OK.

You can change the way WordPerfect marks redlined text. See the section "Using Redline and Strikeout," later in this chapter.

Using Counters

WordPerfect can automatically number pages, lines, paragraphs, and footnotes and endnotes. The Counters feature, new in WordPerfect 6, lets you insert counters for items that aren't automatically numbered— for example, a parts list.

You can use numbers, letters, or Roman numerals, and you can number in increasing or decreasing order. You can hide counters selectively so that the next displayed counter is correctly incremented even though intervening counters aren't displayed.

You can create several levels of counters in a document and increment or decrement each set of counters individually. When you increment, decrement, or set a value for one level, all lower levels are reset to 1.

You can use the Counters feature to edit the system counters Word-Perfect uses to number graphics boxes, lines, and so on.

Creating a Counter

Follow these steps to place a counter in your document:

1. Choose Layout, Character, Counters. WordPerfect displays the Counters dialog box, shown in figure 13.3. Notice in figure 13.3 that the List System Counters check box has been selected. The system counters are displayed in the Counter list preceded by a dot.

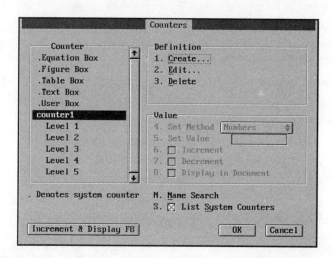

FIG. 13.3

The Counters dialog box.

2. Choose **Create**. WordPerfect displays the Create Counter Definition dialog box, shown in figure 13.4.

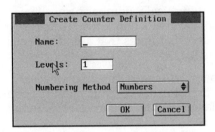

3. Type a name for the counter.

4. To create more than one level for the counter, choose **Levels** and type the number of levels you want.

   If you specify more than one level, WordPerfect displays the counter name and levels in the Counter list of the Counter dialog box. In figure 13.3, notice that Counter1 has four levels.

5. To change the numbering method, choose Numbering **Method** and choose **Numbers**, Lower **Letter**, Upper **Letter**, Lower **Roman**, or Upper **Roman**.

   If you specify more than one level, WordPerfect uses the same numbering method for each level. To change the numbering method for a level, choose **Edit** from the Counters dialog box, as described later under "Editing Counters."

6. Choose OK to return to the Counters dialog box.

7. To change the method or value of the counter, you can choose Set **Method** or Set **Value** from the Counters dialog box. You don't have to use **Edit** unless you want to change the counter's name.

8. Choose **Increment** or **Decrement**.

9. If you want counters displayed (not hidden), choose Dis**p**lay in Document.

10. Choose OK to return to the document window.

WordPerfect inserts the first counter.

Editing Counters

After creating a counter, you can edit the counter and its levels. Follow these steps:

1. Choose **L**ayout, **C**haracter, **C**ounters.

2. In the Counters dialog box, highlight a counter or one of its levels, then choose **E**dit.

   WordPerfect displays the Edit Counter Definition dialog box, which contains exactly the same options as the Create Counter Definition dialog box.

3. Change counter options as described earlier under "Creating a Counter."

Incrementing and Decrementing Counters

When you create a counter, WordPerfect assigns the value *1*, *A*, or *i* to the first counter, unless you set a different value in the Counters or Create Counter Definition dialog box. Follow these steps to insert another counter:

1. Choose **L**ayout, **C**haracter, **C**ounters.

2. Choose a counter or one of its levels in the Counter list.

3. Choose **I**ncrement or De**c**rement.

4. Choose Di**s**play in Document if you want to show the counter in the document screen, or leave the check box blank to create a hidden counter.

5. Choose OK to return to the document.

WordPerfect displays the next counter number if you choose Di**s**play in Document, or inserts a hidden counter if you leave the Di**s**play in Document check box unselected.

Notice in the Counters dialog box that **I**ncrement and De**c**rement are assigned to check boxes, not radio buttons, and can thus both be selected. Choosing both check boxes increments and then decrements the selected counter level, and inserts a counter with the same number as the previous counter.

Changing the Value of Counters

You can change the current value of counters at any time. For example, you may want to count items 1 through 3, then jump to counter number 5. When you change the counter value, WordPerfect increments subsequent counters starting with the new value. For example, if you change the counter value to 5, the next counter will be number 6.

Follow these steps to change the counter value:

1. Choose Layout, Character, Counters.

2. Choose Set Value and type a new value.

3. Choose Display in Document unless you want to create a hidden counter, then choose OK to return to the document screen.

WordPerfect inserts a counter with the new value. Subsequent counters are incremented or decremented from this value.

Creating a Set of Counters

Remember that setting counters is a manual process, requiring that you repeat the following steps to create each counter, as described in the preceding sections:

1. Define a counter and insert the first counter.

2. For each subsequent counter, choose Layout, Character, Counters.

3. Highlight a counter in the Counters dialog box and choose the desired Set Value, Increment, Decrement and Display in Document options; then choose OK.

Using Cross-References

WordPerfect's Cross-Reference feature provides a useful way to refer readers to automatically numbered figures, pages, footnotes, and endnotes. When the automatically assigned number of a figure, page, or note changes, WordPerfect automatically updates the cross-reference as well. For example, See Figure 2. becomes See Figure 3. The Cross-Reference feature has changed in WordPerfect 6, with new options that extend its usefulness.

Creating a Cross-Reference

Follow these steps to create a Cross-Reference:

1. Type optional introductory text such as **See Figure xx**.

2. Choose **T**ools, Cross-Reference (Alt+F5), **B**oth. Choosing **B**oth displays the Mark Cross Reference and Target dialog box, with several new options, as shown in figure 13.5.

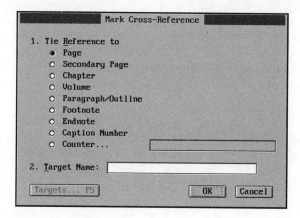

FIG. 13.5

The Mark Cross-Reference and Target dialog box.

3. Choose a reference type from the Tie **R**eference to list. The reference types are explained later under "Reference Types."

4. Type a name in the **T**arget Name box.

5. Press F5 (Targets) and choose a target.

6. Choose OK. WordPerfect inserts a reference code in the document. Now you must mark the target.

7. Move the cursor to the right of the target and press Enter.

WordPerfect inserts a target code. The cross-reference and target are now linked. If the number of the target changes, WordPerfect automatically changes the number of the cross-reference.

You can create multiple cross-references, as in WordPerfect 5.1. To cross-reference a single target with multiple references, create the references and assign the same target name to each.

Marking a Reference Only

If you want to insert a reference mark but you haven't created its target figure, note, or page, you can insert the reference mark only and wait until later to insert the target code. Follow these steps:

1. Type the cross-reference text—for example, **See Figure xx**.

2. Choose **T**ools, Cross-Reference, **R**eference. WordPerfect displays the Mark Cross-Reference dialog box, which contains exactly the same options as the Mark Cross Reference and Target dialog box.

3. Choose a reference type and type a name in the Target Name box. Or press F5 (Targets) and choose a name from the Targets list.

4. Choose OK.

WordPerfect inserts a question mark at the location of the reference until you mark the target and use Generate.

Marking a Target Only

After marking a reference only, as described in the preceding section, you eventually need to mark the target. Follow these steps:

1. Move the cursor immediately after the target.

2. Choose **T**ools, Cross-Reference, **T**arget. WordPerfect displays the Mark Cross-Reference Target dialog box.

3. Type a target name, or press F5 (Targets) and choose a name from the Targets list, then choose OK.

WordPerfect inserts a target code at the cursor. Remember that the reference and target names must match exactly.

Generating Cross-References

After marking references and targets, you need to use the Generate command to number the references. Follow these steps:

1. Choose **T**ools, **G**enerate.

   WordPerfect displays the Generate dialog box, which warns you that existing tables, lists, and indexes will be replaced if you continue.

2. Choose OK.

The **S**ave Modified Subdocuments is discussed in Chapter 9, under "Master Documents." WordPerfect numbers all cross-references in the document.

Using Footnotes and Endnotes

Many features have changed in WordPerfect 6, but footnotes and endnotes have remained essentially the same. The only difference is that dialog boxes replace WordPerfect 5.1 menus.

Creating a Footnote or Endnote

Follow these steps to create a footnote or endnote:

1. Choose Layout, Footnote or Endnote. WordPerfect displays a pull-down menu with the same options as the Footnote and Endnote menus in WordPerfect 5.1 (Create, Edit, New Number, and Options), plus two items that are new in WordPerfect 6: Edit Style in Doc and Edit Style in Note. The Endnote feature includes a Placement option that is also new in WordPerfect 6.

2. Choose Create. WordPerfect displays the Footnote or Endnote editing window, which works exactly the same as in WordPerfect 5.1.

3. Create the footnote text, then press F7 (Exit) to return to the document screen.

WordPerfect inserts the current footnote or endnote number in the text.

Editing a Footnote or Endnote

To edit a footnote or endnote, follow the steps in the preceding section for creating footnotes or endnotes, but in step 2 choose Edit instead of Create.

You can jump from the footnote or editing screen to the next or previous note by pressing PgUp or PgDn.

Specifying Footnote Options

You can change footnote or endnote numbering style and formatting by following these steps:

1. Move the cursor just before the footnotes or endnotes you want to format.

2. Choose **Layout**, **Footnote** or **Endnote**, **Options**. WordPerfect displays the Footnote Options dialog box, shown in figure 13.6.

```
┌─────────────────────────────────────────────────────┐
│▓▓▓▓▓▓▓▓▓▓▓▓▓▓▓ Footnote Options ▓▓▓▓▓▓▓▓▓▓▓▓▓▓▓│
│                                                     │
│ 1. Spacing Between Footnotes:          ┌───────┐    │
│                                        │0.167" │    │
│                                        └───────┘    │
│ 2. Amount of Footnote to Keep Together:┌─────┐      │
│                                        │0.5" │      │
│                                        └─────┘      │
│ 3. Footnote Separator Line...                       │
│                                                     │
│ 4. ☐ Restart Footnote Numbers each Page            │
│                                                     │
│ 5. ☒ Footnotes at Bottom of Page                   │
│                                                     │
│ 6. ☐ Print Continued Message                       │
│                                                     │
│                         ┌──────┐  ┌────────┐        │
│                         │  OK  │  │ Cancel │        │
│                         └──────┘  └────────┘        │
└─────────────────────────────────────────────────────┘
```

FIG. 13.6

The Footnote
Options dialog
box.

Notice in figure 13.6 that the options have changed from the WordPerfect 5.1 Footnote Options menu.

3. Choose options as described in the following paragraphs, then choose OK to return to the document screen.

Notice that the same options are available whether you choose **Footnote** or **Endnote** in step 2. Following are the available options:

■ *Spacing Between Footnotes.* This option is the same as in Word-Perfect 5.1. Notice that WordPerfect 6 doesn't offer Spacing Within Footnotes because you can now set footnote spacing by choosing **Layout**, **Line**, **Line S**pacing from the footnote editing window.

■ *Amount of Footnote to Keep Together.* This option works exactly the same as the Amount of Note to Keep Together option in WordPerfect 5.1.

■ *Footnote Separator Line.* Choosing this option displays the Footnote Separator Line dialog box, shown in figure 13.7.

Notice in figure 13.7 that the dialog box contains new options not available in WordPerfect 5.1. These options are discussed in the following paragraphs.

■ *Line Style.* Choosing this option displays the Line Styles dialog box. To learn more about the options on the Line Styles dialog box, see Chapter 7, where styles are discussed in detail. Styles are used in WordPerfect 6 to perform many formatting chores that are assigned to separate menus in WordPerfect 5.1. You can use the Line Styles dialog box to create and edit line styles for use with footnotes and endnotes.

```
┌─────────────────────────────────────────────┐
│▓▓▓▓▓▓▓▓▓▓▓▓ Footnote Separator Line ▓▓▓▓▓▓▓▓▓│
├─────────────────────────────────────────────┤
│                                               │
│  1. Line Style...        Single Line          │
│                                               │
│  2. Line Alignment                            │
│       ● Left                                  │
│       ○ Full                                  │
│       ○ Center                                │
│       ○ Right                                 │
│       ○ Set Position:    ┌─────────┐          │
│                          │0"       │          │
│                          └─────────┘          │
│  3. Length of Line:      ┌─────────┐          │
│                          │2"       │          │
│                          └─────────┘          │
│  4. Space Above Line:    ┌─────────┐          │
│                          │0.16"    │          │
│                          └─────────┘          │
│  5. Space Below Line:    ┌─────────┐          │
│                          │0.16"    │          │
│                          └─────────┘          │
│                       ┌──────┐  ┌────────┐    │
│                       │  OK  │  │ Cancel │    │
│                       └──────┘  └────────┘    │
└─────────────────────────────────────────────┘
```

FIG. 13.7

The Footnote Separator Line dialog box.

- *Line Alignment.* In WordPerfect 5.1, the line options are No Line, 2-Inch Line, and Margin to Margin. WordPerfect 6 lets you align the footnote/endnote separator line **L**eft, **F**ull (margin to margin), **C**enter, **R**ight, or **S**et Position. The number you type in the **S**et Position box tells WordPerfect how far to indent the separator line from the left margin. To specify the length of the separator line, see the next paragraph.

- *Length of Line.* This option, which isn't available in WordPerfect 5.1, lets you specify an exact length for the footnote or endnote separator line.

- *Space Above Line and Space Below Line.* These options, which aren't available in WordPerfect 5.1, let you specify the amount of space between the footnote or endnote separator line and the text of the footnote or endnote.

- *Restart Footnote Numbers each Page.* This option is the same as the Start Footnote Numbers each Page option in WordPerfect 5.1.

- *Footnotes at Bottom of Page.* This option is the same as the Footnotes at Bottom of Page option in WordPerfect 5.1.

- *Print Continued Message.* This option is the same as the Print Continued Message option in WordPerfect 5.1.

Editing Footnote and Endnote Styles

Follow these steps to change the style WordPerfect 6 uses to print footnotes or endnotes:

1. Choose Layout (Ctrl+F7), **F**ootnote or **E**ndnote, Edit Style in **D**oc or Edit **S**tyle in Note.

   Style in Doc refers to the formatting that WordPerfect applies to footnote or endnote numbers in document text. Style in Note refers to the formatting of footnote and endnote numbers in the notes themselves.

   WordPerfect displays the Footnote (or Endnote) Style in Doc (or Note) dialog box, where you can change the format for footnotes or endnotes.

2. After formatting the note style, press F7 (Exit) to return to the document window.

Changing Endnote Placement

You can override WordPerfect's default printing of endnotes at the end of the document. Follow these steps to specify a new position to print endnotes:

1. Position the cursor where you want endnotes to appear.

2. Choose Layout (Ctrl+F7), **E**ndnote, **P**lacement. WordPerfect asks whether you want to restart endnote numbering.

3. Choose **Y**es to restart endnote numbering, or choose **N**o to bypass this option. WordPerfect inserts a comment box with the text Endnote Placement showing where endnotes will appear.

Numbering Footnotes and Endnotes Manually

WordPerfect renumbers footnotes and endnotes automatically. If you delete or add a note, the remaining notes are immediately renumbered without any action on your part. However, you can set note numbering manually. This capability can be useful for a long document you have divided into several files for more convenient editing. Follow these steps:

1. Choose **L**ayout, **F**ootnote or **E**ndnote, **N**ew Number. WordPerfect displays the Set Footnote Number dialog box. Notice that the same options are available whether you chose **F**ootnote or **E**ndnote.

2. Type the new number in the New **N**umber box. Or, if you just want WordPerfect to automatically increment or decrement the next

number by 1, choose Increment or Decrement. To insert the same footnote or endnote number as the last number, mark both the Increment and Decrement check boxes. You can change the numbering method at this time, without having to choose Layout, Footnote, Edit.

3. Optionally, choose Numbering Method and choose numbering style: Numbers, Lower Letters, Upper Letters, Lower Roman, Upper Roman, or Characters. If you choose Characters, you can choose option 6, Characters, and type a new character for WordPerfect to use for footnote/endnote numbering.

4. Choose Display in Document if you want the next footnote or endnote number to be displayed. If you don't choose Display in Document, WordPerfect hides the next number. (For more information, see the section "Using Counters," earlier in this chapter.)

Positioning Endnotes Manually

WordPerfect prints endnotes at the end of a document by default, but you can specify a different endnote location. Follow these steps:

1. Position the cursor where you want endnotes printed.

2. Choose Layout, Endnote, Placement. WordPerfect asks whether you want to restart endnote numbering.

3. Choose Yes to restart endnote numbering, or choose No to continue the current numbering sequence.

WordPerfect inserts a comment box in the document screen, showing where endnotes will be printed. A hard page break follows the endnote comment box. When you generate endnotes, they are inserted after the hard page break.

Changing Footnote and Endnote System Styles

WordPerfect 6 uses styles for many formatting tasks formerly assigned to formatting commands on feature-specific menus in WordPerfect 5.1. To change WordPerfect's default formatting of footnotes and endnotes, you must edit the corresponding system styles. Follow these steps:

1. Choose Layout, Styles, Options, List System Styles, OK. WordPerfect displays the system styles in the Style List dialog box.

2. Highlight the Footnote or Endnote style and choose **E**dit. Word-Perfect displays the Edit Style dialog box.

3. Choose Style **C**ontents and edit the style as described in Chapter 7, then press F7 (Exit) and choose OK to return to the Style List dialog box.

Notice that because you have changed the style, it's no longer marked in the list with a bullet, indicating that it's no longer attached to a library. The changes you make to the style are applied to footnotes or endnotes in the current document; but if you want the changes to apply to other documents, you must first copy the edited style back into the system styles library. Follow these steps:

1. Highlight the style in the Style List dialog box and choose Co**p**y. WordPerfect displays the Copy Styles dialog box.

2. Choose Shared Library, type the name of a library, and choose OK.

WordPerfect places a bullet beside the style in the Style List box. You can now select the edited style in any new documents. Documents formatted before you change the Endnote or Footnote styles are automatically updated when you retrieve them.

Restoring a Deleted Footnote or Endnote

If you accidentally delete a footnote or endnote number, you can restore it by pressing Ctrl+F7 and choosing Insert Style in Note from the Footnote or Endnote box.

Using Generate

You use the Generate command to update cross-references, tables of contents, tables of authorities, lists, endnotes, and indexes. Follow these steps:

1. Choose **T**ools, **G**enerate. WordPerfect displays the Generate dialog box.

2. Choose OK.

The **S**ave Modified Subdocuments option in the Generate dialog box is used for Master Documents, and is discussed in Chapter 9. WordPerfect updates all the cross-references, tables of contents, tables of authorities, lists, endnotes, and indexes in the document.

Using Hidden Text

Hidden Text is a new feature in WordPerfect 6. The following table shows the differences between Hidden Text and Comments.

Characteristic	Hidden Text	Comments
Prints with document text	Yes (when displayed)	No
Treated as regular document text	Yes (when displayed)	No
Affects page numbering	Yes (when displayed)	No
Enclosed by a box border	No	Yes
Can be created using existing document text	Yes	Yes
Can be converted to document text	Yes	Yes

Creating Hidden Text

Follow these steps to create hidden text:

1. Choose Font, Hidden Text; or press Alt+F5 and choose Hidden Text to display the Hidden Text dialog box (see fig. 13.9).

2. Choose Hidden Text, then choose OK. Deselecting Show All Hidden Text hides hidden text throughout the document.

3. Type the text to be hidden.

WordPerfect places hidden text between [Hidden On] and [Hidden Off] codes. With hidden text undisplayed, only the [Hidden On] code appears in Reveal Codes.

To stop typing hidden text and begin typing normal document text, press right arrow to move the insertion point to the right of the [Hidden Off] code. You can check the insertion point with Reveal Codes (F11 or Alt+F3). Or, press Alt+F5, choose Hidden Text, deselect Hidden Text, and choose OK.

To use Search, Replace, the Speller, Thesaurus, and Grammar Checker on hidden text, the text must be displayed.

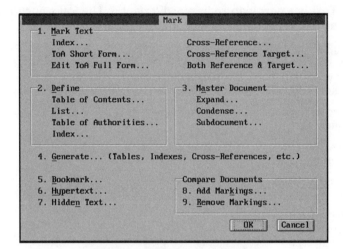

The Mark dialog box.

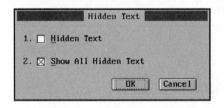

The Hidden Text dialog box.

Formatting Selected Text as Hidden Text

Follow these steps to convert a selected block of text to hidden text:

1. Select the text you want to format as hidden text.

2. Choose Font, Hidden Text; or press Alt+F5 and choose Hidden Text.

WordPerfect places the selected block within [Hidden On] and [Hidden Off] codes.

Converting Hidden Text to Normal Text

To convert hidden text to document text, turn on Reveal Codes (F11 or Alt+F3) and delete the [Hidden On] or [Hidden Off] code.

Creating Indexes

The Index feature in WordPerfect 6 has changed in small ways, with improved options and easy-to-use dialog boxes that replace the WordPerfect 5.1 menus. As before, you create an index in three steps:

1. Mark text to be included in the index (and/or create a concordance file of words you want WordPerfect to include in the index automatically).

2. Make any changes in the default appearance of the printed index.

3. Generate the index.

These steps are described in detail in the following paragraphs.

Marking Text

Follow these steps to mark each word or phrase you want to include in an index:

1. Optionally, select the text you want to include in the index.

2. Choose **Tools**, **Index**, **Mark**. WordPerfect displays the Mark Index dialog box. Selected text is entered automatically in the Heading box.

3. If you don't select document text, you can now type an index entry in the Heading box.

4. To create a subheading, type it in the Subheading box. If you select text in the document and then type a heading in the Heading box, WordPerfect automatically inserts the selected text in the Subheading box.

   You can choose List Index Marks (F5) from the Heading or Subhead box to display a list of index marks you have already entered in the document. To choose an existing index entry mark, highlight it and choose OK. WordPerfect inserts the mark in the Heading or Subheading box.

5. Choose OK to return to the document screen.

WordPerfect places an index entry code at the position of the cursor, or to the left of selected text.

Defining an Index

After marking text you want included in the index, you can tell WordPerfect where in the document to print the index, and how you want the index formatted. Follow these steps to define an index:

1. Move the cursor to the location in the document where you want WordPerfect to insert the index.

2. Choose **Tools**, **Index**, **Define**.

WordPerfect displays the Define Index dialog box, shown in figure 13.10.

```
┌─────────────────────────── Define Index ───────────────────────────┐
│                                                                     │
│   ┌─Level──────Current Style──┐   ┌─Numbering Mode─────────────┐    │
│   │ Heading      Index1       │   │ 1. ○  None                 │    │
│   │ Subheading   Index2       │   │ 2. ○  # Follows Entry      │    │
│   │                           │   │ 3. ○  (#) Follows Entry    │    │
│   │                           │   │ 4. ○  # Flush Right        │    │
│   │                           │   │ 5. ● ...# Flush Right      │    │
│   │  6.  Index Level Styles...│   └────────────────────────────┘    │
│                                                                     │
│   7. ⊠ Combine Sequential Page Numbers (Example: 51-62)             │
│                                                                     │
│   8. Page Number Format...                                          │
│                                                                     │
│   9. Concordance Filename: [                                    ]   │
│                                                                     │
│   [ File List... F5 ]  [ QuickList... F6 ]      [  OK  ] [ Cancel ] │
└─────────────────────────────────────────────────────────────────────┘
```

FIG. 13.10

The Define Index dialog box.

Notice in figure 13.10 that options 6, 7, and 8 are new in WordPerfect 6. Because the Numbering Mode options (options 1 through 5) are the same as in WordPerfect 5.1, they are not described here.

The following paragraphs describe new WordPerfect 6 index options from the Define Index dialog box:

■ *Index Level Styles.* Choosing this option displays the Index Styles dialog box. WordPerfect 6 uses styles to perform many formatting chores that are handled in WordPerfect 5.1 with formatting commands on program command menus. For a full description of the steps to create and edit styles, see Chapter 7.

■ *Combine Sequential Page Numbers.* Choose this option to have WordPerfect format sequential page options with a hyphen. For example, index entries for pages 50, 51, 52, and 53 are entered as 50-53. If you prefer to have numbers printed separately, deselect this check box.

- *Page Number Format.* Choosing this option displays the Page Number Format dialog box. This dialog box lets you set volume, chapter numbers, and secondary page numbers. WordPerfect uses the page numbers in the indexed document unless you choose **Diff**erent from Document. To create a new numbering format, choose **D**ifferent from Document, then choose Number Codes (F5). WordPerfect displays the Page Number Codes dialog box. Next, choose **P**age Number (the default), **S**econdary Page Number, **C**hapter Number, or **V**olume Number. WordPerfect inserts the corresponding code in the **D**ifferent from Document box. When you generate the index, WordPerfect includes a page, secondary page, chapter, or volume number with each index entry.

- *Concordance Filename.* A concordance file contains a list of words and phrases you want WordPerfect to include in an index. To create a concordance file, you type each index entry on its own line and end each line by pressing Enter.

You may want to create a concordance file, for example, if you use the same terms repeatedly in scientific reports. When you generate the index, WordPerfect searches the document for words listed in the concordance file, and includes these words in the index. You can use both index marking methods in the same document: marking some words and letting WordPerfect look up others in the concordance.

To have WordPerfect use a concordance, type a filename in the **C**oncordance Filename text box. WordPerfect generates an index more quickly if you sort the concordance file alphabetically.

Generating an Index

At the location of the cursor when you define an index, WordPerfect inserts a [Def Mark:Index,#,filename] code in the document. The # symbol represents the numbering format you choose for the index, and filename is the name of the concordance file, if any. To generate the index, choose Tools, Generate, OK.

Creating Lists

WordPerfect can automatically number graphics boxes, lines, and paragraphs. You can use the List feature to number other types of information in a document, such as boxes created with Line Draw, or spaces left blank for photographs that will be pasted onto the pages of a sample catalog. Creating a list involves three steps: marking text to be included in the list, telling WordPerfect how to format the list, and generating the list.

Marking Text for a List

Follow these steps to mark each item of text you want to include in a list:

1. Select the text you want to include in the list.

2. Choose **Tools**, **List**, **Mark**. WordPerfect displays the Mark Text for List dialog box.

3. Type a name for the list. If you have already defined lists for the current document, you can press F5 (Lists), highlight a list name, and choose OK.

4. Choose OK.

WordPerfect marks the text for a list.

Defining a List

After marking text for a list, you must tell WordPerfect how to format the list. Follow these steps:

1. Move the cursor where you want the list to be generated, and choose **Tools**, **List**, **Define**. WordPerfect displays the Define List dialog box.

2. Highlight the name of the list you want to define.

3. Choose **Edit**. Or, to create a new list definition, choose **Create**. WordPerfect displays the Edit List or Create List dialog box, depending on your choice in step 3. Figure 13.11 shows the Edit List dialog box.

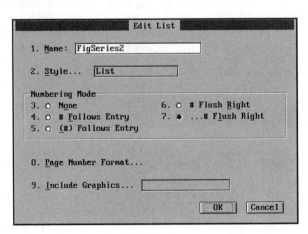

The Edit List dialog box.

The Create List and Edit List dialog boxes contain exactly the same options. If you choose Create, you need to type a name for the new list. If you choose Edit, the list name is inserted for you, but you can choose Name and type a new name in the text box.

4. In the Edit List dialog box, choose Style. WordPerfect displays the List Style dialog box. The List Style dialog box is where you can choose how WordPerfect formats list numbers.

5. Choose Create to create a new numbering style. WordPerfect prompts you for a name. Type a name and choose OK. Or, highlight a style name and choose Edit. WordPerfect displays the Edit Style dialog box or the Create Style dialog box, depending on whether you choose Edit or Create in step 5. Both dialog boxes contain exactly the same options.

6. Type an optional description for the style in the Description text box.

7. Choose Style Type and choose Paragraph Style, Character Style, or Open Style. Style types are discussed in detail in Chapter 7.

8. Choose Style Contents and edit the style format. The steps for editing styles are discussed in Chapter 7. You also find explanations in Chapter 7 for the Show Style Off Codes and Enter Key Action options.

9. After editing the style, press F7 and choose OK, Close to return to the Edit List dialog box.

10. Choose Page Number Format to display the Page Number Format dialog box.

11. Choose OK to return to the Edit List dialog box.

12. Choose Include Graphics if you want to include WordPerfect graphics box captions in the list. WordPerfect displays the Graphics Box Counters dialog box.

13. Highlight a graphics box counter type, and choose Select, OK to return to the Define List dialog box.

Generating a List

In the final step in creating a list, WordPerfect searches through your document for items you have marked for the list and inserts the formatted list at the point where you defined the list. Follow these steps to generate a list:

1. Choose **T**ools, **G**enerate. WordPerfect displays the Generate dialog box.

2. Choose OK to generate the list.

Using Redline and Strikeout

WordPerfect automatically applies redline and strikeout characters to document text that has changed when you use the Compare Document feature, as described earlier in this chapter. You can also apply redlining and strikeout manually to indicate suggested additions and deletions to a document. Follow these steps:

1. Choose **F**ont, **R**edline, or **S**trikeout. Or, select existing text to be redlined or struck out, and choose **F**ont, **R**edline, or **S**trikeout.

2. If you don't select text in step 1, begin typing redlined or struck-out text. If you select existing text in step 1, WordPerfect formats the text as redlined or struck out.

   Redlined text is displayed in red in Graphics mode on color monitors with default screen colors selected. In Text mode, redlined text is displayed in reversed, red type. On black-and-white monitors, redlined text displays as reversed type. Strikeout text is displayed with a line through characters, spaces, and tabs in all views on color and black-and-white graphics monitors.

3. To turn off redlining or strikeout, move the cursor to the right of the `[Redln Off]` or `[StrkOut Off]` code.

Removing Redline and Strikeout

WordPerfect can automatically remove redline marking and delete all strikeout text in a document. For information, see the section "Comparing Documents," earlier in this chapter.

Changing How WordPerfect Displays Redline and Strikeout Text

The steps for editing screen colors are described in detail in Chapter 3, in the section titled "Display." Follow these steps to change the way WordPerfect displays redline and strikeout text:

1. Press Shift+F1 (Setup) and choose **D**isplay, **T**ext Mode Screen Type/Colors.

2. Highlight the color scheme marked with an asterisk and enclosed in brackets ([ ]), and choose **E**dit.

3. Choose **T**ext Attributes and highlight Redline or Strikeout in the Attributes list.

4. If you have installed a color printer, you can choose **C**olor and make any desired changes.

Changing How WordPerfect Prints Redline and Strikeout Text

Depending on your printer model, WordPerfect usually prints redlined text with a shaded background and overprints struck-out characters with a line. Follow these steps to change the way redline and strikeout text is printed:

1. Choose **L**ayout, **D**ocument.

2. Choose **R**edline Method and choose an option from the drop-down list.

   ■ *Printer Dependent.* This option uses WordPerfect's default redlining for your printer. With most printers, redlined text is printed with a shaded background.

   ■ *Left.* This option places redline characters to the left of red-lined text. The default redline character is a vertical bar (|).

   ■ *Alternating.* This option places redline characters to the left of text on left-facing pages and to the right of text on right-facing pages.

   ■ *Right.* This option places redline characters to the right of redlined text.

3. To change the redline character to something other than a vertical bar, choose **L**eft, **A**lternating, or **R**ight in step 2, then choose Redline Character and type a new character in the box.

   To insert a character from the WordPerfect extended character sets, press Ctrl+W with the cursor in the Redline Character box. WordPerfect displays the WordPerfect Characters dialog box, shown in figure 13.12.

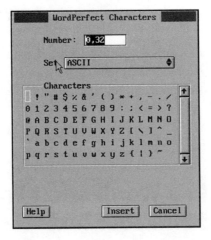

FIG. 13.12

The WordPerfect
Characters
dialog box.

4. Choose **Set**, choose a character set from the list, and double-click a character in the **Characters** box, or highlight a character and choose Insert. WordPerfect inserts the character in the Redline Character box.

5. Choose OK to return to the document screen.

Creating a Table of Authorities

The WordPerfect Table of Authorities feature creates a list that shows where cases and statutes are cited in a legal brief. You can divide the table into separate sections that list cases, regulations, and statutes, and you can format each section differently.

As with other document referencing features, creating a table of authorities requires three steps: mark authorities for inclusion in the table, define the sections of the table, and generate the table. These steps work very nearly as they do in WordPerfect 5.1.

Marking Authorities

You can mark authorities in body text, footnotes, endnotes, graphics boxes, and captions.

To mark a full form, follow these steps:

1. Select the text of the authority, then choose **Tools**, Table of **Authorities**, Mark **Full**. WordPerfect displays the ToA Full Form dialog box.

2. Type a section name in the Section Name box to tell WordPerfect in which section you want to include the authority. If you define several sections, you can choose List Sections (F5), highlight a section name, and choose OK.

3. Type a short form name in the Short Form box.

4. Choose Edit Full Form. WordPerfect takes you into an editing window and displays ToA Full Form in the status line.

5. Edit the citation as you want it to be listed in the table, then press F7 (Exit) to return to the ToA Full Form dialog box.

6. Choose OK to return to the document screen.

To create short form marks, follow these steps:

1. Use Search (F2) to locate other instances of the authority you marked as a full form (see preceding steps).

2. Select the text of the authority.

3. Choose Tools, Table of Authorities, Mark Short. WordPerfect displays the Mark ToA Short form dialog box.

4. Type the short form name in the Short Form entry field. If you have already defined short forms, you can choose List Short Forms (F5) and highlight a short form name in the list, then choose OK.

5. Choose OK to return to the document screen.

Defining a Table of Authorities

The steps for defining a table of authorities are exactly the same as for defining a list, except that you choose Tools, Table of Authorities, Define. Refer to the section "Defining a List," earlier in this chapter.

Generating a Table of Authorities

After you mark entries and define a table of authorities, you can generate the table. Follow these steps:

1. Choose Tools, Generate. WordPerfect displays a message warning that existing tables, lists, and indexes will be replaced if you continue.

2. Choose OK. WordPerfect displays the Generate dialog box and warns you that existing tables, lists, and indexes will be replaced

if you continue. Deselect the **S**ave Modified Subdocuments to have WordPerfect skip the time-consuming process of saving modified subdocuments.

3. Choose OK to generate tables, lists, and indexes.

Creating a Table of Contents

Defining and generating a Table of Contents requires the same steps as in WordPerfect 5.1. Only a few minor aspects of this feature have changed. As with lists and tables of authorities, creating a table of contents involves three steps: mark text for the table of contents, tell WordPerfect how you want the table of contents formatted, and generate the table.

Marking Text for a Table of Contents

Follow these steps to mark text you want to include in a table of contents:

1. Select the word or phrase you want included in the table of contents. If you use WordPerfect's system styles for Heading 1, 2, 3, and so on, the headings are automatically marked for inclusion in a table of contents.

2. Choose **T**ools, Ta**b**le of Contents, **M**ark, type a level number for the entry, and choose OK.

3. Repeat steps 1 and 2 for each table of contents entry.

Defining a Table of Contents

After marking text for inclusion in a table of contents, you can tell WordPerfect where you want it to generate the table, and how you want the table to look. Follow these steps:

1. Place the cursor where you want the table of contents to appear.

2. Choose **T**ools, Ta**b**le of Contents, **D**efine.

3. Choose **N**umber of Levels and type the number of levels (1-5) you want in the table.

4. Choose **L**evel and choose a level from the list, then choose a Numbering mode.

5. If the table of contents has more than one level and you want the last level wrapped flush left, choose **W**rap the Last Level.

6. Choose **P**age Number Format if you want to change the way page numbers are formatted. WordPerfect displays the Page Number Format dialog box.

7. Choose OK, Close to return to the document window.

Generating a Table of Contents

After marking text for and defining a table of contents, you need to generate the table. Follow these steps:

1. Choose **T**ools, **G**enerate. WordPerfect displays a message warning you that existing tables, lists, and indexes will be replaced if you continue.

2. Choose OK. WordPerfect generates tables lists and indexes.

Using Merge

The Merge feature has changed significantly in WordPerfect 6. Primary and secondary files are now called *form files* and *data files*, in keeping with common usage, and you can now store merge data in a table for easier visual reference and proofreading. This means that you can import a spreadsheet into a WordPerfect table and use it as data for merge printing.

Data files and form files are now linked, so you no longer need to remember the name of the data file that you regularly print with a merge form. (You can, of course, remove the link and link the form to a different data file.)

In WordPerfect 5.1, printing merge codes requires a special macro. In WordPerfect 6, you can print out field names without any trouble. A new Blank Remove option automatically omits blank lines from a form when field data is absent, eliminating the need for If Blank and If Not Blank programming statements required in WordPerfect 5.1. Advanced WordPerfect merge programmers will discover 13 new merge commands. System variables can now be entered from a pop-up list, with context-sensitive help. And you can place embedded macros in a merge document, for example to create a dialog box that asks whether you want to print the current data record.

Creating a Data File

WordPerfect 6 can merge data stored in text files, as in WordPerfect 5.1 secondary files, or in tables. The following sections discuss these data file types.

Creating a Text Data File

Follow these steps to create a merge text data file:

1. In a new WordPerfect document window, type the contents of the first data field. Don't add any extra spaces.

2. Choose **Tools**, **Merge**, **Define**; or press Shift+F9.

   WordPerfect displays the Merge Codes dialog box, shown in figure 14.1.

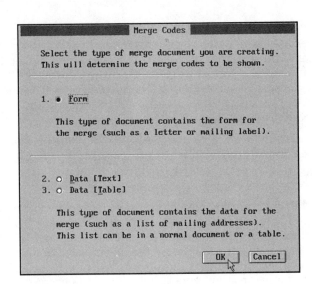

FIG. 14.1

The Merge Codes dialog box.

3. Choose **Data** [Text].

   WordPerfect displays the Merge Codes (Text Data file) dialog box, shown in figure 14.2.

4. Choose End **F**ield.

   WordPerfect returns to the document window and inserts the ENDFIELD code in the text. Make sure that there are no spaces between the field text and the merge code.

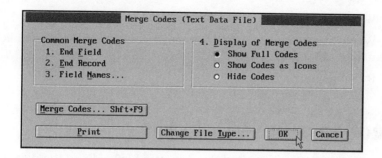

FIG. 14.2

The Merge
Codes (Text Data
File) dialog box.

5. Repeat steps 1 through 4 for the remaining fields in the record.

6. Choose Tools, Merge, Define; or press Shift+F9. And then choose End Record.

   WordPerfect returns to the document window and inserts an ENDRECORD code and a hard page break.

   You can also insert ENDFIELD and ENDRECORD codes with the keyboard. Press F9 to insert ENDFIELD. Press Shift+F9 and choose End Record to insert ENDRECORD.

7. Repeat steps 1 through 6 for each data record.

Naming Data Fields

Naming the fields in a data file makes it easier to refer to the fields when you create forms to merge with the data file. Follow these steps to name fields:

1. Choose Tools, Merge, Define; or press Shift+F9. Then choose Field Names.

   WordPerfect displays the Field Names dialog box.

2. Type a name for the first field and press Enter.

3. Repeat step 2 for all the fields in the data file.

   If you omit a field, highlight the field above the position you want to insert the field and choose Insert Field Name. Type the field name and press Enter.

   To add a field name at the end of the list, choose Add Field Name at the End, type the field name, and press Enter.

   To edit a field name, highlight the name and choose Edit Field Name. Edit the name and press Enter.

4. When you have entered all the field names, choose OK.

   WordPerfect returns to the document screen and inserts the field names at the top of the data file.

5. Save the file.

Creating a Table Data File

Placing merge data in a table makes it easier to proofread the data. It's also quicker to enter data in a table because you don't have to insert ENDFIELD and ENDRECORD codes; instead, you press Tab to move to the next cell or to insert a new record.

Follow these steps to enter merge data in a table:

1. In a new document window, Choose Tools, Merge, Define; or press Shift+F9. Then choose Data [Table].

   WordPerfect displays the Merge Codes (Table Data File) dialog box, shown in figure 14.3.

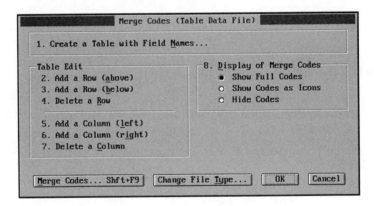

FIG. 14.3

The Merge Codes (Table Data File) dialog box.

2. Choose Create a Table with Field Names.

   WordPerfect displays the Field Names dialog box.

3. Type up to 25 field names. When finish entering names, choose OK.

   WordPerfect creates a table and inserts the field names in the first row. Figure 14.4 shows a table data file with one record.

4. Enter data in the file, pressing Tab to move to the next field and to insert a new row.

You can use WordPerfect's table editing features, for example, to add or delete rows and columns. Notice in figure 14.4 that the table cells are too narrow to accommodate the data without splitting words. To create a wider table, you can select a wider paper size/type definition and use the table editing features to widen the table. Tables are discussed in Chapter 15.

5. Save the file.

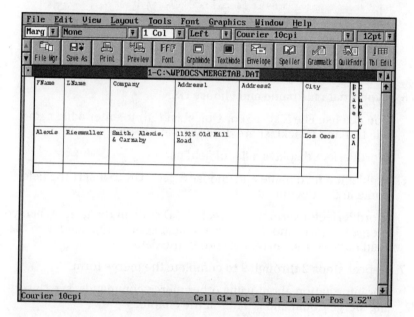

Creating a Form File

A form file (called a primary file in WordPerfect 5.1) is where you type the document to be merged. Follow these steps:

1. In a new document window, type the text of the form document.

2. To insert variable merge data, Choose **T**ools, **M**erge, **D**efine; or press Shift+F9. Then choose **F**orm.

   WordPerfect displays the Merge Codes (Form File) dialog box, shown in figure 14.5.

3. Choose **F**ield.

4. From the Parameter Entry dialog, choose List Field Names (F5) to display the field names in a data file.

```
┌─────────────────── Merge Codes (Form File) ───────────────────┐
│ ┌─Common Merge Codes──────┐  6. Display of Merge Codes─────────┐│
│ │  1. Field               │                                    ││
│ │  2. Keyboard            │     ● Show Full Codes              ││
│ │  3. Page Off            │     ○ Show Codes as Icons          ││
│ │  4. Comment             │     ○ Hide Codes                   ││
│ │  5. Variable            │                                    ││
│ └─────────────────────────┘                                    ││
│                                                                 │
│  ┌Merge Codes... Shft+F9┐  ┌Change File Type...┐  ┌ OK ┐ ┌Cancel┐│
└─────────────────────────────────────────────────────────────────┘
```

FIG. 14.5

The Merge
Codes (Form File)
dialog box.

WordPerfect displays the Select Data File For Field Names dialog box.

5. Type a data file name and choose OK.

   You can use File List (F5) or QuickList (F6) to enter a file name. File List and QuickList are described in Chapter 9.

   WordPerfect displays a list of field names.

6. Highlight a field name and choose Select, OK to insert the field name in the document.

   WordPerfect inserts the correct FIELD code in the form. When you merge the form and data files, the field code is replaced with the field data for the current record in the data file.

7. Repeat steps 2 through 9 to complete the merge form.

   For information about using other merge commands, see "Inserting Merge Commands," later in the chapter.

8. Save the file.

Creating a Form File for an Envelope

You can use the WordPerfect 6 Envelope feature to merge-print envelopes. The Envelope feature is discussed in Chapter 8. Follow these steps to create a merge form file for an envelope:

1. Choose Tools, Merge, Define; or press Shift+F9. Then choose Form, OK.

   Step 1 ensures that the correct dialog box displays later.

2. Choose Layout, Envelope.

3. Choose **R**eturn Address if you want WordPerfect to print a return address on the merge-printed envelopes, then press F7 (Exit).

4. Choose **M**ailing Address.

5. Choose **T**ools, **M**erge, **D**efine; or press Shift+F9. Then choose Field, type a field name, and choose OK.

6. Repeat step 5 for each Mailing Address field.

7. After entering field codes, press F7 (Exit) and choose **I**nsert.

   WordPerfect returns to the document window and inserts the envelope merge definition.

Merge Printing the Files

After preparing form and data files as described earlier, you can merge print the files. Follow these steps:

1. Choose **T**ools, **M**erge, **R**un; or press Ctrl+F9.

   WordPerfect displays the Run Merge dialog box, shown in figure 14.6.

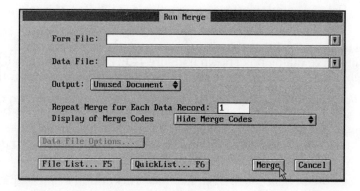

FIG. 14.6

The Run Merge dialog box.

2. Type filenames and paths in the **F**orm File and **D**ata File boxes.

3. Choose **O**utput.

4. Choose an option from the Output drop-down list:

   ■ *Current Document.* This option merges to the current document window.

   ■ *Unused Document (the default).* This option merges to a new document window.

- *Printer.* This option merges to the printer.

- *File.* This option merges to a file. WordPerfect prompts you for a filename.

5. Choose Merge. WordPerfect merges the form and data files and sends the merged data to the output location you specify in step 4.

The following paragraphs describe the remaining options on the Run Merge dialog box:

- *Repeat Merge for Each Data Record.* This option sends the specified number of copies to the output location before proceeding to the next record.

- *Display of Merge Codes.* This option drops down a list with the following options:

  Hide Merge Codes (the default). This option hides merge codes in the form file.

  Show Merge Codes. This option displays merge codes in the form file.

  Show Merge Codes as **I**cons. This option indicates the location of merge codes as graphic symbols.

  Data File Options. This option displays the Run Merge dialog box, shown in figure 14.7.

Notice in figure 14.7 that this dialog box contains the same options as the Run Merge dialog box shown in figure 14.6, but adds options 6 through 9. The following paragraphs describe these additional options:

- *Blank Fields in Data File.* This option pops up a list with two options: **L**eave Resulting Blank Line (the default) and **R**emove Resulting Blank Line. Choose **R**emove Resulting Blank Line to have WordPerfect automatically delete blank lines in the merged document resulting from blank fields in the data file.

- *Page Break Between Merged Records.* This option inserts a page break after each merged record. Deselecting the check box merges data continuously.

- *Generate an Envelope for Each Data Record.* This option displays the Envelope dialog box, where you can enter text and merge fields as described above under "Creating a Form File for an Envelope," earlier in this chapter. When you define an envelope for a merge form, WordPerfect inserts an envelope at the end of the merge document for each record.

- *All Records.* This option merges all records from the specified data file.

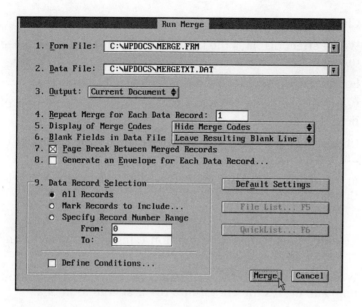

FIG. 14.7

The Run Merge
dialog box.

- *Mark Records to Include.* This option displays the Mark Data Records dialog box.

- *Specify Record Number Range.* Enter starting and ending numbers in the From and To boxes.

- *Define Conditions.* This option displays the Define Conditions for Record Selection dialog box, which is described later under "Defining Conditions for Record Selection."

- *Default Settings.* This option returns all options on the Run Merge dialog box to the defaults.

Defining Conditions for Record Selection

As in WordPerfect 5.1, you can define conditions to select a range of data records to be merged. Follow these steps:

1. Define a merge form and data files as described earlier.

2. Choose **Tools, Merge, Run.**

   WordPerfect displays the Run Merge dialog box.

3. Make any desired selections in the Data Record **S**election area of the Run Merge dialog box.

4. Choose Define Conditions.

    WordPerfect displays the Define Conditions for Record Selection dialog box.

5. For help with entering conditions, choose Example (F4).

    WordPerfect displays the Example of Selection Conditions dialog box.

    Choosing Examples of Valid Entries displays the Examples of Valid Entries dialog box.

6. In the define Conditions for Record Selection, press 1 to select Condition 1.

    WordPerfect displays the List Field Names dialog box.

7. To enter a field name for Condition 1, highlight the name and choose Select.

    WordPerfect inserts the field name above the first Condition column and moves the cursor into the first condition box.

8. Type the first condition and choose OK or press Tab to move to the next condition box.

    Figure 14.8 shows conditions entered for selecting records where the State is CA, AZ, NM, NV, and LName is greater than or equal to N. These conditions select people with last names between N and Z who live in the specified states.

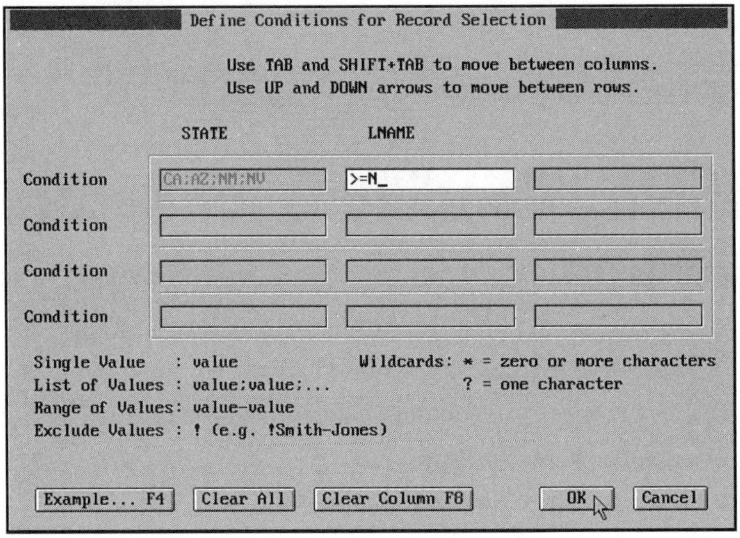

FIG. 14.8

The Define Conditions for Record Selection dialog box with the State field selected for Condition 1.

9. Continue to define conditions, then choose OK and Merge to begin the merge.

Inserting Merge Codes

You can insert merge programming codes in a Merge form file, just as in WordPerfect 5.1. Follow these steps:

1. Choose **T**ools, **M**erge, **D**efine; or press Shift+F9. Then choose **F**orm.

2. Choose **M**erge Codes (Shift+F9).

   WordPerfect displays the All Merge Codes dialog box, shown in figure 14.9.

   Notice in figure 14.9 that when you type the first few letters of a command, the highlight moves to that command in the list. Notice also that WordPerfect displays a brief description of the highlighted command. Press F1 (Help) to see detailed instructions for using the highlighted command.

FIG. 14.9

The All Merge Codes dialog box.

3. Highlight a code and choose Select.

   If the command requires one or more parameters, WordPerfect displays the Parameter Entry dialog box.

   If you choose List Variables with the System command selected, WordPerfect displays a list of system variables, as shown in figure 14.10.

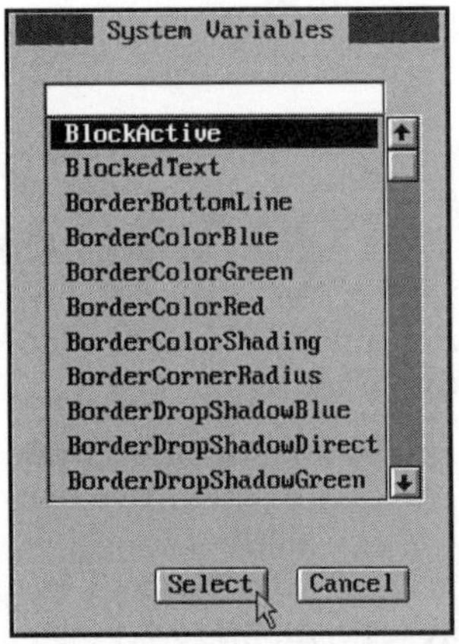

FIG. 14.10

The System
Variables dialog
box.

For detailed instructions on using system variables, press F1
(Help) from the System Variables dialog box.

4. Press Enter to insert the parameter. Finish typing parameters and
   choose OK.

WordPerfect returns to the document window and inserts the
Merge command, where you can edit the parameters as regular
text.

Converting Merge Codes Created with Other WordPerfect Versions

Form and data files created with earlier WordPerfect versions are automatically converted to WordPerfect 6 format during a merge. The
merge will run faster if you convert the files before the merge. Simply
retrieve the form and data files in WordPerfect 6 and save them again.

Using Tables

Numerous improvements have been made to the Tables feature in WordPerfect 6. Most welcome are the improvements in table formatting. For example, you no longer have to select an entire table to format all borders and interior lines. You can use fill styles in table cells, and you can create a three-dimensional effect with table shadows.

If you work with numbers, you will welcome WordPerfect's all-new Spreadsheet feature, which enables you to format a table with math formulas and cell references for what-if analysis. You can even create *floating cells*—single-cell "tables" placed in text that can be referenced in a table.

Creating a Table

The steps to create a table are essentially the same as in WordPerfect 5.1. Follow these steps:

1. Choose Layout, Tables; or press Alt+F7 and choose Tables. Then choose Create. WordPerfect displays the Create Table dialog box.

2. Type the number of columns and rows in the Columns and Rows boxes, or click the arrows to increment and decrement the numbers, then choose OK. WordPerfect creates a table with the specified number of rows and columns and displays it in the Table Editor (see fig. 15.1).

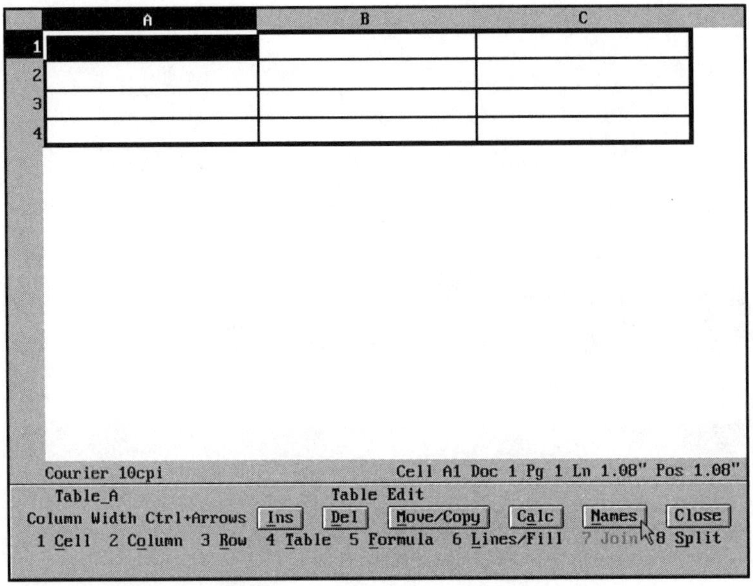

FIG. 15.1

The Table Editor.

3. Use Table Editor options to change the table's formatting, then press F7 (Exit) to leave the Table Editor and return to the document window. WordPerfect displays the formatted table in the document screen.

The WordPerfect 6 Table Editor is similar to the Table Editor in WordPerfect 5.1. The biggest difference is that WordPerfect 6 uses styles to perform most table formatting. You don't have to learn a great deal about styles to do basic table formatting because styles work in the background. But when you decide to change default table formatting options, styles provide a great deal of flexibility and control. For example, you can change the appearance of all the tables in a long document simply by editing table styles.

You can use styles in tables, and you can include a table in a style. To format a table that is included in a style, you must edit the style, then format the table.

Adding Lines, Borders, and Fills

WordPerfect 6 offers a wealth of new ways to change the appearance of a table. You can create table lines and borders with different colors and patterns. You can stack, space, and thicken lines. You can create table shadows for a three-dimensional effect, and you can fill cells with patterns and colors.

The following sections describe the options for formatting table lines, borders, and fill patterns.

Choosing Line and Border Styles

In WordPerfect 5.1, table lines and borders are formatted by using the same commands. In WordPerfect 6, lines and borders are formatted separately. Lines define the basic structure of the table: the column, row, and cell borders. The table border is formatted separately on the outside edges of the table.

Follow these steps to change the border style:

1. Move the cursor into a table and choose **L**ayout, Ta**b**les; or press Alt+F7 and choose Ta**b**les. Then choose **E**dit. WordPerfect displays the table in the Table Editor.

2. Choose Lines/Fill. WordPerfect displays the Table Lines dialog box, shown in figure 15.2.

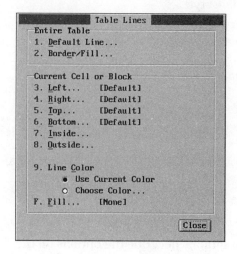

FIG. 15.2

The Table Lines dialog box.

The following paragraphs describe the options on the Table Lines dialog box.

Changing the Default Line Style

Follow these steps to change the default table line style:

1. From the Table Editor, choose **L**ines/Fill, **D**efault Line. WordPerfect displays the Default Table Lines dialog box.

2. Choose Line Style. WordPerfect displays the Line Styles dialog box. To learn how to use style options, see Chapter 7.

3. Highlight a line style and choose **S**elect.

4. Choose Close to return to the Table Lines dialog box.

Changing the Default Line Color

Follow these steps to change the default table line color:

1. From the Table Editor, choose **L**ines/Fill, **D**efault Line, **C**olor.

2. Choose Use Line Style Color to accept the line color defined for the default line style.

   Or, choose **C**hoose Color to display the Color Selection dialog box and choose a color.

The Color Selection dialog box is discussed in Chapter 4, in the section "Paragraph Borders."

Changing the Default Border/Fill

Follow these steps to change the default table border and fill:

1. From the Table Editor, choose **L**ines/Fill, Bord**e**r/Fill. WordPerfect displays the Table Border/Fill dialog box.

2. Choose the options on the Table Border/Fill dialog box.

The following paragraphs describe the options on the Table Border/Fill dialog box:

- *Border Style.* This option displays the Border Styles dialog box. Style options are discussed in Chapter 7.

- *Fill Style.* This option displays the Fill Styles dialog box. Fill styles are discussed in Chapter 4. Style options are discussed in Chapter 7.

- *Customize.* This option displays the Customize Table Border/Fill dialog box. Choosing box borders and fills is discussed in Chapter 12. The options are exactly the same as for table borders and fills.

Choosing Line Options for the Current Cell or Block

You can format lines for individual cells or a block of selected cells, just as in WordPerfect 5.1. Use options 3 through 9 and F on the Table Lines dialog box (refer to fig 15.2).

The options are exactly the same as for changing the default line and border styles, as discussed in the preceding sections.

Formatting Tables

You format tables in WordPerfect 6 using the Table Editor—just as in WordPerfect 5.1. However, formatting cell and table borders and changing the dimensions of columns and rows is much easier, thanks to improvements in Table Edit mode.

 In WordPerfect 6, the Table Editor Join and Split options are exactly the same as in WordPerfect 5.1.

Formatting a Table Cell

With WordPerfect 6, it's much easier to format a table cell than with WordPerfect 5.1 because you can choose all cell formatting options from a single dialog box instead of searching for formatting options in separate menus.

Follow these steps to format a table cell:

1. Place the cursor in the cell you want to format. Then choose Layout, Tables; or press Alt+F7 and choose Tables. Then choose Edit. WordPerfect displays the table in the Table Editor, as shown in figure 15.1, but with the cell that contains the cursor selected.

2. Choose Cell. WordPerfect displays the Cell Format dialog box.

3. Choose text formatting options for cell Attributes and Alignment.

4. Choose a Number Type. Number Type options are discussed later in this chapter.

5. Choose Use Column and mark the Attributes, Justification, and Number Type check boxes to use column defaults to format the cell.

6. Choose **L**ock to lock the cell, as in WordPerfect 5.1.

7. Choose **I**gnore When Calculating to exclude the cell from calculations.

8. Choose OK to return to the Table Editor.

Formatting a Table Column

Follow these steps to format a table column:

1. Place the cursor in the column you want to format. Then choose **L**ayout, Ta**b**les; or press Alt+F7 and choose Ta**b**les. Then choose **E**dit. WordPerfect displays the table in the Table Editor.

2. Choose **C**olumn. WordPerfect displays the Column Format dialog box.

   The Attributes options are the same as for formatting a cell, as discussed in the preceding section. The Alignment options are also the same, except for **D**ecimal Align Position. This option, which is new in WordPerfect 6, lets you specify a decimal alignment position measured from the right edge of a cell.

3. Choose **D**ecimal Align Position, then choose **D**igits or D**i**stance and type the desired figure in the box.

4. Choose Number **T**ype options. Number types are discussed later in this chapter.

5. Choose **C**olumn Margins and type the desired figures in the **L**eft, **R**ight, **W**idth, and **F**ixed Width boxes.

   In the Table Editor, you can also change column width by pressing Ctrl and the right- and left-arrow keys, as in WordPerfect 5.1.

6. Choose OK to return to the Table Editor.

Formatting a Table Row

Follow these steps to format a table row:

1. Place the cursor in the column you want to format. Then choose **L**ayout, Ta**b**les; or press Alt+F7 and choose Ta**b**les. Then choose **E**dit. WordPerfect displays the table in the Table Editor.

2. Choose **R**ow. WordPerfect displays the Row Format dialog box.

3. Choose options and choose OK to return to the Table Editor.

Formatting an Entire Table

Follow these steps to choose formatting options that affect an entire table:

1. Place the cursor in the column you want to format. Choose Layout, Tables; or press Alt+F7 and choose Tables. Then choose Edit. WordPerfect displays the table in the Table Editor.

2. Choose Table. WordPerfect displays the Table Format dialog box.

The Attributes and Alignment options are the same as in WordPerfect 5.1, except for Decimal Align Position, which is described earlier under "Formatting a Table Column." The Number Type options are described later in this chapter under "Spreadsheet."

Inserting Table Rows and Columns

WordPerfect 6 has two new options for inserting table rows and columns. Follow these steps to insert rows and columns:

1. Place the cursor in the table, in the row or column above or below or to the left or right of where you want to insert a row or column. Then choose Layout, Tables; or press Alt+F7 and choose Tables. Then choose Edit. WordPerfect displays the table in the Table Editor.

2. Choose Ins. WordPerfect displays the Insert dialog box.

   The first three options in the Insert dialog box are the same as in WordPerfect 5.1, but the last two options are new in WordPerfect 6 and are described in the sections that follow.

3. Enter the number of columns and rows you want to insert, then choose Before Cursor Position to insert a row above the current row or to insert a column to the left of the current column. Or choose After Cursor Position to insert a row below the current row or a column to the right of the current column.

Inserting and Deleting Rows with the Keyboard

With WordPerfect 6, you can also insert and delete table rows and columns with the following keystrokes:

Keystroke	Action
Ctrl+Ins	Inserts row above cursor
Ctrl++	Inserts row below cursor
Ctrl+Del	Deletes the current row

Deleting Table Columns and Rows

The Delete function works a bit differently in the WordPerfect 6 Table Editor than in WordPerfect 5.1. When you choose **D**el from the Table Editor, WordPerfect displays the Delete dialog box. The **C**ell Contents option is new in WordPerfect 6, but the remaining options are the same as in WordPerfect 5.1.

Moving and Copying Rows, Columns, and Cells

The steps for moving and copying rows, columns, cells, and selected portions of tables are the same in WordPerfect 6 as in WordPerfect 5.1, except that you use a single dialog box instead of separate menus. Follow these steps:

1. Place the cursor in the table. Then choose **L**ayout, Ta**b**les; or press Alt+F7 and choose Ta**b**les. Then choose **E**dit.

2. Select table cells or place the cursor in the table column or row you want to move or copy.

3. Choose **M**ove/Copy. WordPerfect displays the Move dialog box.

4. Choose **B**lock, **R**ow, **C**olumn, or **C**ell, then choose **M**ove or Co**p**y.

5. Move the cursor where you want to move or copy to, and press Enter.

   Or, press Esc, move the cursor where you want to move or copy to, and choose **M**ove/Copy, **R**etrieve.

Combining Tables

In WordPerfect 6, you can create complex tables by creating several tables separately and then combining them. You can do this in

WordPerfect 5.1, but positioning adjacent tables precisely is a tricky process. Follow these steps to combine two tables:

1. Create and format two tables, one above the other with no lines or spaces in between.

2. Place the cursor in the first table, then choose Layout, Tables, Join. WordPerfect joins the tables.

   To split a table into two separate tables, place the cursor in the row above where you want the table to be split, then choose Layout, Tables, Split.

Creating Table Formulas

With WordPerfect 6, you can create formulas in table cells, using 100 functions, and perform spreadsheet what-if analyses. You can reference cells to tables, columns, rows, and floating cells. (Floating cells are explained later in this chapter.)

You can use functions in cells, formulas, and in other functions. Follow these steps to insert a function in a table cell:

1. Move the cursor into the table. Choose Layout, Tables; or press Alt+F7 and choose Tables. Then choose Edit. WordPerfect displays the table in the Table Editor.

2. Move the cursor into the cell (or the first cell in a range) where you want to create a formula, and choose Formula. WordPerfect displays the Table Formula dialog box, shown in figure 15.3.

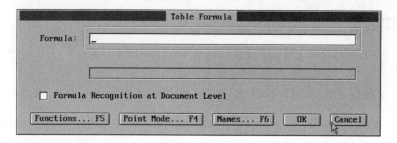

FIG. 15.3

The Table Formula dialog box.

3. Choose Formula.

4. Choose Functions (F5). WordPerfect displays the Table Functions dialog box, shown in figure 15.4. Notice in figure 15.4 that WordPerfect displays a brief description of the highlighted function. To view a list of table functions with detailed descriptions and examples, press F1 (Help).

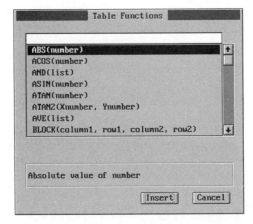

FIG. 15.4

The Table
Functions dialog
box.

5. Highlight a function and choose Insert. WordPerfect inserts the function in the Formula text box of the Table Formula dialog box, with the cursor between the parameters parentheses, if any exist.

6. Type any required function parameters and choose OK.

   The Formula Recognition at Document Level option is described later in this chapter, under "Formula Recognition at Document Level."

   WordPerfect returns to the Table Editor and inserts the function in the cell.

Using Point Mode To Specify a Function Range

For functions that require you to specify a range of cells, WordPerfect can automatically enter the range for you. Follow these steps:

1. From the Table Editor, choose Formula, Functions (F5), highlight a function, and choose Insert.

2. Choose Point Mode (F4). WordPerfect returns to the Table Editor and displays the message: Use arrow keys to define range.

3. Move the cursor to the first cell in the range and choose Start Range (F4).

4. Move the cursor to the last cell in the range and press Enter.

   WordPerfect returns to the Table Formula dialog box and automatically inserts the cell range in the formula.

Naming Cells, Columns, Rows, or Tables

Notice in figure 15.3 that the Table Formula dialog box includes a Names (F6) option. In WordPerfect 6, you can name cells, tables, blocks of cells, columns, and rows. For example, you can name a cell INTRATE. You can then use the named table, cell, block, column, or row in formulas.

Follow these steps to name a cell, column, row, table, or block:

1. Move the cursor into the table. Then choose **L**ayout, Ta**b**les; or press Alt+F7 and choose Ta**b**les. Then choose **E**dit. WordPerfect displays the table in the Table Editor.

2. Move the cursor to the cell or the beginning of the row or column you want to name. To name a block of cells, see the following section "Name a Block of Cells."

3. Choose **N**ames.

4. Choose **C**ell, **C**olumn, **R**ow, or **T**able.

   WordPerfect displays the Create Cell (Column, Row, or Table) Name dialog box. These dialog boxes are the same, except that when you choose **T**able, WordPerfect suggests the table name Table_A, Table_B, and so on.

Follow these steps to name a block of cells:

1. In the Table Editor, select the cells and choose **N**ames.

   Alternatively, don't select the cells; instead, move the cursor into the first or last cell in the block, press Alt+F4 (Block), and choose **N**ames.

   WordPerfect displays the Name Cells dialog box with special options for naming a block, as shown in figure 15.5.

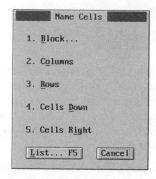

The Name Cells dialog box with block options displayed.

2. If you block cells in step 1, choose **B**lock, type a name, and choose OK.

   Or, if you don't block cells in step 1, choose C**o**lumns, **R**ows, Cells **D**own, or Cells Ri**g**ht.

Using Names in Formulas

You can reference named cells, tables, and so on in formulas. Follow these steps:

1. Define a named cell, table, and so on as described in the preceding section.

2. From the Table Editor, choose **F**ormula and define a formula as described earlier under "Creating Table Formulas."

   After inserting a formula in the Table Formula dialog box, enter the formula parameters using named references for cell, table, column, row, or range parameters.

3. Type the names at the keyboard or choose Names (F6).

   When you choose Names, WordPerfect displays the List Table Names dialog box.

4. Highlight the name of a cell, table, range, row, or column and choose **S**elect. WordPerfect returns to the Table formula dialog box and inserts the selected name in the formula.

   In the List Table Names dialog box, you can choose **E**dit or **D**elete to perform the corresponding operations on cell, block, table, row, and column names.

   Choosing **L**ist all Names in Document includes the current table's name in the list.

Floating Cell Tables

A *floating cell* is a single-cell table you can link to a table so that whenever you calculate the table, the referenced floating cell also changes. For example, a loan calculation table may include a cell that shows the current balance due. You can create a floating cell in a sentence that references the current balance. When you update the table, WordPerfect updates the floating cell.

Floating cells don't look like cells because they aren't formatted with lines and borders. Instead, as in the preceding loan balance example, they look like normal text.

Creating a Floating Cell

To create a floating cell, follow these steps:

1. Place the cursor where you want to create a floating cell.

2. Choose **L**ayout, Ta**b**les; or press Alt+F7 and choose Ta**b**les. Then choose Create **F**loating Cell. WordPerfect displays the Edit Floating Cell dialog box, shown in figure 15.6.

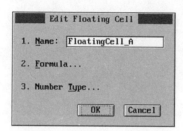

FIG. 15.6

The Edit Floating Cell dialog box.

Notice in figure 15.6 that WordPerfect has automatically entered a name for the floating cell.

3. Accept the name or choose **N**ame and type a new name.

4. Choose **F**ormula. WordPerfect displays the Table Formula dialog box.

5. Enter a formula and choose OK.

6. Choose Number **T**ype. WordPerfect displays the Number Type Formats dialog box, shown in figure 15.7.

   The Number Type Formats dialog box lets you tell WordPerfect how to format numbers derived by a formula in a floating cell.

7. Choose a standard format from the Standard Formats list.

   Notice that when you choose the radio button for one of the Standard Formats, the Preview box shows an example of the numeric formatting that will be applied.

   The following paragraphs describe the choices in the Options box:

   - *Digits After Decimal.* This option is available only for Standard Formats selections that use decimals. Type the number of decimal places you want to display.

   - *Round for Calculation.* This option tells WordPerfect to round numbers to the specified decimal on calculation.

   - *Use Commas.* This option tells WordPerfect to format numbers greater than 1000 with commas (for example, 1,000).

278

```
┌─────────────────────────────────────────────────────────────┐
│                      Number Type Formats                      │
├─────────────────────────────────────────────────────────────┤
│  ┌─Standard Formats──┐    ┌─O. Options─────────────────────┐  │
│  │ 1. ● General      │    │  Digits After Decimal: [0]     │  │
│  │ 2. ○ Integer      │    │  □ Round for Calculation       │  │
│  │ 3. ○ Fixed        │    │  □ Use Commas                  │  │
│  │ 4. ○ Percent      │    │                                │  │
│  │ 5. ○ Currency     │    ┌─Negative Numbers───────────────┐  │
│  │ 6. ○ Accounting   │    │  ● Minus Sign                  │  │
│  │ 7. ○ Commas       │    │  ○ Parentheses                 │  │
│  │ 8. ○ Scientific   │    │  ○ CR/DR Symbol                │  │
│  │ 9. ○ Date         │    └────────────────────────────────┘  │
│  │ T. ○ Text         │    ┌─Currency Symbol────────────────┐  │
│  └───────────────────┘    │  □ On                          │  │
│  ┌─Preview───────────┐    │  □ Align Currency Symbol       │  │
│  │ 0                 │    │    Select... [            ]    │  │
│  └───────────────────┘    └────────────────────────────────┘  │
│   E. Select Date Format...                                    │
│                                            [  OK  ] [ Cancel ] │
└─────────────────────────────────────────────────────────────┘
```

FIG. 15.7

The Number
Type Formats
dialog box.

- *Negative Numbers.* Choose Minus Sign, Parentheses, or CR/DR Symbol to change the formatting of negative numbers.

- *Currency Symbol.* Choose On to display currency symbols for currency Standard Formats types. Choose Align Currency Symbol to align currency symbols in numbers, subtotals, and totals. Choose Select to choose foreign currency symbols from a list.

8. Choose OK, OK to return to the document window.

WordPerfect inserts hidden floating cell beginning and ending codes.

Calculating Tables and Floating Cells

You calculate tables and floating cells just as in WordPerfect 5.1, except that you can calculate without entering the Table Editor. From the document screen, choose Layout, Tables, Calculate; or press Alt+F7 and choose Tables, Calculate All. WordPerfect calculates any formulas in tables and floating cells and inserts the updated results.

Using the Formula Recognition at Document Level Option

You can display addition, subtraction, multiplication, division, and exponentiation symbols in floating cells in the document window and tell WordPerfect to interpret them as mathematical symbols. For example, with Formula Recognition at Document Level turned on, WordPerfect interprets the following as a math problem instead of a phone number: (916) 297-9999.

To turn on Formula Recognition at Document Level, place the cursor between opening and closing floating cell codes and choose Layout, Tables, Edit Floating Cell, Formula, Formula Recognition at Document Level, OK, OK.

Importing and Linking Spreadsheet Data

The Spreadsheet Import and Link features work almost the same as in WordPerfect 5.1. Import copies information from a spreadsheet into a WordPerfect document. WordPerfect can update a linked spreadsheet when the spreadsheet changes in the original application.

You can import and link files from PlanPerfect 3.0 through 5.1, Lotus 1-2-3 Versions 1.0 through 3.1, Microsoft Excel Version 2.0 through 3.0, Quattro, and Quattro Pro.

> You can import or link spreadsheet data of no more than one page in length into a graphics box.   T I P

Follow these steps to import spreadsheet data:

1. Position the cursor where you want to import the spreadsheet, or create a table if you want to import the spreadsheet into a table. WordPerfect automatically creates new rows and columns to accommodate the imported spreadsheet data.

2. Choose Tools, Spreadsheet; or press Alt+F7 and choose Spreadsheet. Then choose Import or Create Link.

   If you chose Import, WordPerfect displays the Import Spreadsheet dialog box, shown in figure 15.8.

   If you choose Create Link, WordPerfect displays the Create Spreadsheet Link dialog box.

   Notice that the options in the Create Spreadsheet Link dialog box are the same as those in the Import Spreadsheet dialog box.

3. Type a filename for the spreadsheet in the Filename box; then type a range in the Range box.

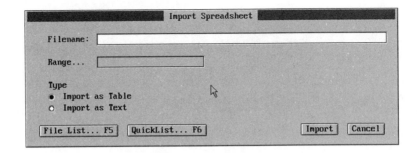

FIG. 15.8

The Import
Spreadsheet
dialog box.

4. Choose Import as Table or Import as Text.

5. Choose Import to import a spreadsheet, or choose Link or Link & Import to link a spreadsheet.

If you choose Link, WordPerfect places a link code in the document but doesn't import the data. When you update the link—as shown in the following two sections—the spreadsheet data is inserted in the WordPerfect document.

If you choose Link & Import, WordPerfect imports and links the spreadsheet data.

Comments in the WordPerfect document window show where linked data begins and ends. You can hide the comments, as explained later under "Hiding Links."

Editing Linked Data

Follow these steps to edit a spreadsheet link:

1. Move the cursor into the linked data.

2. Choose Tools, Spreadsheet; or press Alt+F7 and choose Spreadsheet. Then choose Edit Link. WordPerfect displays the Edit Spreadsheet Link dialog box.

3. Edit link options and choose Link to update the data and return to the document screen.

Updating a Link Manually

Follow these steps to update a link manually:

1. Choose Tools, Spreadsheet, Link Options. WordPerfect displays the Spreadsheet Link Options dialog box.

2. Choose Update on Retrieve, OK.

Whenever you open the document, WordPerfect updates the linked data.

Hiding Links

You can hide the comment box WordPerfect inserts in your document at the location of a spreadsheet link. Choose Tools, Spreadsheet; or press Alt+F7 and choose Spreadsheet. Then choose Link Options, deselect Show Link Codes, and choose OK.

Deleting a Link

To delete a link without removing the spreadsheet information, press Alt+F3 (Reveal Codes); then delete the [Link] or [Link End] code.

Opening or Retrieving Spreadsheet Data as a Table

In WordPerfect 6, you can open a spreadsheet without creating a link or importing the spreadsheet as described in the preceding sections. Choose File, Open, type the name of the spreadsheet, and choose OK. WordPerfect imports the data as a table unless you import it into existing columns, in which case the spreadsheet is imported as text.

Using Outlines

WordPerfect 6 introduces a long-awaited feature: collapsible outlines. When you collapse a WordPerfect 6 outline heading, all its subheadings and body text become invisible. Moving a collapsed heading moves its subheadings and body text as well.

Collapsible headings provide an excellent way to quickly check the structure of a long document and to move quickly between widely separated sections.

Creating an Outline

Follow these steps to create an outline:

1. Choose **T**ools, **O**utline; or press Ctrl+F5. Then choose **B**egin New Outline. WordPerfect displays the Outline Style List dialog box (see fig. 16.1). Style options are discussed in detail in Chapter 7.

2. Choose a style and choose **S**elect, or double-click the style. WordPerfect returns to the document window and activates the selected outline style. If the outline style you selected includes outline numbers, WordPerfect inserts a number for a first-level heading.

Notice in figure 16.1 that WordPerfect includes a Headings outline style with the description Document Headings. When you use this style, WordPerfect doesn't insert heading numbers. However, headings can be collapsed and moved using outline tools, and the outline headings are automatically marked for a table of contents.

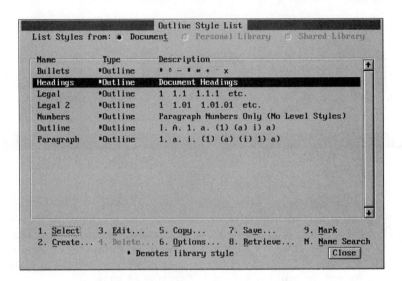

FIG. 16.1

The Outline Style List dialog box.

3. Type the first outline heading.

4. To insert another first-level heading, press Enter and type the heading. To insert a second-level heading, press Enter, Tab and type the heading.

5. To create body text, press Enter to insert a new heading number; then press Ctrl+T or click the T button in the Outline Bar.

6. To convert body text to an outline heading, press Ctrl+T with the cursor anywhere in the body text, or click the # button in the Outline Bar.

You can initiate outline commands in several ways. For example, there are four ways to promote a heading to a higher level:

■ Press Ctrl+O (Outline Edit) and press Shift+Tab.

■ Choose **Tools, Outline**; or press Ctrl+F5. Then choose **Previous** Level.

■ Click the left-pointing arrow button on the Outline Bar. (It's the third button on the left.)

■ Choose **O**ptions on the Outline Bar and then choose **A**djust Levels, **P**revious Level.

This chapter gives instructions for choosing outline commands with the menu bar only. Using the Outline Bar is explained in the following section.

Using the Outline Bar

The Outline Bar provides mouse-click shortcuts for many outline commands. To turn on the Outline Bar, choose **V**iew, **O**utline Bar.

You can use the keyboard to choose commands on the Outline Bar. Press Ctrl+O to turn on Outline Edit mode; then choose Outline Bar commands by pressing their underlined keys. Press Ctrl+O again or press F7 (Exit) to turn off Outline Edit mode.

The following table explains what the Outline Bar buttons do:

Outline Bar Button	Action
#	Change text to a heading
T	Change a heading to text
←	Promote family
→	Demote family
-	Hide family
+	Show family
Show	Choose levels to show from a drop-down list
Hide **B**ody	Hide body text
Sho**w** Body	Show body text
Style	Choose a style from a drop-down list
Options	Display the Outline dialog box

Working with Outlines

WordPerfect 6 turns the Outline feature into a powerful tool for working with documents of all kinds. If you format a document with outline headings, you can collapse the outline so that only the headings are displayed, then reorganize the document with a few simple keystrokes, by moving the headings. In this section you learn how to expand and collapse an outline, hide body text, move, copy, delete, and hide and show outline families.

Hiding Body Text

To hide body text, choose **T**ools, **O**utline with the cursor anywhere in the outline; or press Ctrl+F5. Then choose Hide Body Text.

To reveal body text, choose **T**ools, **O**utline; or press Ctrl+F5 and choose **H**ide/Sho**w**. Then choose Show **B**ody Text.

Moving, Copying, and Cutting an Outline Family

Follow these steps to move, copy, or delete an outline family:

1. Place the cursor in the family.

2. Choose **T**ools, **O**utline; or press Ctrl+F5. Then choose **M**ove Family, Cop**y** Family, or Cut **F**amily.

3. If you are moving or copying a family, move the cursor and press Enter to paste the family. Or, choose **T**ools, **O**utline (Ctrl+F5), **P**aste.

Hiding and Showing an Outline Family

Follow these steps to hide and show an outline family:

1. Move the cursor anywhere in the family and choose **T**ools, **O**utline, **H**ide Family.

2. To show the family again, choose **T**ools, **O**utline, **S**how Family.

Showing Selected Outline Levels

Follow these steps to show selected levels of an outline:

1. Place the cursor anywhere in the outline.

2. Choose **T**ools, **O**utline, Outline Options; or press Ctrl+F5. WordPerfect displays the Outline dialog box (see fig. 16.2).

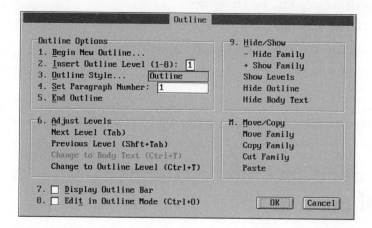

3. Choose **S**how Levels; then choose a number from the drop-down list.

Changing the Style of an Outline

Follow these steps to change the style of an outline:

1. Place the cursor anywhere in the outline.

2. Choose **T**ools, **O**utline; or press Ctrl+F5. Then choose **O**utline Style. WordPerfect displays the Outline Style List dialog box, which was shown in figure 16.1.

3. Highlight a style and choose **S**elect. WordPerfect reformats the outline with the selected style. Styles are discussed in detail in Chapter 7.

Working with Outline Numbers

You may need to leave certain headings unnumbered in an outline. Or, you may have two separately numbered outlines in the same document. This section shows you how to turn off outline numbering, restart outline numbers, and create outline numbers without a style.

Restarting Outline Numbers

Follow these steps to restart outline numbers:

1. Move the cursor where you want to restart the outline numbers.

2. Choose **T**ools, **O**utline, **O**utline Options; or press Ctrl+F5.

3. Choose **S**et Paragraph Number and type a number to restart the numbering.

You must use Arabic numerals separated by commas, spaces, or periods. For example, if you want to start with heading XIX.C.8, type **19.3.8**.

Creating an Outline Number without a Style

You can enter sequential numbers without using the Outline feature. This process is the equivalent of the Paragraph Numbering feature in WordPerfect 5.1. Follow these steps:

1. Choose an outline numbering style.

2. Choose **T**ools, **O**utline, **O**utline Options: or press Ctrl+F5.

3. Choose **I**nsert Outline Level (1-8) and type a number.

   WordPerfect immediately returns to the document window and inserts the heading number.

T   I   P   The keys for moving the cursor in an outline are exactly the same in WordPerfect 6 as they are in WordPerfect 5.1.

Turning Off Outline Numbering

To turn off outline numbering, follow these steps:

1. Choose **T**ools, **O**utline; or press Ctrl+F5.

2. Choose **E**nd Outline.

Using Macros

WordPerfect 6 makes writing and editing macros much less awkward than this process was in WordPerfect 5.1.

In WordPerfect 6, macros record commands rather than keystrokes. Thus, macros are much easier to read and edit. For example, recording a macro that sets left and right margins to 1.5 inches creates the following macro:

```
MarginLeft(1.5")
```

```
MarginRight(1.5")
```

In WordPerfect 5.1, the same keystrokes create this macro:

```
{Format}1m1.5{Enter}1.5{Enter}{Exit}
```

In WordPerfect 6, you can type in macro commands instead of having to pick them from a list. Parameters are enclosed in parentheses instead of tildes—to keep a common programming language convention.

If you share macros with users of WordPerfect 6 foreign language modules, you don't have to translate the macro commands. WordPerfect automatically identifies the foreign language module and translates the macro commands for you.

Although macro programming is beyond the scope of this book, advanced users will be delighted to discover many new conveniences in WordPerfect 6. If you make a macro programming error, the macro no longer just dies, as in WordPerfect 5.1. Instead, WordPerfect 6 displays a dialog box with the type of error and the line of macro code that caused it. Likewise, the Step command no longer displays cryptic messages and command numbers; it now tells you exactly which line the error is on. WordPerfect programmers must check the new and improved Case, Repeat Until, and Use commands, and also note the four new commands for programming dialog boxes: DLGCONTROL, DLGCREATE, DLGEND, and DLGINPUT.

Best of all, the WordPerfect 5.1 macro editor is gone. You can now edit macros in the WordPerfect 6 document screen. You can even interrupt macro recording, make editing changes, and then resume recording. When you turn off macro recording, WordPerfect converts the macro text to program code for fast playback.

You cannot use WordPerfect 5.1 macros in WordPerfect 6. You must re-create them.

Recording a Macro

You can record commands selected with the mouse or keyboard. Follow these steps:

1. Choose **Tools**, **Macro**, **Record**; or press Ctrl+F10. WordPerfect displays the Record Macro dialog box (see fig. 17.1).

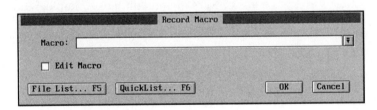

The Record Macro dialog box.

2. Type a macro name. The macro naming conventions are the same in WordPerfect 6 as in WordPerfect 5.1.

   WordPerfect remembers the names of the last four macros you recorded. To edit one of these macros, click the arrow at the right end of the Macro box and choose a name from the drop-down list. As in WordPerfect 5.1, WordPerfect asks whether you want to replace or edit the macro. To bypass the prompt, choose Edit Macro, OK. Editing macros is described later in this chapter in the section "Editing Macros." Choose **R**eplace to replace the macro.

3. Choose OK. WordPerfect returns to the document window and displays Recording Macro in the status bar.

4. Type the text and commands that you want to record. You can choose commands using the mouse or keyboard, but you cannot move the cursor using the mouse. You must move the cursor using the keyboard.

5. When you're finished recording, choose **Tools, Macro, Stop**; or press Ctrl+F10.

WordPerfect saves the macro as program code and displays the normal document window.

> The default (Enter key) macro feature works the same in Word-Perfect 6 as in WordPerfect 5.1. To record a default macro, press Ctrl+F10 (Record Macro), press Enter, type the appropriate keystrokes and commands, and press Ctrl+F10 (Record Macro). To play the default macro, press Alt+F10 (Play Macro) and press Enter.

T I P

Editing a Macro

Follow these steps to edit an existing macro:

1. Choose **Tools, Macro, Record**; or press Ctrl+F10.

2. In the Record Macro dialog box, type the name of the macro to edit.

   You can also press the down-arrow key or click the down-pointing arrow at the right end of the Macro box to list the last four macros you recorded.

3. Highlight a macro and choose Edit Macro, OK. WordPerfect displays the macro in the normal document window with `Edit Macro` in the status bar.

4. Edit the macro, then choose **Tools, Macro, Stop**; or press Ctrl+F10 to save your changes.

Choosing Macro Commands

As in WordPerfect 5.1, you can choose macro programming commands from a list. Follow these steps:

1. Begin recording a macro as described in the preceding section.

2. When you want to insert a command, press Ctrl+PgUp. WordPerfect displays the Macro Control dialog box (see fig. 17.2).

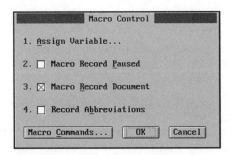

FIG. 17.2

The Macro Control dialog box.

3. Choose Macro Commands. WordPerfect displays the Macro Commands dialog box (see fig. 17.3).

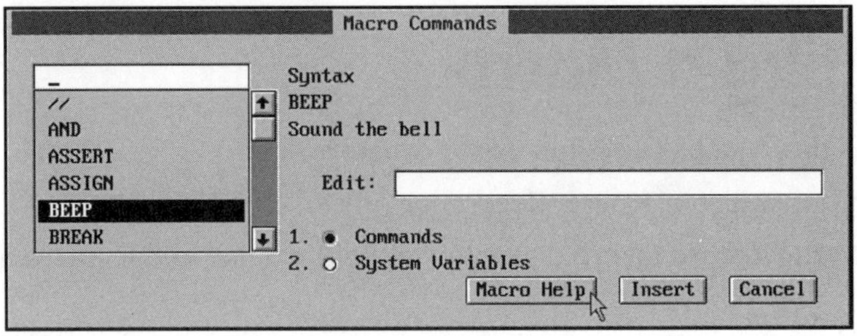

FIG. 17.3

The Macro Commands dialog box.

The Macro Commands dialog box works the same as the macro commands list in WordPerfect 5.1. To highlight a command in the list, type the first few letters of its name.

4. To insert command parameters, choose Edit and then type the parameters.

5. To display system variables in the list box, choose System Variables.

6. Choose Insert to insert the command or variable expression and return to the document window.

Using On-Line Macro Help

Follow these steps to display detailed help for macro commands and variables:

1. Begin recording a macro. Then press Ctrl+PgUp and choose Macro **C**ommands. WordPerfect displays the Macro Commands dialog box.

2. Choose Macro Help. WordPerfect displays the macro Help dialog box (see fig. 17.4).

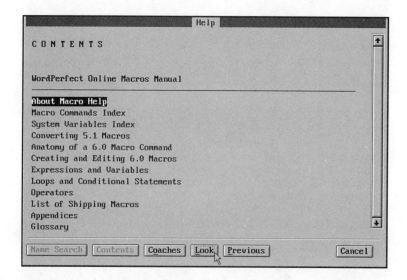

FIG. 17.4

The Macro Help dialog box.

3. Choose Macro Commands Index or System Variables to display help for commands or system variables; then choose **L**ook.

   WordPerfect displays the Macro Commands Index dialog box (see fig. 17.5).

4. Highlight a command and choose **L**ook. WordPerfect displays detailed help for the command (see fig. 17.6).

5. To see a programming example, choose Show Me An Example.

6. Choose **C**ontents to return to the on-line macro help index, or choose Cancel to return to the Macro Commands dialog box.

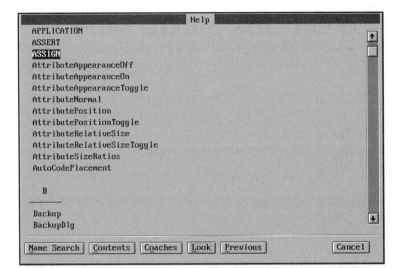

FIG. 17.5

The Macro
Commands Index
dialog box.

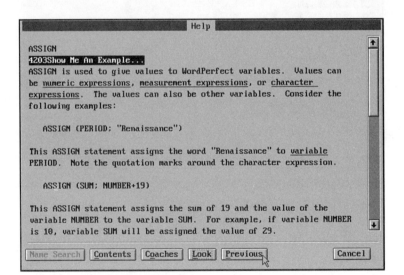

FIG. 17.6

The Help dialog
box for the
ASSIGN macro
command.

Typing a Macro

WordPerfect 6 has no separate macro editor. If you know how to use
macro programming commands, you can enter them in an empty
document window.

Notice that in WordPerfect 6, you can select macro commands from a list, as in WordPerfect 5.1. (See the previous section "Choosing Macro Commands.") You don't have to select them from the macro commands list, however; you can simply type them in the document screen. Selecting them from the list is safer because no risk of misspellings or typos is involved.

Follow these steps to type a macro in the document window:

1. Begin typing commands.

2. If you forget how to spell a command or system variable or if you need help with command syntax, press Ctrl+PgUp to display the Macro Control dialog box.

3. Select Macro Commands and choose Commands or System Variables as described earlier in the sections on Choosing Macro Commands and Using On-Line Macro Help.

4. When you finish typing the macro, save it using the extension WPM.

When you run the macro the first time, WordPerfect compiles it (converts it to a fast macro program code).

Editing a Macro While You Record

If you make a mistake while recording a macro, you can interrupt recording and make changes to the macro's text. Follow these steps:

1. Begin recording a macro as described in the preceding section.

2. When you make a mistake, press Home, 0 (Switch to Document). WordPerfect displays the Switch To Document dialog box (see fig. 17.7).

3. Press 9 to switch to Document 9 (Macro Record).

   This document is where WordPerfect saves the macro code for the keystrokes you type with Record Macro turned on (see fig. 17.8).

4. Edit the macro.

5. Press Home, 0, 1; or press Shift+F3 (Switch) to return to Document 1 and resume recording keystrokes.

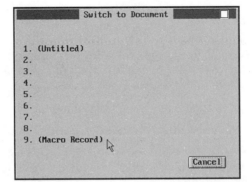

FIG. 17.7

The Switch To
Document dialog
box.

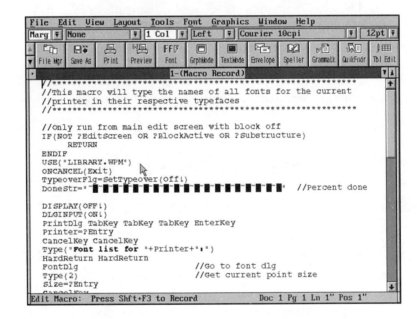

FIG. 17.8

The Document 9
(Macro Record)
window.

Tiling Windows To Watch WordPerfect Create Macro Code

You can watch WordPerfect create macro code for the keystrokes that
you record. Follow these steps:

1. Turn on Record Macro as described in the section "Recording a
   Macro."

2. Press Home, 0, 9 to switch to Document 9, where WordPerfect records macro code.

3. Choose **W**indow, **T**ile. WordPerfect splits the window and displays the Document 9 screen in the top half.

4. Press Shift+F3 (Switch) or click in Document 1, and begin recording keystrokes and commands.

All keystrokes and commands are recorded in Document 9 as macro commands. For example, typing **"This is a macro."** in Document 1 creates the macro code Type("This is a macro.") in Document 9.

This process is an excellent way to learn macro commands so that you can type them in the document screen without selecting them from the macro commands list (see the previous section "Typing a Macro").

Using Macro Controls

Several WordPerfect 5.1 macro commands are assigned to the WordPerfect 6 Macro Control dialog box (refer to fig. 17.2). The following list describes these commands:

■ *Assign Variable.* This option works the same as in WordPerfect 5.1, but now it uses a dialog box instead of a prompt. Follow these steps to assign a variable:

1. Without turning on Record Macro, press Ctrl+PgUp and choose **A**ssign Variable. WordPerfect displays the Assign Variable dialog box (see fig. 17.9).

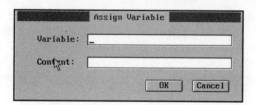

FIG. 17.9

The Assign Variable dialog box.

2. Type a variable name or number in the Variable text box.

3. Type the variable contents in the Content text box.

With text selected, WordPerfect assigns the first 79 characters of the text as the variable contents.

4. Choose OK, OK to return to the document.

298

To insert the variable in a document, press Alt and the number of the variable. You cannot insert named variables using the Alt key.

With the macro recorder turned on, the above steps insert an ASSIGN command in the macro.

- *Macro Record Paused.* This option works the same as the WordPerfect 5.1 macro Pause command.

- *Macro Record Document.* Choosing this check box turns on a WordPerfect 6 feature that automatically turns macro recording back on when you switch from an open document to a macro editing document. With this option deselected, the macro recorder doesn't automatically restart when you switch to the macro editing document, and you must turn macro recording back on by choosing **T**ools, **M**acro, **R**ecord (Ctrl+F10). With this option selected, you can switch back and forth between the macro editing document and the macro recording document by pressing Shift+F3.

- *Record Abbreviations.* When you choose this option, WordPerfect records program commands in abbreviated form; for example, PrinterCtrlGo instead of PrinterControlGo. This creates smaller macro programming document files but doesn't affect the length of compiled macro program files.

Playing Macros

Follow these steps to play a macro:

1. Press the macro's Alt+key combination. You can also choose **T**ools, Macro, **P**lay; or press Alt+F10. WordPerfect displays the Play Macro dialog box (see fig. 17.10).

FIG. 17.10

The Play Macro dialog box.

2. Type a macro name and choose OK.

   Alternatively, click the down arrow at the right end of the Macro text box, or press the down-arrow key to display the last four macros you recorded; then highlight a macro and press Enter.

Using Fax and Sound

WordPerfect 6 includes two entirely new features: Fax and Sound. If you own a fax modem, you can send and receive WordPerfect documents without ever leaving the program.

The Sound feature enables you to embed and play back digital audio and MIDI sound clips in WordPerfect documents. For example, you can record dictation notes and play them back while you type. You can also create multimedia presentations.

Using Fax Services

Before you can fax WordPerfect documents, you must install an appropriate fax device in your computer. For a list of supported fax cards and installation instructions, see the WordPerfect *User's Guide*. You must also install fax software. Note, however, that Microsoft Windows fax programs are not supported. You can use the fax program supplied with WordPerfect (FBMAN.COM), or you can use a program purchased separately. Some options may not be available in WordPerfect's fax-related dialog boxes, depending on the capabilities of your fax software.

Creating a Fax Phonebook

You can fax documents by dialing the fax numbers manually or by selecting them from a WordPerfect phonebook.

Follow these steps to create a phonebook of fax numbers that you use regularly:

1. Choose File, **P**rint/Fax; or press Shift+F7.

2. Then choose Fa**x** Services. WordPerfect displays the Fax Services dialog box (see fig. 18.1).

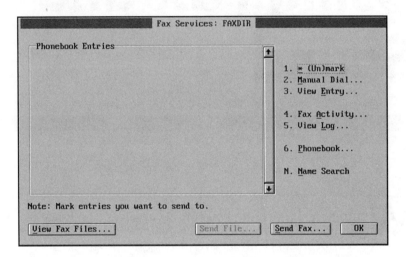

FIG. 18.1

The Fax Services dialog box.

3. Choose **P**honebook. WordPerfect displays the Phonebook dialog box (see fig. 18.2).

4. Choose the appropriate options in the Phonebook dialog box; then choose Close to return to the Fax Services dialog box.

The following list describes the options in the Phonebook dialog box:

- *Create Entry.* This option displays the Create Entry dialog box. Type the recip-ient's name and phone number and choose a resolution in the Destination Fax Machine section, or choose **B**inary, File, **T**ransfer. Then choose OK to return to the Phonebook dialog box.

- *Create Group.* WordPerfect can automatically send a fax to every name and fax number on a list. To create a group from the Phonebook Entries list, choose Create Group. WordPerfect displays the Create Group dialog box. Type a name in the Group Name box; then use Add to Group to add names to the group list. Choose Close to return to the Phonebook dialog box.

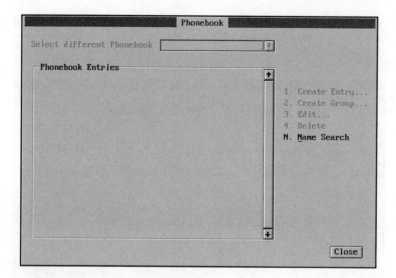

FIG. 18.2

The Phonebook
dialog box.

- *Edit.* This option works the same as Create Entry.

- *Delete.* Highlight a name in the list and choose Delete to delete the
  entry.

Some fax programs do not allow you to add phonebook entries using WordPerfect. However, phone numbers that you
add in the fax program are listed in the Phonebook dialog
box in WordPerfect.

Sending a Fax

After you have set up your fax modem and software, follow these steps
to send a fax:

1. Open the document you want to fax. Then choose File, **P**rint/Fax;
   or press Shift+F7.

2. Choose Fax Services.

3. Highlight a phone book entry and press * to mark it. This entry
   will now receive the fax. Repeat this process for any other entries
   to which you want to send the fax.

   Creating phonebook entries is described in the preceding section,
   "Creating a Fax Phonebook."

4. Choose **S**end Fax, or choose **M**anual Dial if the fax phone number isn't listed. WordPerfect displays the Send Fax dialog box (see fig. 18.3).

```
┌─────────────────────────────── Send Fax ───────────────────────────────┐
│                                                                         │
│ ┌─Fax──────────────────────┐  ┌─Send Options────────────────────────┐  │
│ │ 1. ● Full Document        │   8. ☒ Coversheet... │Default        │  │
│ │ 2. ○ Page                 │                                         │  │
│ │ 3. ○ Document on Disk...   │   9. Send Time... │04-30-93 11:24a │  │
│ │ 4. ○ Multiple Pages...     │   R. Resolution   │Standard      │▼│  │
│ │ 5. ○ Blocked Text      ▷  │   I. Priority     │              │▼│  │
│ │                            │   U. Routing      │              │▼│  │
│ │ 6. ○ Fax on Disk...        │   L. Billing      │              │▼│  │
│ └──────────────────────────┘                                         │
│                                                                         │
│   7. ☐ Save as an image for Fax on Disk                                │
│          Filename: │                                        │          │
│                                                                         │
│              ┌──────────┐ ┌──────────┐ ┌────────┐                     │
│              │Send File...│ │Send Fax │ │Cancel │                     │
│              └──────────┘ └──────────┘ └────────┘                     │
└─────────────────────────────────────────────────────────────────────────┘
```

FIG. 18.3

The Send Fax dialog box.

If you choose **M**anual Dial, WordPerfect displays the Manual Dial dialog box, where you can type the name of a recipient and a fax number to dial; then choose OK to return to the Fax Services dialog box and choose **S**end Fax as in step 4.

5. Choose the appropriate options in the Send Fax dialog box; then choose Send Fax.

The following list describes the options in the Send Fax dialog box:

■ *Full Document, Page, Document on Disk, Multiple Pages, Blocked Text, Fax on Disk.* These options enable you to tell WordPerfect which portion of a document to fax or where the document is located.

NOTE The Fax on Disk option lets you choose a document that you have previously saved on disk as a fax image. Saving a fax on disk is described later in the section "Saving a Fax on Disk."

■ *Coversheet.* This option enables you to create a coversheet for the fax document.

■ *Send Time.* This option lets you specify the date and time that you want WordPerfect to send the fax.

■ *Resolution.* This option enables you to choose a print quality for the fax.

■ *Priority, Routing, Billing.* These options let you specify a priority, routing, and billing.

Saving a Fax on Disk

The Fax on Disk option in the Send Fax dialog box enables you to send a document that you have previously saved on disk in fax format. This option saves time when you need to fax the same document more than once because the document doesn't have to be rasterized (converted to fax format) again.

To save a document in fax format, choose **S**end Fax. Choose Save as an Image for Fax on Disk, type a name for the fax file, and choose **S**end Fax. WordPerfect saves the document in fax format in the default documents subdirectory.

Viewing Fax Files

WordPerfect enables you to view fax documents as they will be printed. Like Print Preview, the View Fax Files option shows you headers and footers. Follow these steps to view a fax file:

1. Choose **F**ile, **P**rint/Fax; or press Shift+F7.

2. Choose Fax Services, **V**iew Fax Files.

3. Type a file name and choose View. WordPerfect displays the View Fax Files screen. The options in this screen are the same as for Print Preview, which is described in Chapter 10, "Printing."

Sending a File in WordPerfect Format

You can send a WordPerfect document using a modem without converting it to fax (rasterized) format. However, your modem must be able to transfer binary files. Follow these steps:

1. Choose **F**ile, **P**rint/Fax; or press Shift+F7.

2. Choose Fax Services.

3. Mark the phonebook entries that you want to receive the file. Alternatively, choose **M**anual Dial, type a name and phone number, and choose OK.

4. Choose Send File. WordPerfect displays the Send Files dialog box (see fig. 18.4).

5. In the Filename box, type the name of the file that you want to send; then choose Send File.

WordPerfect transmits the file to the remote modem.

Cancelling a Fax

Follow these steps to cancel a fax that is being sent:

1. In the Fax Services dialog box, choose Fax Activity.

2. Choose Cancel Current Fax. WordPerfect cancels the fax and returns to the Fax Services dialog box.

Checking Fax Activity

While WordPerfect is sending a fax, you can view the status of the job. Start the fax transmission; then choose Fax Activity in the Fax Services dialog box. WordPerfect displays the Fax Activity dialog box (see fig. 18.5).

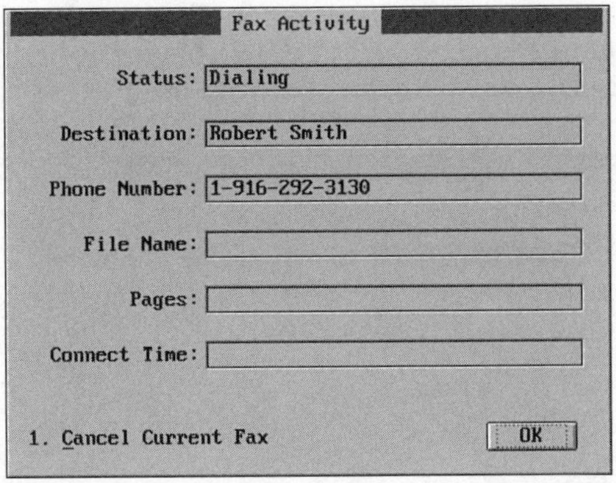

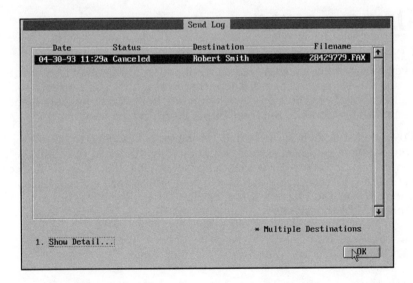

FIG. 18.5

The Fax Activity
dialog box.

Viewing the Fax Log

WordPerfect keeps a record of the faxes that you send and receive.
Follow these steps to view the Fax Log:

1. Choose View Log from the Fax Services dialog box; then choose
   Send Log or Receive Log.

   WordPerfect displays the Send Log or Receive Log dialog box
   containing a list of the faxes you have sent or received (see
   fig. 18.6).

FIG. 18.6

The Send Log
dialog box.

2. To view detailed information about a fax, highlight its entry and choose **S**how Detail. WordPerfect displays the Send Log (or Receive Log) Details dialog box (see fig. 18.7).

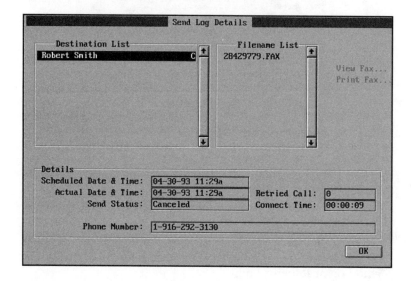

FIG. 18.7

The Send Log Details dialog box.

3. Choose OK until you return to the Fax Services dialog box.

Using Sound

Using WordPerfect 6, you can embed voice notes, sound effects, and even music in your documents using digital or MIDI sound files. You could, for example, create a macro that runs a business presentation including voice notes. You can also dictate notes and then play them back while you transcribe them into a WordPerfect document.

To embed sounds in WordPerfect documents, you need to have a sound device installed in your computer, and you need to install the device with the WordPerfect Install program. Installation is discussed in Chapter 1. To record voice notes, your sound card needs a microphone. If you don't have a sound card, you can play back (but not record) MIDI sound files through your computer's internal speaker.

Setting Up Your Sound Card

After installing a sound device in your computer and selecting it with the WordPerfect Install program, you need to install it again from within WordPerfect. Follow these steps:

1. Choose **T**ools, **S**ound Clip; or press Ctrl+F7. Then choose **S**ound Setup. WordPerfect displays the Sound Setup dialog box (see fig. 18.8).

FIG. 18.8

The Sound Setup dialog box.

2. Choose **T**ype. WordPerfect displays the Setup Sound Type dialog box (see fig. 18.9).

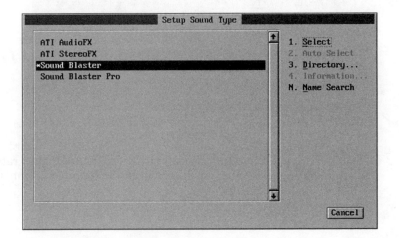

FIG. 18.9

The Setup Sound Type dialog box.

3. Highlight a device in the list and choose **S**elect. WordPerfect returns to the Sound Setup dialog box.

4. Choose **H**ardware Setup. WordPerfect displays the Hardware Setup dialog box (see fig. 18.10).

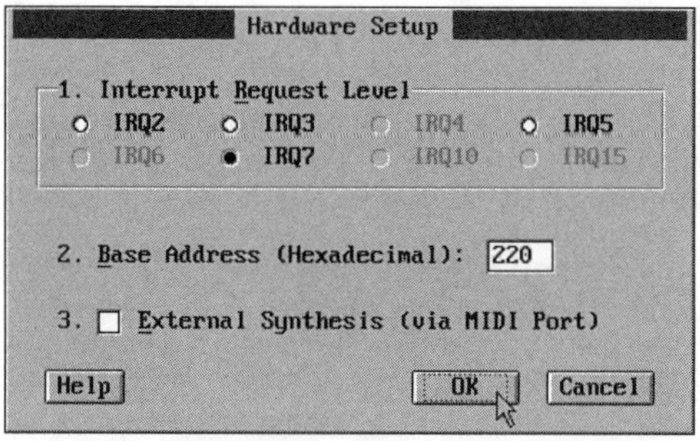

FIG. 18.10

The Hardware
Setup dialog
box.

5. Refer to your sound card's documentation in order to choose the appropriate options in the Hardware Setup dialog box. Then choose OK to return to the Sound Setup dialog box.

6. Choose **R**ecording Quality Setup. WordPerfect displays the Recording Quality Setup dialog box (see fig. 18.11).

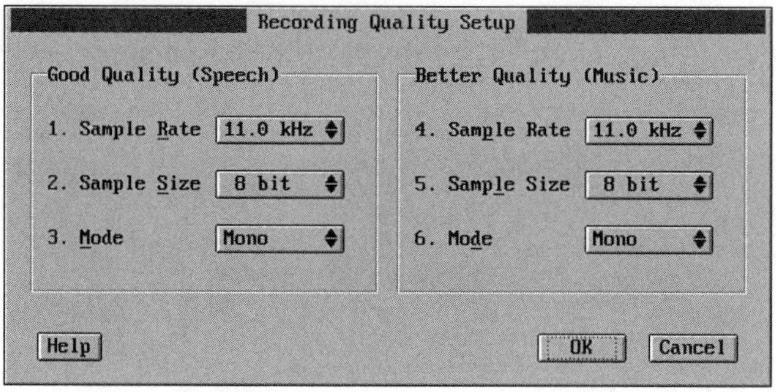

FIG. 18.11

The Recording
Quality Setup
dialog box.

To improve the quality of sound recording, increase the Sample **R**ate and Sample **S**ize settings. Be aware, though, that higher rates use more disk space. Choosing Stereo from the **M**ode list doubles the size of each sound file.

7. Choose OK, Close to return to the document window.

Using Sound for Dictation

After installing a sound card in your system, follow these steps to record dictation notes:

1. Choose **T**ools, Sound **C**lip; or press Ctrl+F7. Then choose **R**ecord, or press Ctrl+D. WordPerfect displays the Record Sound Clip dialog box (see fig. 18.12).

FIG. 18.12

The Record
Sound Clip
dialog box.

2. Adjust the settings for V**o**lume and Recording **Q**uality, if desired. The following list describes the V**o**lume and Recording **Q**uality options:

   ■ *Volume.* This option sets the recording and playback volume.

   ■ *Recording Quality.* You normally choose Good (Speech) for dictation, and Better (Music) for music. Choosing Other displays the Other Recording Quality dialog box.

   In this dialog box, setting a higher Sample **R**ate and Sample **S**ize results in better sound quality but creates bigger sound files. Likewise, choosing Stereo under **M**ode doubles a sound file's size.

3. Choose **R**ec and begin recording the sound.

4. Choose **S**top to end the recording, and choose Insert to insert the sound clip and return to the document.

5. To save the sound clip on disk, choose **T**ools, Sound **C**lip (Ctrl+F7), **P**lay. Highlight the sound clip in the Clip Description list and choose **S**ave, type a file name, and choose OK.

6. Choose Insert. WordPerfect returns to the document window and inserts the sound clip in the document. On-screen, you see a box with musical notes and a tag, such as Sound (Ctrl+S): Clip #1.

Playing Back and Transcribing a Sound Clip

Follow these steps to play back and transcribe a sound clip that you have inserted in a document:

1. Place the cursor just before the sound clip. Then choose **Tools**, **Sound Clip**; or press Ctrl+F7. Then choose **Play** or press Ctrl+S.

   WordPerfect plays back the sound and displays the Listen and Type dialog box.

2. As the sound clip plays, type the text and use the **Stop**, **Repeat**, and **Play**/Pause controls.

3. Choose Exit to return to the document window.

Adding a Saved Sound Clip to a Document

Follow these steps to add a sound clip that you have saved on disk to a document:

1. Choose **Tools**, **Sound Clip**; or press Ctrl+F7. Then choose **Add**. WordPerfect displays the Add Sound Clip to Document dialog box (see fig. 18.13).

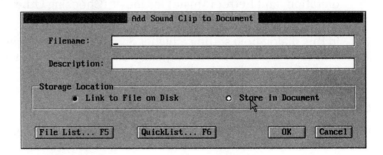

FIG. 18.13

The Add Sound Clip to Document dialog box.

2. Type a filename.

3. Choose **Link** to File on Disk or **Store** in Document.

Choosing **Link to File on Disk** inserts the sound clip in the on-screen document. However, the sound clip is stored in a separate file. This option saves disk space if you want to attach the clip to several documents. If you give the file to other WordPerfect users, you must remember to copy the linked sound clip file as well.

Choosing **Store in Document** saves the sound clip with the document, resulting in a larger document file.

INDEX

Symbols

E

G

H

halftones (graphics images), 218
handing indents, 78
hard returns, 113
hardware setup (sound cards), 307
Header/Footer/Watermark command, 80-81
headers
   creating, 80
   displaying, 30
   positioning, 80
   spacing below, 80
headings (outlines), 284
Help, 15-20
   About Help, 18
   context-sensitive, 20
   F1 function key, 15
   Glossary, 17
   How Do I, 16
   hypertext buttons, 16
   Index, 16
   Keystrokes, 18
   macros, 19-20, 293
   Shortcut Keys, 18
   System Information, 20
   topics, 16
hidden menus, 11
hidden text, 239-240
   converting to normal, 240
   creating, 239-240
   formatting as, 240
hiding
   body text in outlines, 286
   comments, 225
   links, 281
   menu bar, 11

Outline Bar, 11
outline families, 286
HLS (Hue Luminosity Saturation) color, 51
horizontal scroll bar, 27
How Do I (Help dialog box), 16
hypertext, 91
   activating, 93
   appearance, 92
   buttons
      creating, 91-92
      Help, 16
      jumping to documents, 93
      moving to, 95
      running macros, 94
   jumps, 95
   links, 91, 94
   styles, editing, 96
Hypertext command, 91
hyphenation defaults, 43

I

Image Editor, 215-219
   cropping images, 218
   flipping images, 219
   rotating images, 219
   scaling images, 219
   tools, 216-218
   WP Presentations program, 216
images, *see* graphics images
Import option (Spreadsheet command), 279
importing
   graphics images in graphics box, 204
   spreadsheets, 279-281

L

N

Que Has WordPerfect 6 Books
for All Types of Users!

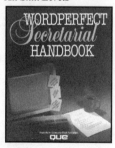

Learning is Easy with Easy Books from Que!

Que's Easy Series offers a revolutionary concept in computer training. The friendly, 4-color interior, easy format, and simple explanations guarantee success for even the most intimidated computer user!

Easy WordPerfect 6
Version 6

$16.95 USA
1-56529-087-9, 256 pp., 8 x 10

Easy DOS, 2nd Edition
Through Version 6

$16.95 USA
1-56529-095-x, 200 pp., 8 x 10

Easy 1-2-3, 2nd Edition
Releases 2.4

$19.95 USA
1-56529-022-4, 224 pp., 8 x 10

Easy Macintosh
All Macintosh Computers

$19.95 USA
0-88022-819-9, 200 pp., 8 x 10

Easy Quattro Pro
Version 4

$19.95 USA
0-88022-798-2, 200 pp., 8 x 10

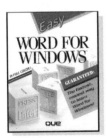

Easy Word for Windows
Versions 1 & 2

$19.95 USA
0-88022-922-5, 224 pp., 8 x 10

Easy Quattro Pro for Windows
Version 5.1 for Windows

$19.95 USA
0-88022-993-4, 224 pp., 8 x 10

Easy Windows
Version 3.1

$19.95 USA
0-88022-985-3, 200 pp., 8 x 10

Easy WordPerfect for Windows
Version 5.2 for Windows

$19.95 USA
0-88022-126-3, 208 pp., 8 x 10

 To Order, Call: (800) 428-5331 OR (317) 573-2500